Illinois Terminal
The Electric Years

By Paul H. Stringham

Interurban Press
Glendale, California

Library of Congress Cataloging-in-Publication Data

Stringham, Paul.
    Illinois Terminal, the electric years / by Paul Stringham.
       p.   cm.
    Includes bibliographical references.
    ISBN 0-916374-82-3
    1. Illinois Terminal Railroad Company. 2. Railroads—
Illinois   I. Title.
TF25.I422377 1989
385'.09773—dc20   89-37338
                                                  CIP

ILLINOIS TERMINAL • *The Electric Years*

1989
© by Paul H. Stringham

No portion of this book may be used or reproduced without written permission from the publisher, except in brief quotations used in reviews.

ISBN 0-916374-82-3

Published by INTERURBAN PRESS
P.O. Box 6444
Glendale, California 91225

Design and Production
Brueggenjohann/Reese Creative Services

Typography
Roc-Pacific, Los Angeles, CA
Express Type Co., Simi Valley, CA

Printing and Binding
Walsworth Publishing, Marceline, MO

ENDSHEET PHOTOS

Front: The second section of an early Illinois Traction Shop Employees Special pauses at Clinton. Motor 353 was originally an AC-powered car, built for service on the lines from Peoria to Bloomington and Decatur, and Peoria to Springfield.
          Illinois Traction, Dale Jenkins Collection

Rear: Three runs met and exchanged passengers at Mackinaw Junction in the morning, in the late 1930s. Motor 275, at left, heads up St. Louis-bound train 91; to the right of the tower, car 274 has just come north from Springfield as train 62, pulled around the east leg of the wye, and backed to the station where it is ready to depart as train 101. Beyond the 272 and not in view, car 1200 is about to depart for Peoria as train 40. The date was May 15, 1938.
          Paul H. Stringham

FRONTISPIECE

Illinois Traction, and later Illinois Terminal, passenger cars all were a fine place for rail enthusiasts to ride. Here, Bill Janssen inspects the right-of-way through an arched front window, while Bob Mehlenbeck records the scene for all time. The date and location are unknown; what is known is that the world lost something special when it lost passenger service on the Illinois Terminal.

Final Page Photo

"Good Bye," waves this beautiful lass, from the rear platform of an Illinois Traction parlor car. She was stylized from H.E. Chubbuck's daughter (McKinley's right-hand man) and featured on IT playing cards, as well as this promotional poster—a fitting end to this book about The Road of Good Service.
          Illinois Traction, John Hubbard Collection

Table of Contents

Acknowledgements *7*
Introduction *9*
In the Beginning *11*
Passenger Services 1901–1958 . . . . *33*
Suburban Services *59*
The Valley Division *73*
The Alton Line *85*
Illinois Terminal Railroad *95*
The Belt Lines and Freight Services 1906–1981 . . . . *101*
Accidents *125*
A Ride Over the Line *133*
Illinois Traction System Stations *167*
Shops and Carbarns *193*
Cars of the Illinois Traction System *203*
A Colorful Interurban *233*
Appendix A *249*
Appendix B *252*
Appendix C *255*
Appendix D *255*
Appendix E *256*
System Map *191*
Bibliography *256*
Index *257*

The final run of train 92 took place on March 12, 1955, with car 277 doing the honors. Here, she waits in front of the East Peoria station for the carbarn crew to run her into the barn. Tomorrow, and for all future times, things will be quiet at this time.
Paul H. Stringham

Acknowledgements

Very few people can write a book alone; the more assistance that is offered, the more complete the story will be. I have been very fortunate in receiving a great deal of help from quite a number of friends and acquaintances, and I wish to express my gratitude to each and every one of them.

Mr. Walter Cassin, President of the Illinois Terminal, made it possible for me to go through the hundreds of files of records, and Mr. Ray Wehmeyer, who was in charge of those records, was very helpful in helping to locate the things of value.

Lee Roten, a commercial photographer for many years in Peoria, did a beautiful job in making up the many enlargements which are reproduced in this volume.

William C. Janssen, Robert V. Mehlenbeck, George Fehl III, Robert Merriman, Richard Deller, Jim Barrick, Dr. John Hubbard, and John Leisenring were all very generous in the loan of photographs or negatives, maps, etc., of almost every period in the Traction's existence.

Jim Buckley put in many tedious hours of work on the roster. Dale Jenkins supplied many details from the information in his files on the operation of the line. George Wynn filled in many details of some of the operations in the Danville area. Gill Siepert furnished information on the Homer branch, and on the ITS operation of the Kankakee & Urbana Traction. George Hadaller sent me many details of the operations in the Granite City area.

Mr. E.E. Kester, Passenger Traffic Manager of ITS, supplied me with many company publications over the years.

Motormen L.K. McCrillis, William Simmons and Elmer Ruff, and Conductors Frank A. Bergschneider and George Kauffman furnished me with many details of the early years of the line's operation.

The Staff in the Reference Department of the Peoria Public Library, especially Miss Molly Lanke and the late Ms. Jane Burch, Ms. Sandra M. Stark of the Illinois State Historical Library, and Tom Kilton of the University of Illinois Library, were all very helpful in locating items of importance.

I sincerely hope that I have not overlooked any of those who were so helpful; if I have, please accept my sincere apologies.

Paul H. Stringham
October 1989

Introduction

From humble beginnings at the turn of the century, the Illinois Traction System — or "the Traction," as it was known by those who rode it — was destined to become the largest interurban electric line in the Midwest. It ran from St. Louis to Peoria, from Springfield to Danville, and from Decatur to Bloomington and Mackinaw; along the way, it also operated suburban service on numerous branch lines and local service in several on-line cities.

For most of its life, it operated with big, distinctive arch-window interurbans and freight locomotives. It was one of the few electric interurban systems in the country to operate both parlor-car and sleeping-car services, and these services lasted longer on the IT than just about anywhere else.

It should come as no surprise, then, that the Illinois Traction System, later known as the Illinois Terminal Railroad, is one of America's best known and most oft-remembered electric railways. Just because it was one of the biggest, and offered more services than most other interurban electric lines did? No, it was much more than just that. The big, arch-window cars each had a personality of their own, and the friendly employees — trainmen, station agents, shopworkers — and the friendly little towns along the way, all added a little something to the aura of that which was the Illinois Terminal. And when the Illinois Terminal's passenger service ended in 1958, a way of life did, as well.

Illinois Traction car 234 (1st) leaves Henry Siding, near Morton, in 1910. This photo was taken to publicize the new automatic block signals, which protected passengers on "The Road of Good Service." Illinois Traction, John Hubbard Collection

In the Beginning
Danville, Paxton & Northern

It was an unlikely place for a major interurban system to originate, yet in Danville, Illinois, one of the world's finest traction lines began. A city of 16,354 in 1900, Danville is 125 miles south of Chicago, close to the Indiana state line. Railroads and coal mining played a significant role in Danville's history. Four railroads centered there: the Chicago & Eastern Illinois, the Big Four, the Wabash and the Peoria & Eastern. West and south of the city were hundreds of thousands of acres underlain with coal; by the turn of the century these coalfields were under development.

Although four railroads already served the city, mine development meant there was room for more, and the incorporation of the Danville Paxton & Northern on December 2, 1899 was a move in that direction. Plans called for a steam road from the south line of Vermillion County (in which Danville is located) north and northwest to Paxton.

The proud crew stands by with office car 233 as Mr. H.E. Chubbuck, Vice President of Illinois Traction (in the straw hat), and Mr. Brown of the Mexico City Tramways pose for the photographer. Mr. Chubbuck was taking Mr. Brown on a tour of the IT on this date, October 12, 1910; the location is Emery, which boasted the fine combination station/substation building used here as a backdrop.   Illinois Traction

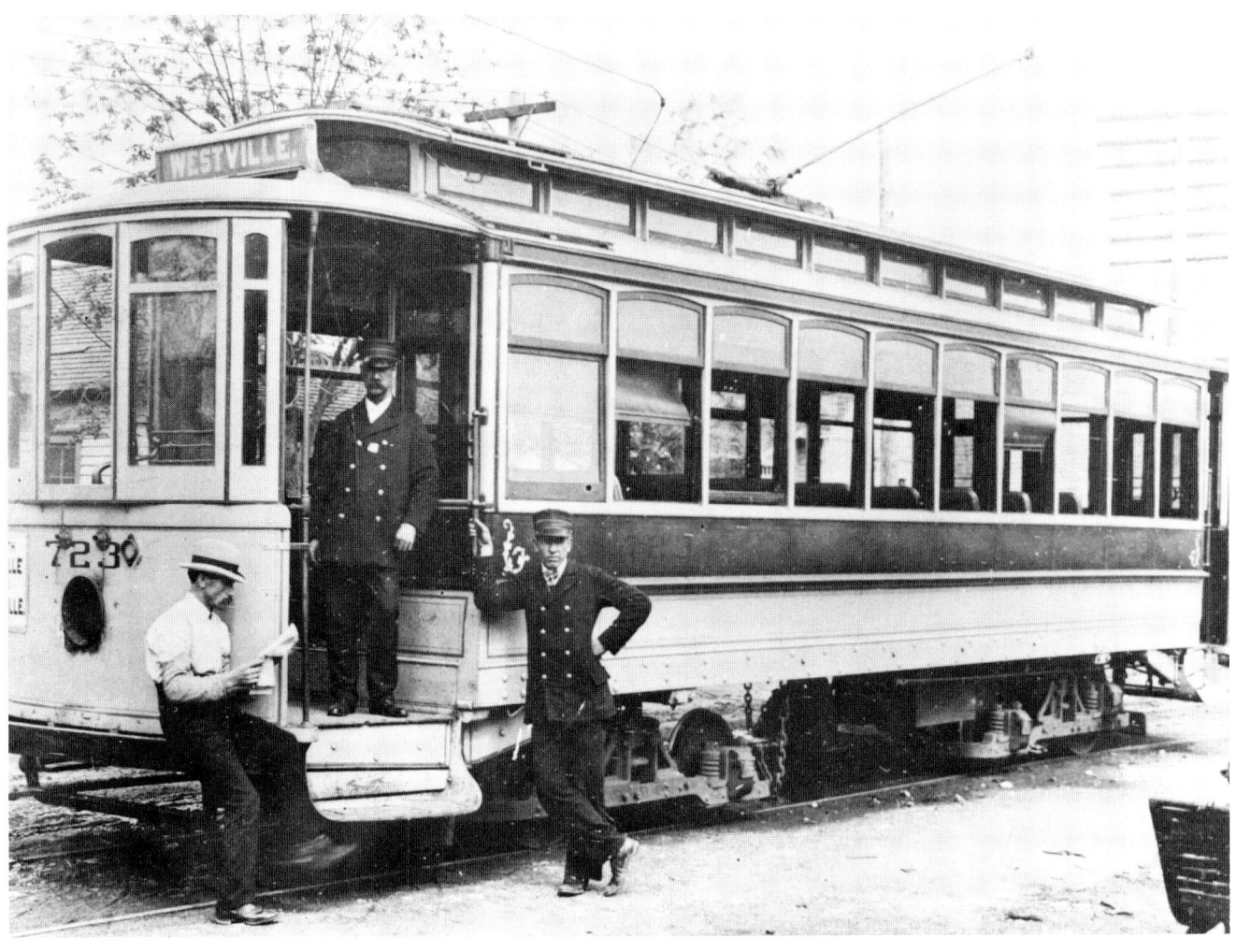

Car 723 came to the Danville Paxton & Northern from Washington, D.C., where it carried the same number. This type of car opened the DP&N; it is shown here at Danville in 1902 or 1903. The "maximum-traction" wheelsets were unsuitable for interurban service and were soon replaced. This series of cars was renumbered in the 140s after the Danville Urbana & Champaign took over.
Charles Gammell Collection

Before construction began, however, the incorporators decided an electric line was a wiser choice, for it would better provide passenger service to both mines and towns.

The first section of the DP&N was to connect with city streetcars at West Main and Gilbert Streets, Danville, cross the high Gilbert Street bridge over the Vermillion River, run south on Danville's Main Street, over the Wabash Railroad and then west to a point near the section line between Georgetown Road and the Cairo line of the Big Four Railroad. From there it would go directly south to Westville. However, though franchises were obtained from Danville and the Vermillion County Board, the company couldn't post a $25,000 performance bond, and the project came to an abrupt halt.

Enter William B. McKinley. His McKinley Syndicate, already heavily involved in public utilities, bought the Danville Street Railway & Light Company on July 18, 1900. Work at once began on rehabilitating the property. By late spring 1901, it was in first-class condition. McKinley then investigated the defunct DP&N, bought it and resumed work late in May by strengthening the Gilbert Street bridge. On July 13, excavation for the track in South Danville began and by August 8, track was complete to the Wabash Railroad's South Danville viaduct site.

At 2:00 p.m., September 16, 1901, the first car left downtown Danville with a load of dignitaries running to the Wabash viaduct, then under construction. Beyond the viaduct the track was complete almost to Westville. Next day, service began from Danville to the viaduct. On September 29, a car was taken south of the viaduct and put on the track. Its first run was as far as Kelley's store, with passengers transferring at the viaduct. By October 8, the track was finished into Westville.

With tracks leveled and sidings put in, the Danville-Westville line opened October 20, 1901, with Danville city car 18 making the first trip. Over 2,000 people rode on opening day, even though the transfer at the viaduct was still necessary. Not for long, though. Steel erection began October 25, and was complete November 19. On that day, through Danville-Westville service began. A week later, three double-truck cars bought from the Metropolitan Street Railway of Washington, D.C. arrived, soon replacing the single-truck Danville trolleys. The new cars were numbered 723, 725, and 726 and were painted yellow.

Just before the Westville line was finished, Catlin residents asked that a branch be built to their village. Nothing was done until April 1, 1902, when a gang began erecting poles. By the 15th a large force was grading, and track was laid by month's end. The only opposition was in South Danville, which wanted double track in its village in exchange for a franchise. Instead the company side-stepped the issue, bought about 300 feet of land alongside the street in question, and laid track on its own property.

Car 725 made the first trip on May 25, and on May 29 regular service began on the four miles between Danville and Catlin. So popular was the interurban, that on June 6, the Wabash Railroad discontinued its miners' train since the miners now rode the electric cars.

Georgetown residents had expected that the extension from Westville to their village would be built before the Catlin branch, and when they saw the latter under construction, they decided to form a new company and build the line themselves. They sold $22,000 in stock and by May 10, 1902 had bought most of the right of way. At that point they decided to offer the property and franchises to the DP&N since, after all, none of them had any experience in building or operating an electric line. The offer was accepted and construction began on June 25.

A problem in Westville was the refusal of the Chicago & Eastern Illinois to allow its tracks to be crossed; ironic since the C&EI a few years later was the first steam road to have freight connections with the interurban. On August 5 a Danville car was pulled across the railroad and put on the finished track. By August 15, track was finished to the Georgetown limits, with linemen just a short way behind. A trial run was made to Georgetown August 25, and on the 27th, regular service was started. Danville city car 22 handled Westville to Georgetown service, passengers transferring at the crossing.

However, the dispute was resolved, the crossing was installed, and on September 3 through Danville-Georgetown service began. Half-hour service was provided, and 4,000 patrons rode on opening day. Express service began March 20, 1903, with three daily round trips.

Construction was not complex. The country was fairly level and no heavy cuts or fills were needed. The one deep ravine at the Vermillion River was already bridged at Gilbert Street, so the only sizeable bridge needed spanned the Wabash Railroad in South Danville. Danville-Georgetown was 10.63 miles, Danville-Catlin 6.4 miles. Cars on both lines used the same tracks for a mile to the junction in South Danville. This was the last line built by the DP&N, which on April 24, 1903 was transferred to the Danville Urbana & Champaign Railway under a deed of sale.

MR. MCKINLEY'S RAILROAD…Danville Urbana & Champaign

William B. McKinley was from Champaign, 30 miles west of Danville, and maintained a home there until he died. In 1900, Champaign had 9098 residents and Urbana 5728, plus the nearby University of Illinois had its thousands of students. The Illinois Central and the Peoria & Eastern Railroads had shops in Champaign, and the area between Danville and Urbana was thickly populated. Conditions were right for an interurban between the two towns.

On July 31, 1902, the Danville Urbana & Champaign Railway was incorporated. An Urbana-St. Joseph route was defined, and work began at once. How to get from St. Joseph to Danville, however, was not as clear. One alternative was to extend the Catlin line to Homer, then to Urbana; another was to run west from Danville alongside the Peoria & Eastern Railroad. Since this route was seven miles shorter, it was the winner and an Ogden-Homer branch was built.

Urbana granted the franchise August 11, 1902; by August 20, all right of way to St. Joseph had been acquired. On August 29, grading began. Near the Salt Fork River, just west of St. Joseph, a fill eight feet high and six hundred feet long was under way with 24 teams and scrapers at work. By mid-September over 50 teams and scrapers were at work. Urbana & Champaign

Railway single-truck city cards 16, 31, and 32 were overhauled and repainted to be ready when the line was finished to St. Joseph.

The first rails were laid October 13, at the east end of the Main Street pavement in Urbana. Six days later, at 3:00 a.m., the Wabash crossing in Urbana was put down, with no opposition. On November 2, McKinley took a carload of employees and their families on the 4.9 miles completed to Mayview, and on the seventh, cars 31 & 32 made trial runs to the end of track three miles east of Mayview. On November 9, 1902, the first revenue trip left Urbana with 35 passengers. It ran to the end of track, two miles west of St. Joseph; the round trip took 55 minutes. Two more cars were put into service by noon and 1200 people had ridden by day's end. In addition, there were crowds lining the track.

The Salt Fork bridge was completed by November 12, and the last half-mile into St. Joseph finished November 21. Two days later the overhead was finished and a switch put in at Mayview, and Urbana-St. Joseph service began. Two motors and a trailer were used on opening day, when about 2500 rode. Full service began a few days later when ballasting was finished. Two-hour service began Thanksgiving Day (November 27).

Things were quiet during the winter, but on March 15, 1903, a grading crew began working east from St. Joseph, while another crew cleared brush and trees at Possum Trot, where the line crossed the Vermillion River's Middle Fork, a few miles west of Danville. By month's end two gangs of track layers were working, one toward Danville from the Western Brick Co., the other west. A large force was doing the heavy grading at Possum Trot, and a trestle across the river was about to be started.

On May 3, 1903, cars from St. Joseph began running through Urbana on the street railway track into Champaign, eliminating the transfer and adding 2.3 miles to the route. A steam construction locomotive was put to work east of St. Joseph at this time. The track layers were working about two miles west of Ogden.

The first section at the Danville end was ready May 10, and Danville single- truck car 121 was pulled across the Big Four Railroad bridge with a steam locomotive. At Oakwood Avenue it was transferred to the interurban track. At 6:00 a.m. the next day, service began from the west end of the uncompleted Vermillion River bridge at Ellsworth Park to Vermillion Heights. Passengers to and from Danville city cars crossed on a temporary footbridge.

In August 1903, cars 136 and 137 were delivered to the Danville Urbana & Champaign, the first true interurban cars on the line. One of the two is shown here crossing the Vermillion River at Ellsworth Park in Danville. The date of the photo is unknown, but apparently the car had been repainted Pullman green, which would place the photo sometime after 1907. On November 7, 1903, these cars inaugurated the first "Limited" runs, relegating older cars to local service.

Charles Gammell Collection

Champaign-St. Joseph runs were extended east to Ogden May 10, making a 15.6 mile run, too long for a single-truck car. On May 20, interurban 134 was shipped from Danville to Champaign via the Peoria & Eastern as a replacement. Track was already in for some distance east of Ogden, but at Possum Trot heavy grading on both sides of the trestle was holding back progress.

Service to Fithian, 20 miles from Champaign, began June 21; by July 1, all grading was complete except for Possum Trot. Early in August interurbans 136 and 137 were delivered from the American Car Company in St. Louis. These were the first true interurban cars on the line: combination passenger-baggage cars with railroad roofs and arch windows.

The first Danville-Champaign run was August 29, 1903, but the Fithian substation was incomplete. Regular service began September 6, cars running to Fithian from Champaign and Danville until Fithian substation was complete. At this time a short stub was built on Walnut Street in Champaign to serve as a terminus, going into service September 18.

Fithian substation was finished October 5, and the next day Champaign-Danville service began, with a formal opening two days later in which three cars left Champaign for Danville carrying company officials and dignitaries from the towns on the line.

Danville's elite, too, were treated to a special Danville-St. Joseph run. However, the new interurban cars didn't go into service until November 6 and 7, and then were assigned the Limited runs. Smaller streetcar types were used on locals, and on December 12, express service was begun, using a car newly-built in the Company's shops.

In early May 1904, property was bought in St. Joseph for a station and for lengthening two sharp curves near the town's west end. The first industry served by the new line was a St. Joseph coal yard. Service began September 26. In December the McKinley syndicate bought 13,000 acres of coal land near Danville from the Kelly Coal Company. Most of the coal mined was destined for the powerhouse, but some was retailed to the public. Some 25-ton coal cars were bought and an electric locomotive was being built at Danville.

Grading for the five-mile Homer branch began October 1904. By the end of April 1905, the bridge over Salt Fork was nearly finished. The branch was in service May 25, car 130 (just turned out of the Danville shop) leaving Danville at 6:00 a.m., arriving Ogden at 7:00 a.m. and Homer at 7:30 a.m. Regular service was every two hours initially, but cars were always crowded; in June, service became hourly.

As the Homer line progressed, Ridge Farm residents petitioned the McKinley Syndicate to extend the Georgetown line to that point. The Syndicate had already considered this and in a remarkably short time work was under way, tracklaying starting July 27. On September 28, it was complete except for the Clover Leaf Railroad crossing at Ridge Farm. On September 30, a car was dragged across the Clover Leaf track so the Company could keep its promise to have the line running by October 1.

This attractive brick station was built in Homer, so arranged that cars could be loaded and unloaded under cover. The penny scales, bulletin board, and baggage truck help to add a little atmosphere to this scene, date unknown. Charles Gammell Collection

Early October 1, a crew was on hand to install the crossing, but the railroad had a locomotive blocking it. Since it was on a public street, the locomotive was frequently moved to unblock traffic. A group of residents, anxious to see their interurban completed, drove a wagon onto the track as the locomotive cleared the crossing, defying the enginemen to bother them. That took care of the problem, the crossing went in quickly, and by 11:00 a.m. the first car crossed the railroad.

The crossing of the Vermillion River at Danville is shown here in 1929.   Illinois Traction, Dale Jenkins Collection

Regular service began immediately, with a small Danville car running Georgetown-Ridge Farm while ballasting was completed. On December 31, 1905, through Danville-Ridge Farm operations began.

With this line, the Danville Urbana & Champaign reached its peak, with a 33.7 mile Danville-Champaign main line, a 5.5 mile Ogden-Homer branch, a 16.23 mile Danville-Ridge Farm branch, and a 5.40 mile Danville-Catlin branch. The main line left Danville, dropping sharply into the Vermillion River Valley, and after crossing the river climbed out of the valley and continued west along the Peoria & Eastern Railway for several miles. At Possum Trot the line dropped sharply into the Middle Fork Valley and returned sharply to high ground. These deep ravines were trouble spots throughout the line's life. West of Possum Trot was level ground with slight grades at Stone Creek (west of Bronson) and at Salt Fork (west of St. Joseph). Street trackage was used in Danville, St. Joseph, Urbana, and Champaign; the rest of the line was on private right-of-way.

Except for the Little Vermillion Bridge near Georgetown, the Ridge Farm line was mostly level. So were the Catlin and Homer lines (except for slight grades on the Homer branch at Salt Fork Bridge). Street track was used in Westville, Georgetown, Ridge Farm, Tilton and Catlin. Otherwise these branch lines were side-of-road with little private right of way. The Homer branch ran on the east side of the road, but on Company land.

ON TO ST. LOUIS....St. Louis & Springfield Railway

Originally known as the Decatur Springfield & St. Louis Railway, this company was incorporated May 28, 1903 to build from Decatur to St. Louis. Almost its first move was to buy a nearly-complete roadbed east of Springfield (between Riverton and Niantic) from the Everett-Moore syndicate, which had run out of cash.

In June, the DS&STL acquired the Decatur Street Railway & Light Company, thus assuring access into Decatur. Grading between Springfield and Riverton began in July; by early September four miles of grade were finished and crews were working on a heavy fill west of the Sangamon River, with the Riverton Bridge a-building. Two miles of track were laid by October 15, but on November 30, construction ceased for the winter.

Clearly the McKinley Syndicate had had second thoughts about funding the entire Decatur-St. Louis project through just one company. The new Illinois Central Traction Company therefore took over the Springfield-Decatur section December 10, (the same day on which it was incorporated for that very

An early view of the Decatur Electric Railway Company at Water and Condit Streets. The Decatur Springfield & St. Louis acquired the Decatur Electric in June of 1903.
Illinois Traction, Dale Jenkins Collection

Another view of Decatur shows an interurban car closely following a city car on Main Street. Date unknown.
Illinois Traction, Dale Jenkins Collection

purpose), while the truncated Decatur Springfield & St. Louis continued south of Springfield. To better reflect this state of affairs, the company's name was changed on December 28, 1903, to the St. Louis & Springfield.

South of Springfield, the original survey contemplated a line via Bunker Hill, not Staunton, but the Staunton route was decided upon when farmers on the proposed Bunker Hill line began asking $999 an acre. It was evidently decided to concentrate on the Springfield-Staunton section first, and leave Staunton-Granite City for later, since grading on that section did not begin until September 1904. Even at that late date surveys were still being made between Edwardsville and Granite City. Clearly this part of the line was another candidate for splitting off into a separate company, an act accomplished on December 22, 1904, when the St. Louis & North Eastern was established for the purpose.

The St. Louis & Springfield was now left with the Springfield-Staunton route.

Grading had begun June 8, 1903, (under the Decatur Springfield & St. Louis banner) in southwest Springfield and about 25 miles was finished September 7. Late in February 1904, agreement was reached with the Springfield Consolidated Railway for use of its Springfield tracks. A downtown office and station were established at 520 East Monroe Street shortly thereafter. By April 15, grading and bridges to Auburn (by-passed when a franchise to run through was refused) were finished and track nearly so. On June 5, regular Springfield-Auburn service began with two-hour service using newly-delivered cars 200-203.

Crews pushed on through Virden and Nilwood, reaching the latter July 25, not without opposition at the Virden crossing of the Jacksonville & St. Louis Railroad. Although a locomotive blocked the crossing, it had to be moved periodically to clear the street. On one such movement, interurban crews piled ties under the locomotive and tender, immobilized it and installed the crossing, to the glee of several hundred villagers. Similar problems were encountered with the Chicago & Alton Railroad at North Carlinville, but were not so easily resolved. In fact, it took 18 months to gain entry to Carlinville. In the meantime, service began September 18 as far as a wye at North Carlinville. Tracks, however, were complete within Carlinville itself before construction shut down for the winter.

In order to hold its franchise in Carlinville, the company had to operate on the city track by May 31, 1905. With the crossing problem still unresolved, a car was hired from the Springfield Consolidated Railway, pulled across the Chicago & Alton tracks and on that last day of May put into service within Carlinville, as far as the crossing site. Passengers walked across the railroad to board the Springfield car.

Other crossing problems proved more amenable to reason, and tracks were virtually complete by August. On August 13, the construction locomotive pulled several flat cars loaded with 400 Gillespie residents down to Staunton and back. The last rail was laid on September 3, and another excursion was made September 4 when the construction locomotive hauled 300 riders to Carlinville. The overhead was finished shortly after and on September 24, a Springfield car took a Carlinville group to a Gillespie baseball game.

Only the Chicago & Alton gap remained to be closed, and in the meantime several interurban cars were dragged across the gap to start Carlinville-Gillespie services September 30. The small Springfield car continued to shuttle from Carlinville Station north to the disputed crossing. Meanwhile, the company decided to deal with the problem by building an underpass; Surprisingly, the Chicago & Alton didn't care for that approach either, at one point dumping 16 carloads of dirt into one of the cuts.

It was surprising because at the very same time the C&A, building a Springfield- Murrayville line, needed to cross the St. Louis & Springfield by means of a viaduct at Iles. The situation quickly resolved itself. No underpass? Very well, no viaduct. The C&A quickly capitulated and both projects were completed without further hindrance.

The St. Louis & Springfield was now free to put in a temporary Carlinville crossing of the C&A at grade, so that interurban cars could be moved between the northern and southern sections. On November 20, two-hour service began from Carlinville to Staunton. By February 9, 1906, a work train made the first traverse of the new underpass, a wye was installed at Carlinville Station February 14, and the same day cars began to run through from Springfield. Two days later, full Springfield- Staunton service began.

Meanwhile the St. Louis & North Eastern had been building north from Granite City to Staunton and a connection with the St. Louis & Springfield. Except for a grade crossing problem over the Wabash Railroad at Worden, they, too, were in operation by this time. Again the crossing isssue was settled by building an underpass; with that complete on March 13, 1906, through Springfield-Granite City service awaited only completion of ballasting.

Office car 233 passes Wall Siding, near Staunton, in this December 1, 1910, view. The city can be seen in the background. Note the unusual semaphore switch target to the left of the car, and the white painted pole in the foreground, which signaled an approaching switch during times of reduced visibility.
Illinois Traction, John Hubbard Collection

On March 16, several officials made a trip over the line, finding it ready throughout, except for ballasting. New cars had been bought, some to be used in *Corn Belt* limited service. *Missouri* was one such car, and on May 22 it made a trial Granite City-Springfield run in 3 hours 23 minutes, losing 13 minutes to delays and taking 50 minutes to traverse a still-unballasted section between Staunton and Carlinville.

The *Corn Belt Limited* trains made their first runs June 4, 1906, connecting at Granite City with Terminal Railroad Association (TRRA) suburban trains for St. Louis.

This was a fairly easy connection to make; the Granite City interurban station was adjacent to the TRRA station on Neidringhaus Avenue. On August 11, the *Corn Belt Limited* schedule was cut to three hours even, in each direction. A new station was opened at Monroe and Eighth Streets, Springfield (replacing the old), while on November 1, the twice-daily *Limited* runs were increased to four daily in each direction.

Leaving Springfield, St. Louis & Springfield cars used street railway tracks to Spring and Cedar, continuing on ITS track along Spring to Laurel and Walnut and then onto ITS right of way. It was level ground for some miles, but at Lick Creek there was heavy grading, before reaching more level ground south to Carlinville. There were many coal mines en route, mostly served by the Chicago & Alton, but the interurban also built up a large ridership of commuting miners.

Just south of Carlinville, the line dropped into Goat Hollow (so named after a work train was derailed by a herd of goats) where heavy grades and curves were encountered. Upon reaching high ground again, the way was level until the Cahokia Creek Valley was reached just north of Staunton. Track was on company right of way throughout, except for street running in Virden, Girard, Nilwood and Carlinville. The three smaller towns had less than 3000 people each in 1900, while Carlinville had less than 5000. All were coal mining communities, though Carlinville was also home to Blackburn College.

CREATING A TRACTION HUB....Illinois Central Traction

It would seem logical that, with the completion of the Danville Urbana & Champaign, the next step would have been a Champaign-Decatur line. But when the McKinley Syndicate opted to move its construction headquarters to Springfield, it shifted its focus to lines radiating from Springfield, and the Danville-Champaign line remained an isolated segment for some time. The Decatur Springfield & St. Louis was the big project of 1903; the size of the intermediate cities, together with their future prospects, made good fiscal sense. When the project was carved up, and the Illinois Central Traction was formed on December 10, 1903, the Springfield-Decatur segment was also logical.

In addition to being the Illinois capital, Springfield in 1900 had a population of 34,159 and was a coal mining and industrial center. The Chicago & Alton, Illinois Central, Cincinnati Hamilton & Dayton, the Wabash, and the Chicago, Peoria & St. Louis all served the city. Decatur had a population of 20,754 and was a manufacturing and grain processing center, served by the Illinois Central, Wabash, Cincinnati Hamilton & Dayton and Vandalia railroads. Between the two cities were several rural towns and some of the finest farming lands in the Midwest, plus some coal deposits.

Car 202, just in from Mechanicsburg, waits at Mechanicsburg Junction for a car on the Springfield-to-Danville run in this early-day view.
Harry Hagaman Collection

Once Illinois Central Traction took over the existing project from the Decatur Springfield & St. Louis (and winter ended) work resumed. A signal system was installed on this line, with semaphores at Starnes, Hessar, Cantrall, Pinson and Wycles. It was arranged so a dispatcher could set the semaphore at stop: when the car reached the signal the motorman could plug in a telephone and talk directly to the dispatcher. On May 18, 1904, car 203 made a trial run from East Springfield to the west end of the Sangamon River bridge. On May 22, regular service to that point began from the Springfield Consolidated Railway connection in East Springfield; some 3700 rode that day.

The Springfield franchise was awarded June 15, giving trackage rights to Illinois Central Traction over the Springfield Consolidated Railway, but the Illinois Central Railroad protested the interurban installing a crossing on Capitol Avenue to connect with the streetcar tracks. At 1:00 a.m. on June 26, fifty men assembled at the Monroe Street car barn and were taken to the site of the crossing. A few men distracted a watchman long enough to keep him from reaching a phone, while the rest of the crew laid the crossing. As soon as the crossing was in, a car was run across and the affair legalized. From that day, interurbans ran through to the Company offices on Monroe Street and looped around the square in downtown Springfield.

The first car crossed the Sangamon River bridge at 2:00 p.m. on July 10, and on August 27 the line was complete as far as Dawson, the first car arriving there at 9:00 a.m.

Passenger-baggage combines 250-257 were delivered August 31; one was sent to Danville, while the remainder stayed on this segment, the first car running to Illiopolis the next day with regular service beginning September 3. There was no wye at Illiopolis, so front trolley poles had to be installed so the cars could back up. On Labor Day, September 5, it took all seven cars to handle the crowds.

At 4:00 p.m. September 17, 1904, car 250 arrived in Decatur, the first to operate through from Springfield. It had been a slow trip, since the track was still only partially ballasted. Upon arrival at Decatur, the McKinley Syndicate party on board the car went to the St. Nicholas Hotel for a celebration. The car in the meantime was opened to the public and 700 walked through. Doubtless they were impressed, for the red and yellow 28-tonner had leather upholstered seats, rather than the cane seats of earlier cars, and could hit speeds of 65 m.p.h.

It was hoped that regular hourly service would start the next day, but 3.5 inches of rain fell and service was postponed so the line could be spruced up in time for the State Fair. Regular service began September 25th, with five cars in operation.

Springfield to Decatur was 2 1/2 hours, with meets at Riverton, Long Point, and Harristown. By September 28, hourly service between the two towns was established. The Decatur ticket office and waiting room was in the Transfer House, downtown. Express cars were put into service about January 15, 1905, but packages had already been handled for some time before this, using the baggage compartment of the passenger cars.

Some 3.5 miles south of the main line was the farming town of Mechanicsburg. When the Wabash Railroad was built, the town had been missed, and in 1882, A. T. Thompson headed a group which built the Mechanicsburg & Buffalo Railroad, a horse line with one car, half of which was for passengers, the other half an open freight platform. It came directly south from Buffalo, then east into Mechanicsburg.

When the Illinois Central Traction was built, McKinley was approached by Mechanicsburg residents anxious for a connection. Agreement was quickly reached; grading began in May of 1905; on August 9, the first cars ran from the Junction to the Chautauqua Grounds at Clear Creek, with regular service following September 16. Seven days later, service reached downtown Mechanicsburg. A one-car shuttle was used, meeting the main line cars at the Junction.

Illinois Central Traction was 39 miles long. It used Springfield Consolidated Railway track to reach its own tracks at Capitol and Twentieth, then headed north and northeast to Starne, then east to the Sangamon Valley. Here were steep grades on both sides of the river, after which was flat land through to Decatur, except for heavy grades at Stevens Creek, just west of town. The line was on private right-of-way except in Riverton, Buffalo, and Illiopolis, where street running was required. The Mechanicsburg Branch, too, was on company right-of-way, except for Main Street in Mechanicsburg. Its only grade was at Clear Creek.

St. Louis & North Eastern Railway

This McKinley Syndicate Company was incorporated on December 22, 1904, to take over from the St. Louis & Springfield the construction of the

Just south of Worden, the St. Louis & North Eastern crossed a county highway directly under the Big Four Railroad (New York Central) line from St. Louis to Indianapolis. By the time this photo was taken, on March 20, 1957, the arch had changed somewhat in appearance, but the essence of this curious crossing was still very much intact.   Paul H. Stringham

Granite City-Staunton section. By March 1, 1905, grading was ready for the track and on March 20, a switch was laid from the Litchfield & Madison into Hillsborough Road in Edwardsville. Two days later the Company signed an agreement with the Madison County Highway Commissioners under which the Company paid $3250 for the right to use the arch under the Big Four Railroad near Worden. Since the track would cross the highway inside the arch, making a totally blind crossing, each car would be required to stop before entering the arch.

On April 7, a free-for-all took place near the Court House in Edwardsville, when an attempt was made to put in a crossing with the Alton Granite & St. Louis Traction. A squad of police had to be called to end the fight, and City authorities closed down the work. It took three days for a truce to be arranged and track crews gotten back to work. By mid-month, track was down from Edwardsville almost to Worden. South of Edwardsville, there were grading crews almost every mile. There was a one-mile stretch on that section in which 90,000 yards of dirt had to be moved.

Two trainloads of merrymakers pause for their pictures in Granite City, probably en route to Center Grove Park, near Edwardsville, from St. Louis. The date of the photo is unknown, sometime after 1910. Several parks were located along the line before paved highways became common.
George Hadaller Collection

By May 1, track was complete to Staunton, except for a short stretch at the Wabash Railroad underpass just north of town. South of Edwardsville was a seventeen-foot fill which continued to impede progress until September; and track laying in Granite City didn't begin until June 28. East St. Louis at this time refused Illinois Traction System the franchise it wanted. So did the Terminal Railroad Association of St. Louis, who had been approached for trackage rights over their Merchants' Bridge into St. Louis. Since Granite City officials took the opposite view, offering the Company use of their streets, the planned route on the East Side was modified. Now it would go through Granite City and East St. Louis to cross the Mississippi on the Terminal Railroad's Eads Bridge, and gain access to St. Louis in that manner.

A feature of the line which brought much passenger business for years was Center Grove Park, south of Edwardsville. Construction of the park began early in September 1905, and by October 31, the track from Granite City to Edwardsville, and from Edwardsville to Staunton (with the exception of the Wabash crossing at Worden) was complete. The Worden problem was solved by building an underpass. The first car ran into downtown Edwardsville on December 29, 1905; two days later regular Edwardsville-Worden service began, connecting there with Worden-Staunton cars, pending completion of the underpass.

On January 5, 1906, officials learned that the Big Four Railroad planned to tear up track and wire at the underpass. The reason is not known, since it had been there for over two years and did not in any way interfere with railroad operations.

Superintendent B. D. Smith ordered the power lines loaded to the limit, 33,000 volts was sent out over the high tension line and the Big Four management warned. A railroad crew showed up anyway, but after listening to the hum of 33,000 volts, retreated without controversy. Nine days later they returned and tore up 300 feet of track, cutting several wires also, but that damage was restored the same afternoon.

Edwardsville-Granite City service was inaugurated at 2:20 p.m. on January 29, 1906, when two cars set out, loaded with Company brass and civic dignitaries from towns en route. At 19th and D Streets, Granite City, the guests got off and were taken to Lauff's Hotel where a light lunch was served before they returned to Edwardsville at 4:30 PM. Regular service began February 2. Granite City-Springfield service began on February 16, with passengers transferring at the Worden underpass. The first through car operated on March 13, and through service was initiated by June, featuring *Corn Belt Limited* service, already discussed in the St. Louis & Springfield Railway section.

With East St. Louis still adamant in its refusal to allow the McKinley lines their own tracks in the City, alternative arrangements were made to get cars into the city.

These were completed by mid-October, 1906, when trackage rights were granted over the almost-complete line of the Alton Granite & St. Louis Traction Company, from Granite City (Neidringhaus and Madison Avenues) to East St. Louis. That line, after a few blocks of street running, used private right-of-way along the east side of Madison and Venice and entered East St. Louis at Willows Viaduct at the north edge of town. A short distance beyond the viaduct, street trackage was used to reach Third and Broadway in downtown East St. Louis, next to the new station of the Alton Granite & St. Louis Traction.

However, gaining access to St. Louis remained problematic. In addition to the continued hostility of the East St. Louis authorities (before even getting within sight of the Mississippi River) there was the formidable barrier of the River itself to hurdle. The Eads Bridge and downtown St. Louis weren't far away from the Alton Granite & St. Louis Traction's East St. Louis station, but the Terminal Railroad (TRRA) objected to what it felt were overweight interurban cars running on its bridge.

This objection was never lifted; for four years St. Louis-bound passengers had to transfer to East St. Louis cars which could cross the Eads bridge.

Operation into East St. Louis had been further blocked for some time by the Louisville & Nashville Railroad, which refused a crossing at Seventh and Bowman Streets.

Finally, after a favorable ruling was handed down by the courts, a crossing was installed and on November 14, 1906, the first cars ran downtown. A reverse curve at Seventh, St. Clair, and Collinsville Avenue was excessively sharp and had to be relaid. Thus, only on November 16 did the first car actually make it to the Third and Broadway (passenger) Station in East St. Louis. A McKinley System freight house was opened in a former East St. Louis Railway carbarn near Collinsville and St. Clair Avenues.

After a year or so, the access route to East St. Louis was changed when on December 29, 1907, all McKinley cars, and Limited cars of the Alton Line began to use a new south approach to Willows Viaduct, which led down onto Lynch Street, Thirteenth, and St. Clair, before rejoining the old route.

Leaving Staunton, the St. Louis & North Eastern was level (except for the Worden underpass) to Edwardsville, where north and south of the town heavy grading was needed. Once down from the bluffs south of Edwardsville, the line was level into East St. Louis, except for the Willows Viaduct ramps. There was street running in Staunton, Edwardsville, Granite City and East St. Louis, but otherwise the line was all on private right-of-way.

Construction proceeded on the Staunton-Hillsboro section all through 1905; Staunton to Litchfield was opened by November 29, 1905. The remainder should have been complete by the end of the year, but malfunctioning track-laying machinery and cloudburst-induced track washouts combined to delay the opening until the spring of 1906. A trial run was made May 23, and on June 4, 1906 — the same day the *Corn Belt Limited* began through service to Springfield — the full Hillsboro branch opened, originally running through to Granite City.

The Hillsboro courthouse loop was completed on January 25, 1907, and a crossing at Litchfield on February 16, allowing cars to run around Library Square. At the same time, runs were cut back from Granite City to operate Hillsboro-Staunton only, passengers transferring there to main line cars. From Staunton to Litchfield, the line was level, but beyond

IN THE BEGINNING • 23

and into Hillsboro the country was rough, with high fills and deep cuts needed. In Staunton, Mt. Olive, Litchfield and Hillsboro, street running was required; otherwise, private right-of-way was used.

Springfield and North Eastern Traction

Although the McKinley Syndicate intended to build north from Springfield to Lincoln, they were outfoxed by the Springfield, Lincoln, Bloomington, Pekin & Peoria Electric Railway when that body was incorporated March 7, 1904. However, although the SLBP&PE moved quickly to survey and begin grading, (changing its name on December 23, 1904 to the Springfield & North Eastern Railroad), progress began to bog down for lack of money; it wasn't until September of 1905 that even the Springfield-Lincoln grading appeared close to completion. Then, on September 10, 1905, the L. E. Myers Construction Company shut down the whole project for lack of cash.

Some behind-the-scenes activity ensued; on February 15, 1906, the McKinley Syndicate acquired the property and franchises of the S&NE, reorganizing it on April 28 as the Springfield & North Eastern Traction. Grading resumed in May of 1906, with crews working north from Springfield and south from Lincoln. The first tracks were laid later that month.

By the end of August, the line was virtually complete at both the Lincoln and Springfield ends. Then there was a slight change of plan. At that time, track was complete to Springfield's Sangamon Avenue, but was never extended beyond that point since the Chicago Peoria & St. Louis Railroad refused permission to cross its line. Instead, McKinley decided to build a belt line, leading the main line at Ridgeley Junction, running due south to Starne, where it joined the Springfield-Decatur line.

At Starne, the Wabash and the Illinois Central caused some delay, but as the interurban would cross both lines at an already established interlocking plant, permission was granted. This new section of line, therefore, (not requiring heavy grading) went in rapidly and on December 13 track was completed to Starne. Thus, what was to have been a belt line became instead the main line, while the intended main line to Sangamon Avenue was leased to the Springfield Consolidated Railway for their Smelter route.

The first car left Springfield for the Illinois Central crossing just south of Lincoln about 5:00 p.m. on December 14, 1906, and regular service began next day with a car every two hours. However, the Illinois Central continued to obstruct entry into Lincoln until January 1907 and Lincoln itself did not grant a franchise until April 1. As a result, the first car into downtown Lincoln did not arrive from Springfield until 8:19 p.m. on October 21, the same day the carbarn was put into service. On January 1, 1908, the Company opened a ticket office in Alvey's Drug Store at Broadway and Chicago Streets in Lincoln.

The Springfield & North Eastern was one of the McKinley Syndicate's alternating current lines, but was not operated as such until August 13, 1907, when the four cars assigned for the line were ready. Almost all the line was on level ground except for a short stretch of rough country at the Sangamon River, a slight climb over "Mt. Fulcher" (a twenty-foot high ridge near Elkhart), and at Salt Creek just south of Lincoln. The line was on private right-of-way except for street running in Springfield, Williamsville, Elkhart, Broadwell and Lincoln. Springfield and Lincoln, the latter with a population of about 10,000, were the only two towns of any size on the line.

Chicago Bloomington & Decatur

This optimistically-named operation, incorporated April 19, 1905, was in fact assigned the Decatur-Bloomington segment, ground being broken in Clinton on June 10. By October 10, track gangs were working between Decatur and Forsythe, between Forsythe and Emery and between Emery and Maroa. A connection with the Decatur city car tracks was made October 16, and a trial run to Forsythe was made with Decatur car 42 on October 29.

Regular two-hourly service began November 1.

Heavy grading near Salt Creek and the Vandalia Railroad underpass at Maroa slowed completion of the remainder, and it wasn't until December 31, 1905 that car 150 made the first Decatur-Clinton run; even then, ballasting was not complete. Clinton didn't care though; its citizenry was out en masse, cannons were fired, and a big celebration was held.

Regular service to Clinton (population 5,000) began January 4, 1906, while the track layers advanced north from Clinton and south from Bloomington. With the Kickapoo Creek bridge finished on July 3, the first car ran from Bloomington (population 25,768) to Clinton, with regular service starting the next day. Passengers had to transfer at the Illinois Central Railroad in Clinton, until an interurban crossing was completed on July 15. The Bloomington loop, from Madison via Monroe, Center, and Jefferson was complete July 21; on July 27, a party of Company officials made the first through run from Springfield to Decatur and Bloomington on car 230. Regular service began August 1.

A 15-car Plasterer's Union special tours the line north of Decatur, circa 1910.
Illinois Traction, John Hubbard Collection

From Decatur to Salt Creek, the line was level, but a steep descent into and ascent out of Salt Creek Valley was needed, and at the south edge of Clinton was another dip, where the line made three crossings of Coon Creek and went under the Illinois Central.

North of Heyworth, the line dipped into the Kickapoo Creek Valley, but was then nearly level into Bloomington. The line was on private right-of-way, except for street running in Decatur, Forsythe, Maroa, Clinton, Heyworth and Bloomington.

Peoria Bloomington & Champaign Traction

Incorporated April 19, 1905, this was an extension of the Decatur-Bloomington project to Peoria. However, not until January 1, 1906, when the McKinley Syndicate bought the Central Railway Company of Peoria, did the Company have any practical means of getting to the city's heart.

Grading began in East Peoria on March 8, construction of the Illinois River Bridge on April 25, and by mid-May four crews were working between Peoria and Morton. This was very rough country, where the line climbed out of the Illinois River Valley. A 32-foot deep cut and a 52-foot high fill were needed, along with numerous other heavy cuts and fills, and a concrete arch was needed to span one 65-foot-deep ravine.

By June 1, over 230 teams were working on the grading between Peoria and Bloomington and progress was steady through the remainder of the year. On December 28, a work car made the first run from

The first interurban in regular service to East Peoria pauses at Morton on April 13, 1907. W.C. Janssen Collection

Bloomington to Danvers and regular two-hour service began January 6, 1907, using Bloomington double-truck city car 52.

On April 6, 1907, the first of 10 a.c.-d.c. cars (numbered 350-359) arrived from the American Car Company in St. Louis. The first run with one of these new cars was on April 12, from Bloomington to within 400 feet of the Farm Creek Bridge in East Peoria.

Regular service to the east end of the bridge began next day. Two days later an electric locomotive got into East Peoria and on April 16, it was the first piece of equipment across the Illinois River Bridge and into downtown Peoria, where it was inspected by hundreds.

The bridge was a classy affair, with four through truss spans each 142 feet 10 inches long, and a bascule span 141 feet long. Piers 1 and 6 were on pilings driven to bedrock; other piers rested on bed rock. West of the river were several through girder spans carrying the line over the railroads and Water Street. West of Water Street were short deck girder spans. Peoria's big day was April 20, when at 2:10 p.m., the first passenger car crossed the bridge to be displayed downtown. Next day regular service began.

This was built as an a.c. line. Power was generated at Peoria powerhouse at 2300 volts, stepped up to 33,000 volts and fed to the transmission line. At substations it was reduced to 3,300 volts and fed to the trolley wire. Each car was equipped with a transformer, bringing the voltage down to 250, with a compensator tap changer for starting.

As we've already seen, the Springfield & North Eastern became an a.c. line August 13, and when the Peoria Lincoln & Springfield was opened a little later, it too was an a.c. operation; indeed for a short time all lines from Peoria to Bloomington and Springfield were a.c. However, a.c. was not the success anticipated; on July 8, 1909, all a.c. lines were switched to normal d.c. traction current.

Leaving Bloomington, cars used the Bloomington & Normal street railway track to the west edge of town, where they gained their own tracks. It was rolling country to Danvers, where the terrain leveled off. West of Danvers was a long up-and-down grade at the west branch of Sugar Creek, after which the country was level almost to Mackinaw. On each side of the Mackinaw River, some heavy grading was encountered, but from Allentown west the line was level, with many long curves to keep atop a ridge. A few miles west of Morton, the line descended the bluffs using high fills and deep cuts until it reached level ground in the Illinois River Valley.

Peoria, with a 1900 population of 66,950, had distilleries and breweries, agricultural machinery manufacturers, grain elevators and the Toledo Peoria & Western Railroad's shops. Bloomington, whose 1900 population was 25,768, was a college town with many industries and the Chicago & Alton Railroad's shops. Morton, Mackinaw and Danvers were farming villages.

St. Louis Decatur & Champaign Railway

Incorporated by the McKinley Syndicate April 25, 1906, this line would connect the isolated Danville Urbana & Champaign with the rest of the system. Grading began on May 15, and after some months of hassle, the Decatur City Council issued a franchise in mid-June, assuring an entry from the east. Until that was done, there was a chance the line would have to be built west from Champaign to Clinton to connect with the Chicago Bloomington & Decatur, and then enter Decatur from the north, a much longer route.

On January 31, 1907, Danville Urbana & Champaign Railway single-truck car 42 made the first run from Champaign to Seymour, and regular service began later that day. On February 11, interurban car 142 was brought from Danville and runs were extended to White Heath. Ten days later, operations were extended to Monticello from Champaign, although a shortage of power required use of a single-truck car from Whiteheath to Monticello.

On June 2, the first car ran from Monticello to Bement, while regular service began a few days later. On June 14, a portable substation was moved into Bement to correct some of the power shortages. The next day ITS General Manager L. E. Fischer left Champaign in his private car to make a through run to Decatur. Regular service began June 16 when car 306 left the transfer house at Decatur. Since the Bement viaduct was not quite finished, passengers transferred there for a few days.

Express service between Decatur and Danville began September 18, the Garfield Avenue belt line was under construction, together with several of the substations, and ballasting was being completed. By January 1, 1908, all was sufficiently in order to begin through Springfield-Danville runs; on that day car 238 made the first eastbound run and 239 the first westbound.

Cars leaving Champaign used the local street railway tracks to the west edge of town, then their own tracks on level ground to Camp Creek (just west of White Heath) where some heavy grading was needed. West of Monticello, the line was level, with a hump

Locomotive 102 working the Heyworth gravel pit, probably in 1907 or 1908 as the Peoria and Mackinaw Junction-Lincoln lines were being completed. The 102 later became the 1559. In the background stretches a line of wooden gondola cars. Dale Jenkins Collection

over the Wabash Railroad in Bement. Beyond that point, the land was level again to the Sangamon River. Heavy grading was needed at that point, and then the grade leveled off again all the way to Decatur. Entering Decatur, the cars used local street railway tracks to enter downtown.

The line was on private right-of-way, except for street running in Decatur, Oakley, Cerro Gordo, Milmine, Monticello and Champaign. Decatur in 1910 had a population of 31,140, Champaign, 12,421, and Monticello, 1,981. All the other towns on the route were small farming communities.

Peoria Lincoln & Springfield Traction

Before the Peoria Bloomington & Champaign Traction project was complete, the McKinley Syndicate announced it would build a line from near Mackinaw to Lincoln, closing the gap separating Peoria from Springfield and giving Peoria a direct route to St. Louis, via Lincoln, Springfield and Staunton.

William Evans of Lincoln, a large landowner, was anxious to have an interurban line through his property. In mid-February 1907, he guaranteed the Syndicate a long stretch of right-of-way across his land free of charge, and across the land of other owners who wanted the interurban as badly as he. That was an offer that couldn't be refused.

On March 26, surveys began, some weeks before the April 18 incorporation of the Company.

Grading was begun soon after and was finished by July 1; later in July, track laying began. In Lincoln, the Company ran into grade crossing problems when the Illinois Central and Chicago & Alton Railroads refused to let crossings be installed.

The City of Lincoln had given a franchise for tracks on Davenport and Logan Streets, and the Lincoln Street Railway already had a track on Davenport Street which crossed the Chicago & Alton. This company allowed the interurban trackage rights over the crossing, the Illinois Central reluctantly agreed to a Logan Street crossing, and so the problem was at least temporarily solved. At 3:40 p.m., December 31, 1907, the first car from Peoria left Mackinaw Junction, arriving at the site of the Illinois Central Crossing at the north edge of Lincoln about 6:30 p.m. Regular two-hour service began next day, only to be temporarily cut to two cars each way daily for a short period, while workmen applied finishing touches to the tracks.

The original Mackinaw Junction station was built in 1908 in the center of the wye at the junction. In 1909, it was moved to the point where the Springfield and Bloomington lines joined. It was totally destroyed by fire on January 8, 1925, and was replaced by a two-story brick structure. For many years, the dispatcher's offices were on the second floor. W.C. Janssen Collection

On March 18, a work car crossed the Illinois Central tracks at Logan Street; at noon that day, the first passenger car came into the Lincoln ITS station from the north.

Through Peoria-Springfield service was planned for May 3, but incessant spring rains persisted throughout the month, further delaying the opening. Indeed, on June 3, the already-truncated service was further cut to one car a day until ballasting could be finished.

On July 4, an excursion train made the first Peoria-Springfield through run. On July 15, Limited runs were started, with a three-hour-ten-minute timecard. Local service began a few days later. In addition to the Peoria-Springfield service, there were four Limited runs from Springfield to Bloomington via Mackinaw Junction.

The line began at a connection with the Peoria Bloomington & Champaign at Mackinaw Junction at the east end of the Mackinaw River bridge. It made a long curve from east to south, dipped into a cut beneath the Vandalia and Peoria & Eastern Railroads, then made a long climb out of the Mackinaw Valley. After attaining high ground at Summit, some of the fastest track on the whole ITS system was reached. It was mostly level except for the hump just north of Mindale where the Chicago & Alton was crossed.

There was a long downgrade into the Sugar and Kickapoo Creek Valleys, but otherwise the remainder of the route into Lincoln was level. The entire line was on private right-of-way, except for Lincoln street trackage.

St. Louis Electric Terminal Railway

The shortest, most expensive and undoubtedly the most important section of the McKinley system was that from Granite City to downtown St. Louis.

The McKinley lines wanted very much to gain access to St. Louis; for other than Chicago (still out of reach) this was by far the biggest plum within the system's grasp. Nearly 700,000 people lived in St. Louis at that time, with an additional 100,000 in St. Louis County. As the region's main industrial center, it had no peer.

But as we've seen, the ITS was confined to East St. Louis after being denied the use of both the Merchants and Eads bridges by the TRRA.

What to do? Perhaps cars could be ferried across the river to St. Louis. In 1905 and early 1906, such a scheme was seriously considered. The Danville & Edwardsville Terminal Railroad was incorporated by the Syndicate to build a line from the south limits of Madison to the Venice ferry landing, mostly on private right-of-way, a site which would put the road directly opposite St. Louis's Salisbury Street.

A few weeks later, on March 8, 1906, the St. Louis Electric Terminal Railway was incorporated in Missouri to build a line from downtown St. Louis to the river, and then from Venice and Madison to a connection with the St. Louis & North Eastern in Granite City. The question of a river crossing was left open for the moment.

Early in September 1906, construction began on State Street in both Granite City and Madison. By late November, a suburban service was begun from the south limits of Madison to Granite City's business district. On January 3, 1907, the Syndicate bought a line running from the Venice Ferry landing, along Main Street and Broadway Avenue in Venice to Madison Avenue. A short piece of track was then built to connect the State Street track with Broadway. This new purchase was originally built by the Venice Madison & Granite City Railway, and was acquired by Alton Granite & St. Louis Traction on September 8, 1904. This route eliminated any need for the Danville & Edwardsville Terminal Railroad; that Company was then deeded to the St. Louis & North Eastern.

More to the point, the ferry option had been weighed in the balance and found wanting.

Specifically, McKinley could see no way in which it could be profitable, even if it were a temporary situation prior to the opening of a bridge. It was a bridge to which the Syndicate was inclining; on January 4, 1907, the day after buying the Venice ferry landing line, the Syndicate announced that it would escape the "Bridge Arbitrary" (as the TRRA had been dubbed by the St. Louis *Post-Dispatch*) by building its own. McKinley bought 24 acres of land at the foot of Salisbury Street in St. Louis, where the west approach would be built, plus seven acres of land in Venice at the eastern bridge landing.

In the meantime, after just six months of through service to East St. Louis (the line into downtown East St. Louis was opened on November 16, 1906) the Granite City Station was on May 3 put on wheels and pulled by an interurban car from its old location at Neidringhaus and A Streets to a new location at Neidringhaus and 22nd Streets, since the old location would no longer be served.

After a few skirmishes, a crossing of the TRRA was made in Venice May 8, 1907, and a special car chartered from the Alton Granite & St. Louis to take McKinley officials to Collinsville, where an injunction was obtained to keep the TRRA from molesting the crossing. With the crossing completed, the ITS now had a through track from Decatur to the east bank of the Mississippi River. The first express car from Springfield arrived in Granite City on May 7, and was the first revenue car to use the crossing. A few hours later regular passenger service began. Local cars ran from the Venice ferry landing to the Granite City business district.

State Street was too narrow for double track, so a franchise to build on paralleling G Street was obtained, and a single track built there for northbound cars. G Street was not then continuous; some parcels of land had to be acquired. A related piece of work was the building in mid-July of a loop track to connect with the State Street track in Granite City. It continued along State Street to 23rd, to A Street, then back on A Street to a connection with the old track on Neidringhaus, which completed the loop.

In July, plans for the McKinley Bridge across the Mississippi river were approved by the U.S. Government. Preliminary work began on August 22, 1907. It was to take three years. The bridge was to be 8000 feet long, including a 2700-foot approach at the west end. There would be three through truss spans, the center 523 feet long, the others 521 feet long.

Two 150 feet deck truss spans approached the west shore and one 150 feet long deck span approached the east shore. Structural steel elevated approaches spanned several railroad tracks and some low-lying ground. The bridge deck width was 65 feet, with a

The McKinley Bridge, as viewed from the south side, looking east. It had a heavier carrying capacity than any other Mississippi bridge at the time it was built. It was completed in September 1910.   Illinois Traction, Dale Jenkins Collection

double-track interurban line between the girders of the through spans and a one-lane roadway outside the girders on each side. Carrying capacity was 12,000 pounds per lineal foot, heavier than any other Mississippi bridge at that time, and the cost was $4,500,000.

On the Missouri side, work did not begin on the St. Louis street trackage until June 9, 1909, concurrent with work on the Granite City freight belt line, and on G Street in Granite City. Most of that year and much of next was taken up with constructing the other facilities needed, such as freight houses and yards, and some $200,000 was spent on ancillary facilities. An ice gorge wrecked 300 feet of falsework under the bridge January 10, 1910, throwing 69 men into the river (all of whom were saved), causing a quarter-million dollars in damage and setting back completion several months.

The franchise from St. Louis allowed the Company until September 30, 1910 to have the line running. A franchise run (completed by having a construction locomotive tow interurban 221 over the bridge) was made at 2:25 p.m. on September 21. At Broadway Station, the locomotive came off, the pole went up and the car continued on to Twelfth and Lucas. The first car across the bridge and into St. Louis wholly under electric power was office car 233, which made the run September 30.

The next day, the St. Louis to Granite City bridge cars began their regular runs without ceremony. There were 20 motors (900-919) and ten trailers (950-959) used for the service, and two days later they were joined by interurban cars. For that week only, some runs continued to East St. Louis, but on October 10, all interurban service was switched to the McKinley Bridge. A huge opening celebration was slated for November 10, and on the due date it all passed off

Another view of the McKinley Bridge looking east, this time from trackside.
Illinois Traction, Dale Jenkins Collection

without a hitch, the papers full of news and happy editorials about the new age dawning with the coming of the electric railroads. President Taft was invited, but declined; otherwise there was a full complement of Illinois and Missouri dignitaries, from the respective governors down to McKinley System officials. The bridge was blessed by Archbishop (later Cardinal) John Glennon. Julia Mattis of Champaign (McKinley's niece), escorted to the middle of the bridge by the two Governors, then raised the U.S. flag to the bridge's highest pinnacle, to the accompaniment of the Star-Spangled-Banner. Following that, there was a banquet for 700 at the Planters' Hotel in St. Louis and a good many speeches.

Late in November, the freight and express building in St. Louis was opened. On December 14, the Madison County Ferry between Venice and St. Louis was discontinued, its traffic now crossing overhead on the bridge. The ITS yard under the west approach was not opened until March 20, 1911, but it was a huge affair, able to hold 100 cars.

Southbound cars used State Street through Granite City and Madison. Northbound cars used G Street. Just inside Venice, southbound cars curved onto Broadway Avenue to Main Street, curved left a short distance, then climbed a steep ramp onto the bridge.

West of the bridge, the tracks used Ninth Street, a short stretch of private right-of-way, and then Twelfth Street to the terminal at Lucas. At the station was a large loop with six stub tracks and two through storage tracks within the loop. East of the loop were three stub-end tracks to serve the freight house.

At this time, the population of St. Louis was 687,000; Granite City, 9,903; Madison, 5,096; and Venice, 3,718. The whole area was heavily industrialized.

Passenger Services 1901–1958

As originally planned, the McKinley System was exclusively a passenger carrier, although this narrow view of the interurban's role was quickly modified. For years, however, the principal source of income was passenger operation. With the coming of paved highways, a steady decline set in, which persisted tenaciously until, in the end, the only business left was freight.

During the construction years, passenger service began as soon as a town was reached.

On several segments of line, the first passenger runs were made with borrowed single-truck city cars, which bounced along on unballasted track. Did the riders complain? They did not! In fact, they filled the

This Illinois Traction publicity shot was staged on July 23, 1912, to draw attention to the fast, frequent service. The car is signed as a Decatur-Bloomington Limited; note the marker lamp and flags. The location is Decatur.
Illinois Traction, John Hubbard Collection

Cars 136 and 137 were the first true interurban cars on the system, delivered in 1903. Here, car 137, practically brand new, models the curious two-window front of these cars, resplendent in red and yellow. This scheme did not last long as the colors faded rapidly; Pullman green became standard beginning in 1907.
Charles Gammell Collection

cars to overflowing. The frequent service, as compared to the steam roads, gave passengers the chance to go (when they wanted) to and from a wide variety of destinations. By contrast, the typical steam railroad ran two or three round trips daily--and some of these did not stop at the smaller towns.

Moreover, wagon roads were only of use in getting to and from the nearest town. In summer, they were ankle deep in dust; in wet weather they were bottomless mud holes.

The crude services which opened the McKinley lines did not last long. Initially, a number of double-truck former city cars were modified for interurban service, but it wasn't long before interurban cars were acquired, and the Syndicate turned to long-haul services. By the time the Danville-Champaign line was completed in 1903, the first true interurban cars on the system, Nos. 136 and 137 had arrived, inaugurating the first "Limited" runs on November 7, 1903, and relegating older cars to local service.

In 1904, cars 200-203 arrived, double-end low-floor vehicles more like suburban cars, which were used to open both the Springfield-Riverton and Springfield-Auburn lines.

Soon after, interurbans 250-257 replaced the smaller cars, which then were demoted to suburban and branchline service.

The Staunton-Granite City line opened with Nos. 220-225, double-end low-floor cars, but when the line was opened through from Springfield to Granite City,

226-232 were on hand. These cars, together with all but one of Nos. 250-257, served the Springfield-Granite City and Springfield-Decatur lines. The missing car was sent to Danville for the Champaign run. Until 226-232 were delivered with their fancy plush seats, all cars had rattan seats.

In 1906 the three cars *Missouri, Illinois* and *Indiana* arrived, large 62-foot long interurban cars with a small cafe section. On June 4, 1906 they went into *Corn Belt Limited* service, taking 3½ hours on the Springfield-Granite City run. In August, when the ballasting was more complete, these runs were cut to an even three hours, and on October 31st service was doubled to four daily round trips. However, though the service was immensely popular, cafe service was not; the run was too short to be profitable. In fall 1906, the ITS bought two sleeping cars from the Holland Palace Car Company of Indianapolis. Built by the Harlan & Hollingsworth Company, they could be used as either parlor or sleeping cars. Several Indiana interurban companies had tried them without positive results. Immediately after the cars arrived on the ITS, they were taken to the Bloomington shop to be rebuilt,

One of the two Holland Palace Car sleepers is seen in this view, circa 1908, to the right of the downtown station on Monroe Street, near Ninth, in Springfield. Originally a carbarn of the Springfield Consolidated Railway, Peoria-to-St. Louis trains loaded and unloaded in the street, while cars from Danville used tracks into the rear of the station, off the street.   Bill Janssen Collection

repainted and tested. On February 14, 1907, the sleeper *Decatur* left East St. Louis and the sleeper *Springfield* left East St. Louis on their first trips, arriving at their respective terminals in the early morning of February 15. Between Springfield and East St. Louis, the service was well used, but the Decatur section was not, resulting in an August 19 cutback of sleeper service to the Springfield-East St. Louis section.

New cars in 1907 included Nos. 350-359 for the a.c. Bloomington-Peoria line, 233-239 for the d.c. lines and 240-249, some of which were dual-equipped. All came in the dark green color scheme; in August 1907, the ITS announced that the older cars in red and yellow colors would also receive the dark green.

With completion of the missing Decatur-Champaign link, the Springfield-Danville *Capital City Limited* began operation on January 1, 1908. On July 15, limited Peoria-Springfield runs began. Locals were scheduled between Limiteds to take care of smaller towns, stopping at nearly every crossing or other location denoted by signs.

Once the a.c. power system between Peoria and Bloomington was eliminated, through service between Peoria and Decatur became possible, beginning August 25, 1909.

The Holland sleepers were popular, but as self-propelled units, the noise from the motors and air compressors was annoying. In 1909 therefore, two trailer sleepers were ordered, being delivered in the early spring of 1910. They were put on exhibition all along the line between March 13 and 27, staying in the larger cities all day and in the smaller localities just a few hours; but even the smallest places had at least an hour to inspect them. Interurban sleepers were uncommon, and the exhibition attracted thousands of curious people who toured the cars.

The new sleepers *Peoria* and *St. Louis*, which made their first regular runs April 1, 1910, had ten sections permanently installed. Berths were longer than a standard Pullman berth, and each upper berth had a small window. There were safety deposit boxes for valuables, the passenger retaining one key and the porter the other. Rolls and coffee were served at no charge just before final destinations were reached. Porters were not allowed to accept tips.

The Holland sleepers continued their nightly runs between Springfield and East St. Louis until the small hours of May 20, 1910, when the *Springfield* was wrecked. Leaving Gillespie northbound, and approaching Loveless siding, the motorman noticed

Sleeping car Springfield *was one of the first two sleeper trailers which replaced the Holland Palace Cars. It is shown here at the Decatur shops on August 10, 1925.* Bill Janssen Collection

Here is what the interior of one of the sleeper trailers (504 Springfield*) looked like, before the bunks were made up with bedding. This particular car has been preserved at the Illinois Railway Museum; the view was taken in 1987.* Donald R. Kaplan

the southbound express had already passed the siding where it was supposed to be in the clear. He immediately brought the car to a halt and had just started reversing when express motor 1059 struck the sleeper. Fire broke out, but the sleeper crew managed to get the bruised (but unhurt) passengers out. However, the *Springfield,* the express motor and two trailers were destroyed. The crew of the express car was trapped and burned to death.

This left the ITS with one sleeper on the East St-Louis-Springfield run; an order was immediately placed for two more sleeper trailers. Until those were received, the northbound East St. Louis-Peoria train lay over several hours in Springfield to allow those detraining there to get almost a full night's sleep. The remaining Holland car took care of southbound traffic, until new trailers *Springfield* and *Decatur* (the same as the Holland cars) arrived, to go into service on Springfield-St. Louis set-outs. The Holland sleeper Decatur was then numbered 272 and converted to a coach.

The porters on President Taft's special train pose at Decatur with office car 233 just prior to the run on February 11, 1911.
Illinois Traction, John Hubbard Collection

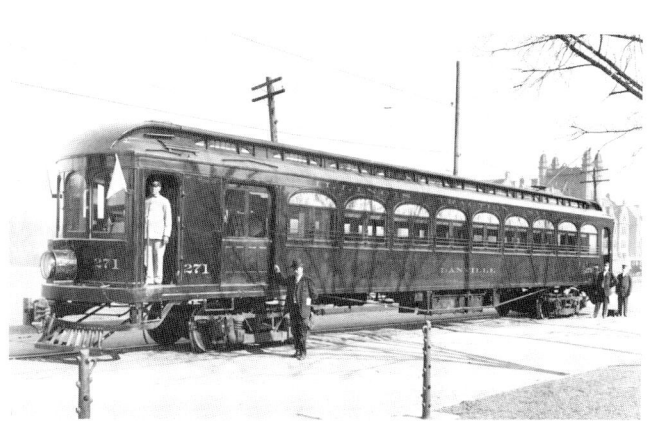

Car 271, acting as pilot car, preceded the President's special by 10 minutes with company officials and journalists aboard. It was posed here in front of Milliken University in Decatur just prior to the run. Illinois Traction

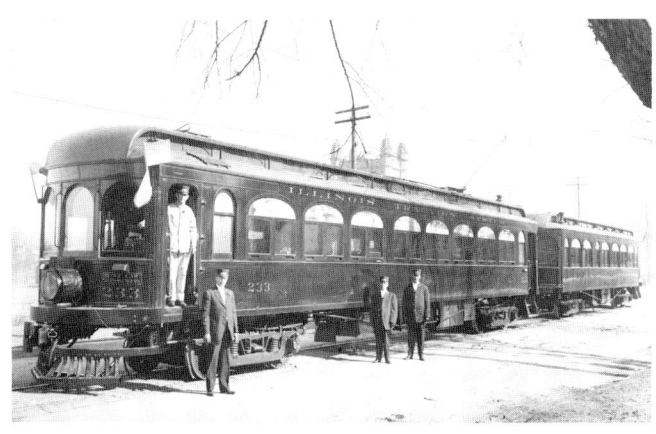

Office car 233 and private car Champaign *struck a similar pose in front of Milliken University on the morning of President Taft's special run over the Illinois Traction. This is the train aboard which the President rode.* Illinois Traction

The special train has just made a safe arrival in Springfield, and President Taft is barely visible in the center window as throngs of well-wishers greet the train. When the trip began, the President's overstuffed chair was back about 10 feet for safety's sake, but he would have none of that; he wanted to be right up front where the action was. James T. Ratcliffe Collection

One of the most memorable trips in Illinois Traction's history took place on February 11, 1911, when President William H. Taft, at the invitation of McKinley, rode from Decatur to Springfield on a tour of Illinois. No. 271 acted as pilot car, preceding the special by 10 minutes; it carried several Company officials and journalists. The special itself consisted of office car 233 and private car *Champaign*. All switches were spiked, a flagman was stationed at every highway crossing, and the track patrolled over the entire distance. Opposing trains were held at Springfield from the time the special left Decatur, and no train followed from Decatur until the special left Mechanicsburg Junction.

Parlor-observation service debuted July 16, 1911, on the Illinois Traction. On July 23, 1912, this promotional view was taken of country girls boarding parlor car 514.

Illinois Traction, John Hubbard Collection

Another promotional view of parlor car service. This one was recorded in 1914 at Matheny Cut, Caldwell Hill, east of Peoria.

Illinois Traction, John Hubbard Collection

W. C. Janssen Collection

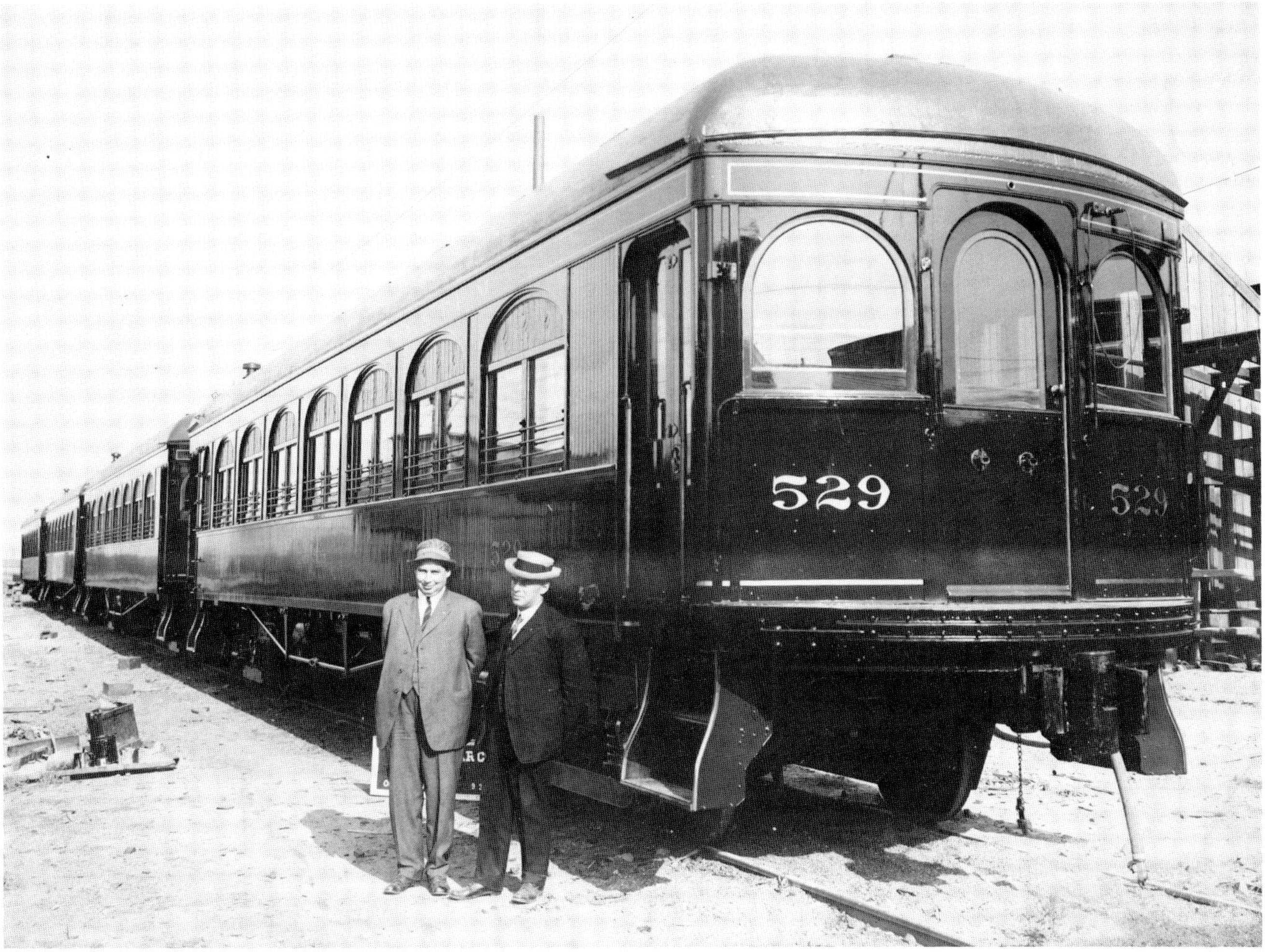

J.M. Bosenbury, Superintendent of Motive Power for the Illinois Traction, is at right, next to the Superintendent of the St. Louis Car Co. The date was April 12, 1912, location, the St. Louis Car plant in St. Louis, as four new trailers for the IT were completed.
Illinois Traction, Dale Jenkins Collection

Parlor-observation trailer cars debuted July 16, 1911, making two daily round trips between Springfield and Danville. On July 20, two more entered service on the Peoria-St. Louis run. A few days later a third began Peoria-Decatur runs. However, this last was too short to sustain parlor car service and it was soon discontinued. The trailers were luxuriously fitted and boasted brass-railed observation platforms.

The final large purchase of cars was in 1913, when Nos. 273-283 were ordered. In 1914, 284 was bought to replace 279, which had been destroyed by fire when only a few months old. The final car of the series was No. 285, bought in 1916. All of these cars handled the best runs for years, 284 bringing IT main-line passenger service to a close in March, 1956.

Through Peoria-St. Louis runs began November 20, 1913, with six trips each way, daily, taking about 6½ hours. With these runs in place, passenger services remained largely unchanged until 1924. In that year, 280-285 were overhauled at Decatur shops, having their cross seats replaced by parlor car chairs, and being painted tangerine orange. Faster schedules were instituted, with the Peoria-St. Louis running time reduced to 5 1/4 hours. There were four "Tangerine

Illinois Terminal Railroad Company
PASSENGER'S CHECK. To be retained by passenger to identify accommodations.
FROM STATION STAMPED ON BACK TO
SPRINGFIELD, Ill.
Seat No. 17 Car
Train No. 97 , M.
CURRAN-ST. LOUIS
3154
Form 12 B

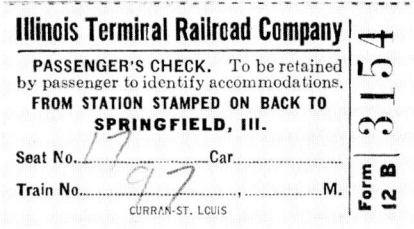

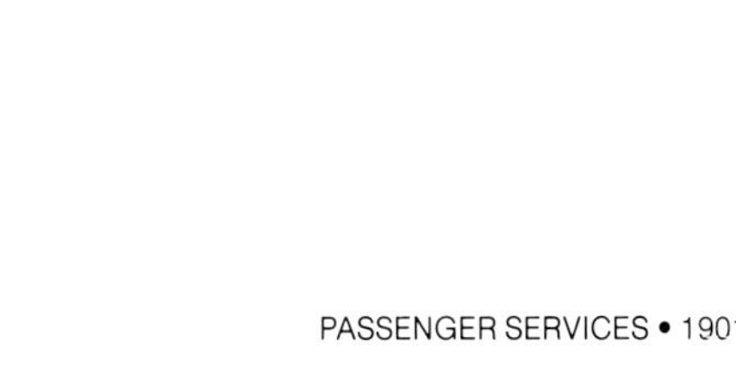

W. C. Janssen Collection

Interior view of coach-trailer 518, built by St. Louis Car Co. in 1911. This car has also been preserved at the Illinois Railway Museum, where it was photographed in 1987. Donald R. Kaplan

Dale Jenkins Collection

It was hard not to know about the Illinois Traction System, as the company developed an extensive publicity campaign beginning in 1909, which included billboards such as this one which was photographed in St. Louis in 1913. Illinois Traction, John Hubbard Collection

This classic photo shows car 251 on Adams Street at Main, in front of the Peoria Court House, circa 1917. World War One was in progress, as evidenced by the "Food Will Win the War" billboard on the lawn of the Courthouse. Judging from the ladies' clothing, it must be cold outside today.

W.C. Janssen Collection

A special four-car train consisting of Class B motor 1578 pulling coach 531, sleeper Edwardsville, *and parlor car* Clinton *ran from St. Louis to Indianapolis on February 27-28, 1922, to the convention of the Central Electric Railroad Association. Here, the special train poses in Crawfordsville, Indiana, in front of the interurban station of the Terre Haute, Indianapolis & Eastern.*

Illinois Traction, Dale Jenkins Collection

Beginning in late 1924, schedules were tightened and several name trains introduced on the Illinois Traction. One of these, the Owl, *is pictured here circa 1925, having just arrived in Granite City. Quite likely the motor car and two sleeping cars left Peoria, and at Springfield the Springfield-St. Louis sleeper and the* Champaign, *from Champaign, were picked up.*   Illinois Traction

Flyers," a parlor car train *Capitol Limited,* and the sleeper train *Owl* each way daily, beginning November 9, 1924.

On the same day, the *Illini* sleeper was inaugurated between St. Louis and Champaign with three round trips per week. Mondays, Wednesdays, and Fridays the cars ran from Champaign to St. Louis. Tuesdays, Thursdays and Saturdays they operated between St. Louis and Champaign; a late arrival in this direction obligated serving a light breakfast at no charge. On June 26, 1927, this train was put on a seven nights per week schedule, but was taken off entirely in 1928.

ITS bus service began March 7, 1926, with nine daily round trips between Edwardsville and St. Louis. In September 1928, it was expanded to take in five daily round trips between Staunton and Hillsboro, in addition to the seven round trips made by interurban cars between those two points. On the same day, five round trips began between Springfield and Mechanicsburg, replacing rail service between Mechanicsburg and the Junction, which had ceased the day before. Again, on the same day, four daily round trips were made by buses between Carlinville and St. Louis in addition to the interurban cars.

Illinois Traction began bus service in 1926; the city bus fleet is pictured here at Granite City circa 1930.   Illinois Traction, Glenn Knight Collection

A close-up view of bus 216, also at Granite City.   Illinois Traction, Jack Henry Collection

Car 270 is pictured here before its 1928 rebuild, in Danville-Springfield Limited service.
Illinois Traction, Dale Jenkins Collection

The interior of car 270, after the 1928 rebuild. Note the wicker chairs, also the ad over the doorway for Sleeping Car Service.
Illinois Traction, Dale Jenkins Collection

The Illmo Limited *is stopping at the Walnut and Washington Street station in Peoria, circa 1928. At the time the photo was taken, the trains still ran about a half mile further, into the heart of downtown Peoria.*
Bill Janssen

Modernized cars 270 and 271 entered Danville-Springfield service on February of 1928.

The baggage compartment became a smoker, the center section now had wicker chairs, a floor covering was installed, and the cars were painted orange.

The 10 a.m. Peoria-St. Louis "Tangerine Flyer" was replaced by the *Illmo Limited* on March 1, 1928, carrying a parlor car, now fitted with one motorized truck and multiple-unit controls. The parlor seats in the "Tangerine Flyers," however, reduced capacity too much; from late 1928 to early 1929, these cars were refitted with standard seats. In 1930, ITS decided to repaint all cars orange in place of dark green, a more attractive color which gave better visibility at grade crossings.

Dale Jenkins Collection

PASSENGER SERVICES • 1901–1958 • 45

The Peorian *is headed down Spring Street in Springfield, headed for St. Louis in 1930. The building in the left background is the Illinois State Capitol; during the years that the ITS operated through Springfield, the cars passed the north and west side of the Capitol.* Bob Mehlenbeck

The Owl *is standing on Hamilton Street, just below the Peoria station, after its arrival from St. Louis. Although the train arrived in Peoria at 6:25 a.m., passengers could remain aboard the sleeper until 8 o'clock. The photo is circa 1930.* Bill Janssen

Between September 1934 and February 1935, parlor cars were relettered to become "reserved seat coaches." Anyone with a coach ticket could ride, whereas a first-class ticket was necessary in addition to a parlor car seat before then. Here, the southbound Capitol Limited *has just left the Mackinaw Junction station en route to St. Louis, during the summer of 1935. Parlor car* Cerro Gordo *has been relettered to a reserved seat coach. The next summer, closed-in observation cars were on the run.*   Bill Janssen

On February 5, 1930, the *Peorian* replaced the 1:00 p.m. Peoria-St. Louis "Tangerine Flyer," bringing parlor car service back to three trains each way daily. On May 7, the first rebuilt parlor cars went into service and it was not long before all three trains had the rebuilt cars. A parlor car and a trailer were rebuilt to sleeping cars, with nine individual rooms along one side of the car and an aisle on the other. Each room had a bed, hot and cold water, a toilet and writing desk. The first car left Peoria on the Owl at 11:40 p.m., August 5, 1930.

Many trains were accelerated with the schedule introduced on October 1, 1931. The *Peorian* and *Illmo Limited* now took four hours, twenty-five minutes instead of five hours, five minutes, and the Capitol Limited just 15 minutes more. Between Springfield and Danville some Limiteds were cut to three hours, 35 minutes from four hours even. Additionally, Peoria-Decatur Limiteds were speeded up by a few minutes.

United States Mail Limited trains between Peoria and Decatur, and between Springfield and Champaign, began on March 13, 1932. The Peoria-Decatur run was scheduled to meet both eastbound and westbound runs at Decatur, which made for a good distribution of the mail. Only closed pouches

On May 15, 1938, a fan trip was run from Peoria to Springfield, Decatur, Bloomington, and back to Peoria using arch-window motor 273 and parlor car 514, which was the last parlor car to have an open end observation platform. The train was backed onto the Sangamon River overflow bridge, north of Springfield, for this shot; the bridge in the background is the Alton Railroad's northbound main.
Paul H. Stringham

After 1932, ITS trains entered and left St. Louis almost entirely on private right-of-way, some in a subway, some on an elevated structure, and some along the Mississippi at ground level. Here, car 102 on the St. Louis-to-Alton division rolls over city streets in St. Louis on the elevated; many minutes were saved with each trip once these improvements were completed.
Bob Mehlenbeck

On September 21, 1945, with nearly half the mainline equipment in Peoria, the Illinois River bridge was knocked out of commission by a boat. When it was found that it would take two to three weeks to get the bridge back into service, the IT made arrangements with the Peoria & Pekin Union to tear out a part of one of the platforms at the Union Station and build a short connection between the streetcar track and the railroad. A P&PU diesel handled the cars, and one by one they rounded the sharp curve under their own power, to be coupled into a train which was hauled across the P&PU bridge and returned to IT rails at P&PU siding, not far from Farm Creek yard. Here the diesel has 14 cars, with a few more to go, in front of Peoria's Union Station. Lee Roten Studio

were handled; ITS was never able to get Railway Post Office contracts. Passengers were allowed to ride in the main compartment.

Set-out sleeper business on the Springfield-St. Louis route fell off in the early 1930s, to be discontinued entirely on August 5, 1934. Through St. Louis-Peoria service continued until 1940, when on July 31, last runs were made. *Missouri* made the final southbound trip and *Illinois* the last northbound. *Illinois* was taken back to Granite City on Train 95, on August 1.

Between September 1934 and February 1935, the parlor cars were relettered to become reserved seat coaches. By using this name, anyone with a coach ticket could ride these cars, whereas on a parlor car, a first-class ticket was necessary in addition to the parlor car seat.

Train 91, the fastest on the main line, was cut to four hours ten minutes on May 31, 1935, and when later in the year trains were rerouted around Madison and Venice via McKinley Junction, the time was cut again to four hours even. With twelve regular stops and five conditional stops, plus several safety stops at unprotected railroad crossings, this 171-mile four-hour schedule meant the crews who handled this run had to be full-fledged "ballast scorchers." In 1936, all equipment used on the name trains went into the shops once more for refurbishing. A more radical remodeling was performed, with the observation cars receiving closed-end platforms, and all cars having their arch windows blocked off and (remarkably) air-conditioning equipment fitted on many cars.

A device to encourage ridership was the excursion fare. Each weekend, the price of a one-way ticket plus 25 cents was good for a roundtrip ticket. Occasionally a one-day excursion fare would be offered

Within three or four minutes train 92, with parlor car Monticello *bringing up the rear, will be at its destination in the Peoria station; it has just entered the east side of the Illinois River bridge. Note the closed-in observation car, remodeled from an open platform car. The draw span of the Toledo Peoria & Western bridge may be seen below the IT bridge. The date: November 18, 1946.*   Paul H. Stringham

on which the fare was even cheaper than the regular one-way fare. Such low rates kept cars full on weekends; for several years, trains 92 and 97 operated with four cars on Sundays, all well-filled.

Early in 1942, a large munitions complex was built near Illiopolis, about halfway between Springfield and Decatur. Labor in the immediate vicinity was non-existent, and since gasoline was now scarce, some way of getting workers from Springfield and Decatur had to be devised. In October 1942, therefore, no less than 55 cars were bought from New York's Sixth Avenue Elevated, modified at ACF Industries to be used on the IT as trailers and soon went into service pulled either by Class B locomotives or cars 280-282 which were geared for power rather than speed. They ran throughout the war but once peace came, they were scrapped.

Detailed plans for new Peoria-St. Louis streamlined trains were being developed at war's end, but owing to strikes and huge order backlogs at the manufacturers, the three combination passenger-baggage cars, three reserved seat coaches, and two regular coaches weren't delivered until 1948-49. By that time, passenger traffic was already falling away from its wartime highs and the new IT President had no interest in keeping passenger service any longer than necessary.

Car 284 models the final rebuild appearance for most IT equipment, in which arch windows were covered over in an effort to modernize the fleet. Air conditioning was fitted to many cars at the same time. This particular paint scheme, nicknamed "mustache," was short-lived, to be replaced by blue.
Paul H. Stringham

The interior of car 284 as modified. Considering the car's 1914 vintage, the modernization was a success—but it could only do so much. This view was taken at Springfield in February 1955.
Donald R. Kaplan

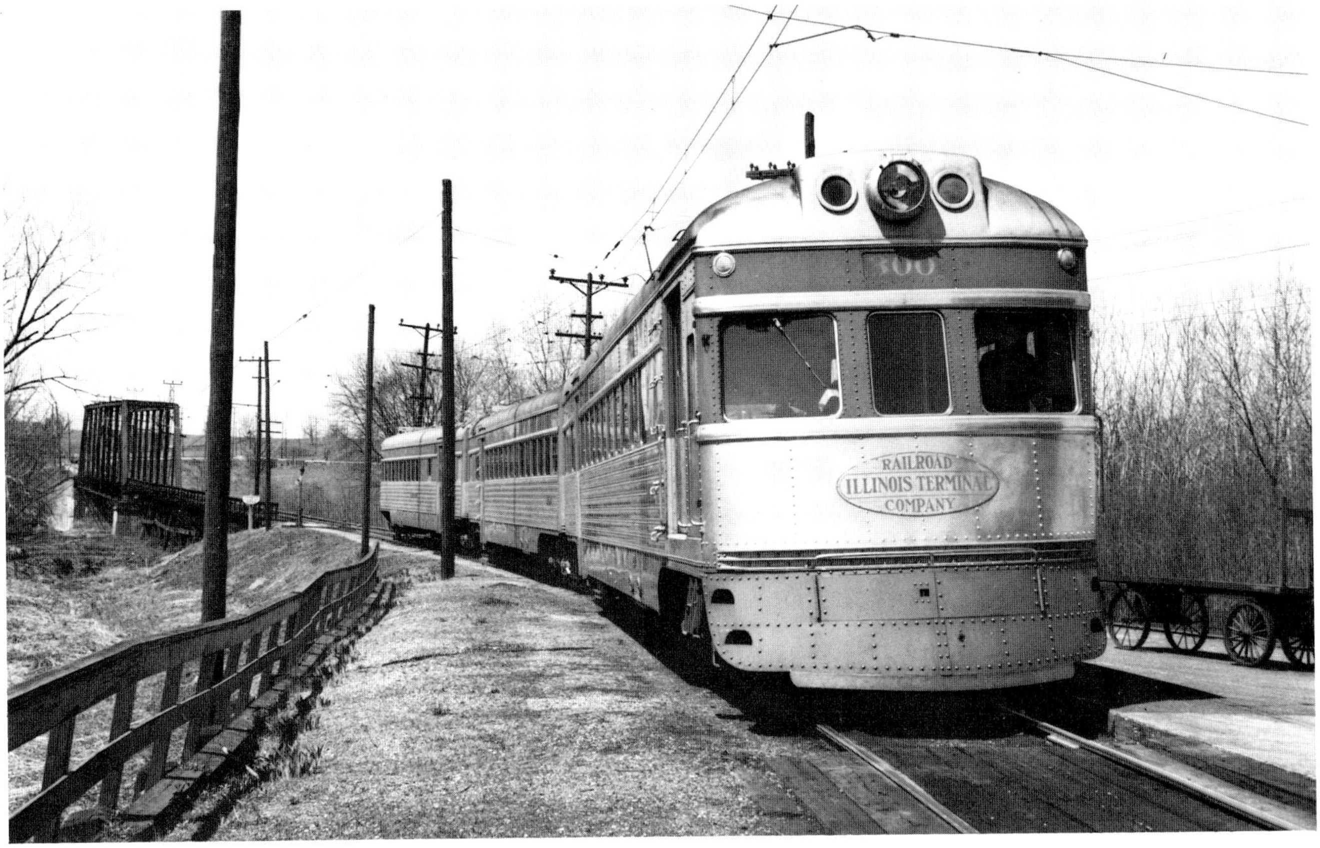

Motor 300 heads a three-car streamliner on a trial run at Mackinaw Junction in October 1948, en route to St. Louis.
Bill Janssen Collection

ILLINOIS TERMINAL RAILROAD COMPANY

RESERVED SEAT COACH

1946-47 No. RSC

ISSUED TO

RAILROAD ILLINOIS TERMINAL COMPANY

This pass, when presented with pass covering transportation, will be honored for seat fare on Reserved Seat Coach.

Valid When Countersigned by MYSELF, W. J. SULLIVAN or C. A. MATZAT

COUNTERSIGNED

A. P. Titus

PRESIDENT AND GENERAL MANAGER

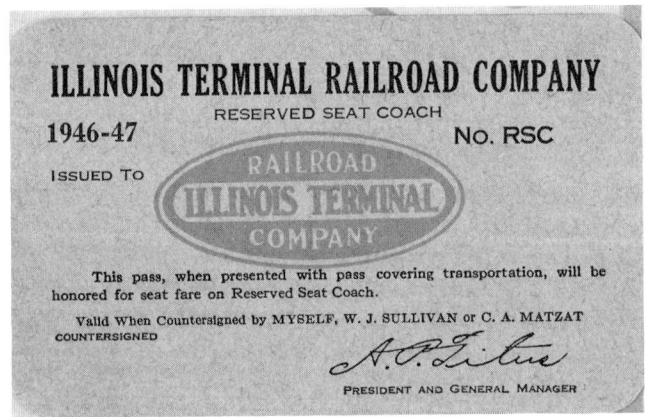

Dale Jenkins Collection

After an exhibition tour of the system, the two-car *City of Decatur* began Decatur- Springfield-St. Louis service on November 7, 1948. The old *Illmo Limited* and *Capitol Limited* were renamed *Fort Creve Coeur* and *Mound City*, although for the moment they were still using old equipment. Schedules were cut to four hours until February 27, 1949, when the new cars replaced old equipment on the East Peoria-St. Louis *Fort Creve Coeur*.

The schedule went back to 4 hours 30 minutes, with an extra ten minutes for the shuttle from East Peoria to Peoria. The new cars could not make the final few hundred yards over the bridge into Peoria because of severe curvature. The *Mound City* was still using old equipment at this time, but it too was cut back to East Peoria on this day, even though new equipment was not assigned to the run until April 15. All other runs continued through to Peoria until on January 15, 1950, they too were cut back to the new East Peoria station, leaving the shuttle to take passengers into town. A St. Louis & Alton center-entrance car was initially used on

The interior of one of the regular coach streamlined cars, No. 301, as seen at Springfield in December 1955.
Donald R. Kaplan

Only once did a streamliner cross the Illinois River bridge and come into the Peoria station. Some trouble was encountered at the sharp dip where the bridge met the street, and more trouble occurred when the train was run into the station on the track with the sharp reverse curve. The date was October 21, 1948; it was the beginning of the end for passenger service. Things worked out perfectly for the company to abandon the bridge and station.
Peoria Journal-Star

Car 405 was brought to Peoria from the St. Louis-to-Granite City line, to be used as a shuttle car between the Peoria and East Peoria stations during the time that all runs originated or terminated at East Peoria. Here, the 405 descends the west approach of the Illinois River bridge, into Peoria.
Paul H. Stringham

Soon after the Peoria station was closed, the City of Decatur *streamliner was transferred to the East Peoria-St. Louis run as a third streamlined run, and renamed the* Sangamon. *It is seen at the Springfield station in September of 1950.*
Bill Janssen

A northbound streamliner erupts from the St. Louis subway on the first stage of its fast run to Peoria, on September 4, 1950. Very few traction lines could offer a scene like this. Bill Janssen

the shuttle, and later a St. Louis-Granite City lightweight, but the shuttle ceased June 7, 1950 and the fine Peoria station was closed. Soon after, the *City of Decatur* streamliner was transferred to the East Peoria-St. Louis run as the *Sangamon*. The streamlined trains had a new stainless steel and blue color scheme. The blue paint scheme was applied to other cars as they needed repainting, but since passenger service ceased before all were done, many remained in orange until scrapped.

For years there were six daily round trips between Peoria and St. Louis, six between Peoria and Decatur, and six between Springfield and Danville. On November 12, 1950, Peoria-Decatur and Springfield-Danville runs were cut to four daily, followed on September 30, 1951 with a cut in the East Peoria-St. Louis service to four round trips daily, although an additional round trip between Springfield and St. Louis remained.

Reserved seat coaches were abolished at this time and train names were dropped.

Dale Jenkins Collection

A Hyman-Michaels dismantling crew takes up the rails of the Mackinaw Junction-Forsythe line near Mackinaw, on July 7, 1953. A G.E. center-cab diesel heads the scrap train, pulling a flatcar with a large winch, a mill gondola, and a flatcar with ramps to the gondola at one end and a ramp to ground level at the other. Rails were dragged up the ramps, several at a time, to drop with a terrific crash into the gondola. It was a sad sight. Paul H. Stringham

All passenger and freight service between DeLong and Danville ceased April 26, 1952, when that section of line was abandoned, as it was on February 21, 1953, when the 60 miles between Mackinaw Junction and Forsythe was discontinued. On April 25, 1953, four round trips were discontinued from East Peoria to Mackinaw Junction and from Decatur to Forsythe (remnants of the Mackinaw Junction-Forsythe abandonment), and all passenger service from Champaign to DeLong was dropped. At the same time, Champaign-Decatur service was cut to three round trips daily, with four daily round trips between Decatur and Springfield. One of those was dropped June 28, 1953, leaving only three between Springfield and Champaign.

Even the sky was shedding tears as train 83, pulled by motor 277, prepared to leave East Peoria on its final run, on June 11, 1955. After that date, the IT was a freight-only railroad north and east of Springfield. Paul H. Stringham

This abbreviated service was unchanged until March 12, 1955, when the Champaign-Springfield and East Peoria-Springfield services were each cut to one daily round trip, and Springfield-St. Louis was cut to two. Only the latter was left after the other lines closed June 11, 1955, and the two daily round trips between Springfield and St. Louis carried on until March 3, 1956, when the last passenger trains operated.

Dale Jenkins Collection

Suburban Services

In the early years, a few suburban runs operated on the interurban lines, examples being Peoria-Morton, Danvers-Bloomington-Heyworth, Decatur-Cerro Gordo and East St. Louis-Edwardsville. They were really commuter services designed to keep short-distance riders off the long distance through runs. However there were two big suburban operations on the ITS. These were the Danville lines, running to Hillery, Georgetown and Catlin, and the St. Louis-Granite City route.

Illinois Terminal P.C.C. car 456 approaches the Broadway and North Market station in St. Louis, en route to Granite City on September 4, 1950. This fine grade-separated line cut considerable running time from both suburban and through trains of the Illinois Terminal; the old surface route followed several narrow streets with a number of sharp curves. Bill Janssen

SUBURBAN SERVICES • 59

This photo was evidently taken to show the congestion caused by IT cars at the Catlin station. The car is one of the 400-403 series, and the photo was taken in 1928, just before the Catlin-Tilton line was abandoned. Paul H. Stringham Collection

W. C. Janssen Collection

A suburban car heads across the Vermillion River bridge at Danville in 1929.
Illinois Terminal, Dale Jenkins Collection

Car 302 crosses the Vermillion River bridge at Danville, en route from Georgetown, circa 1934. The 302 was formerly Chicago & Illinois Valley (ITS Valley Division) car 67.   Bill Janssen

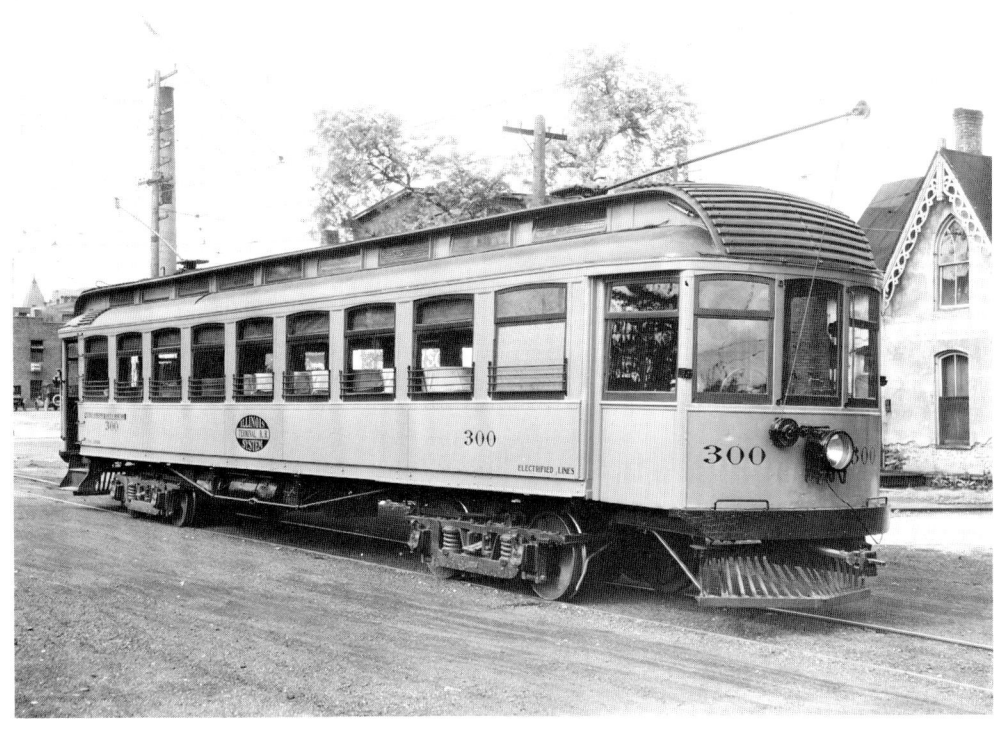

Car 300 was one of IT's earliest cars, used mainly in branchline and suburban service. At the time of this photo, it was in service on the Danville-Ridge Farm line, which places this view circa 1930. The sign at rear advises "Westville & Georgetown, Olivet & Ridgefarm." The car was later reconfigured for one-man operation on the Staunton-Litchfield line. Illinois Terminal, Dale Jenkins Collection

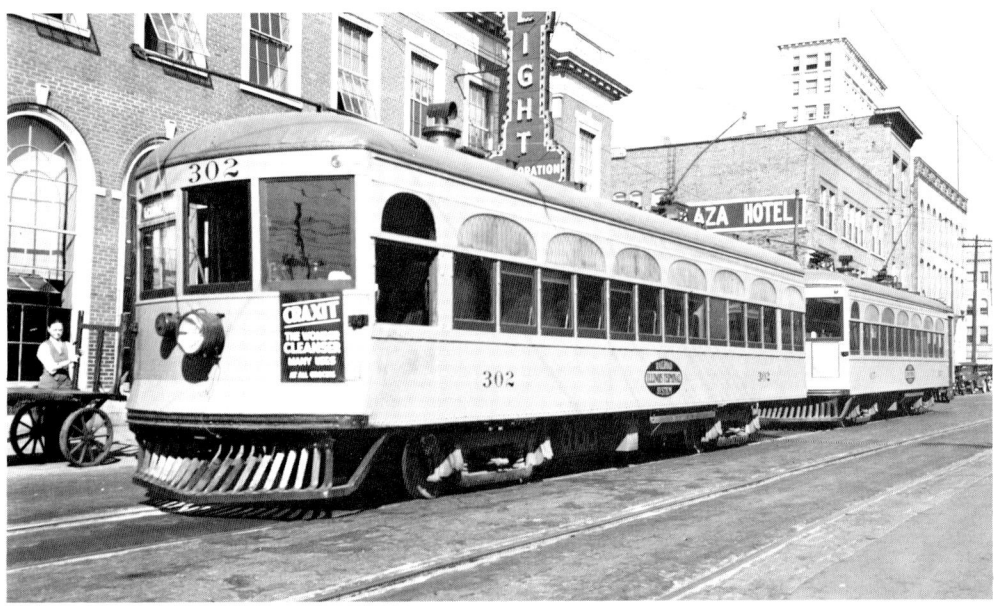

Car 302 at the Danville Station on a Danville-to-Georgetown run; it was a single end as there was a wye at Georgetown and a loop at Danville. Behind it, car 415 had been rebuilt for double-end operation, and was on a Tilton-Danville-Hillery run. Both cars were former Chicago & Illinois Valley cars. The view was photographed in 1935. Bill Janssen

Coming in from a suburban run to Hillery, car 415 rolls onto the Vermillion River bridge circa 1939. After a short stop at the Danville station, the car will continue on to Tilton.
Bill Janssen

In Danville, the suburban services provided hourly schedules most of the time and a variety of equipment, the earliest being rebuilt city cars later sold to the Danville Street Railway. Later, the heavier 300 class suburban cars were used for many years, being replaced in turn by light city cars from Danville. For the last few years of operation, cars from the Chicago & Illinois Valley were used — the best of all cars used on Danville suburban runs so far as the passengers were concerned, yet they couldn't hold the business. Catlin-Tilton was discontinued January 31, 1928, Ridge Farm-Georgetown September 30, 1933, Georgetown-South Danville Junction April 26, 1936, and Tilton-Danville-Hillery on July 19, 1939.

Dale Jenkins Collection

Illinois Traction motor 903 and trailer 958 round the corner from Ninth Street to the McKinley bridge in St. Louis. These were the original cars used in St. Louis-Granite City suburban service. This part of the street running in St. Louis was eliminated when the elevated line was built.
Bill Janssen Collection

Once the McKinley Bridge opened, a St. Louis-Granite City suburban service began. Save for a short loop near the St. Louis station, the Bridge cars (as they were known) used the interurban track all the way to Granite City, branching off to make a figure-eight loop through downtown Granite City (not served by the interurbans) to return to St. Louis. Twenty motors and ten trailers were bought new for this service, large city cars in design without high speed equipment, unnecessary for this non-interurban service. For years they were painted dark green to match the interurbans, but in 1924, they were repainted bright red below the belt rail and cream above.

Suburban car 412 emerges from the subway in St. Louis, headed for Granite City circa 1934. At the far right, the track enters 12th Street for two blocks before climbing onto the elevated structure.
Bill Janssen

In the early 1930s, they were replaced by lightweight cars from the Chicago & Illinois Valley. The new St. Louis subway had just been opened, and a wye had replaced the former loop, and it would have been inconvenient to wye the frequent suburban runs, so, before the lightweights entered St. Louis suburban service, they were converted to double-end cars. Moreover, even though they were always run as one-man cars up north, they required both a motorman and a conductor in Granite City service. They were painted orange.

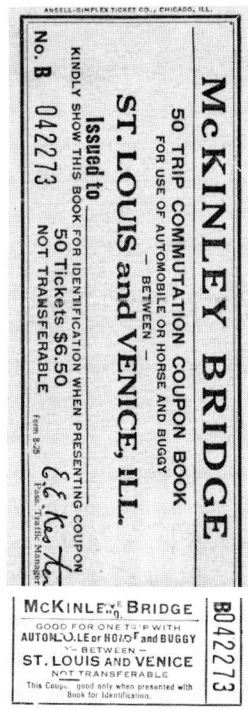

Dale Jenkins Collection

Heading towards Granite City, car 409 passes over the Broadway line of the St. Louis Public Service Co. in 1934. The elevated line passed over a number of railroad tracks in St. Louis. Bill Janssen

Car 404 pauses at State and Niedringhaus in Granite City, en route to St. Louis in the late 1930s.
Bill Janssen

Cars 472 and 471, pictured here on Niedringhaus Avenue in Granite City on October 15, 1936, were among several bought from the East St. Louis & Suburban Railway.
Bill Janssen

In 1948, the IT painted one of its ex-East St. Louis & Suburban cars running on the Granite City suburban line maroon, as an experiment. Evidently it was not satisfactory, as it was soon repainted, and no other cars got this treatment. Here, car 473, in maroon, is on Madison Avenue in Madison, headed for St. Louis.   Bill Janssen

On certain holidays, through runs were made between St. Louis and Litchfield. A brief stop was made on the viaduct over U.S. Highway 66 near Staunton so this photo could be made. Car 100 was normally only seen on the St. Louis-Alton line.   Bill Janssen

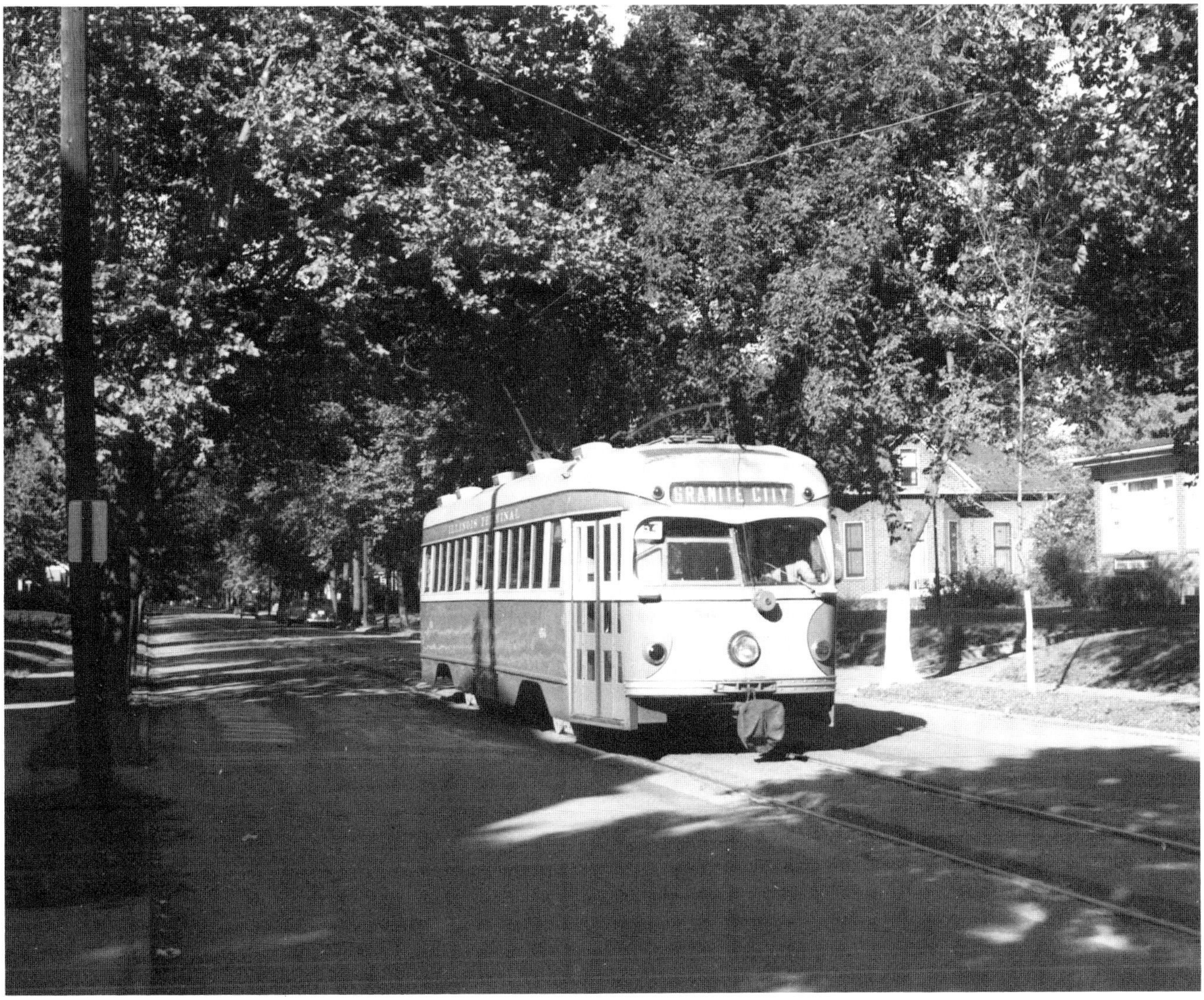

Double-end P.C.C. car 456 glides along beautiful State Street in Granite City, on September 3, 1950. From this placid scene, the car will soon be racing along the high-speed elevated line, into St. Louis. Bill Janssen

3

Chicago, Ottawa & Peoria Railway Co.

Date Waybill No. 57 Car No.

FROM TO

Consignor Consignee

C. L. Ref. Address

Via

No. Pkgs.	ARTICLES	WEIGHT	RATE	FREIGHT	ADVANCES	PREPAID
	TOTAL TO COLLECT					

Delivery Receipt

Delivered the above property 192

Delivery Clerk

RECEIVED in good order, the above described property

Signature Consignee

Per

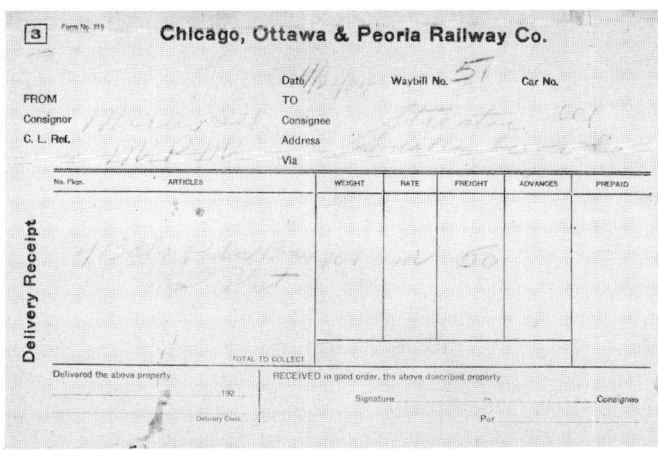

W. C. Janssen Collection

Illinois Terminal 451 rolls along on Niedringhaus Ave. in Granite City, circa 1955. Harre W. Demoro

In addition, there were several heavier center-entrance cars, bought from the East St. Louis & Suburban Railway, also in an orange paint scheme. In the 1950s, some of both types of car were repainted light green, and one of the center-entrance cars was for a short time painted maroon.

In 1949, eight double-end suburban PCC cars were delivered, in a light green paint scheme, allowing most of the ex-Chicago & Illinois Valley lightweights to be retired. These cars remained in service for only nine years, completing their last runs in the early hours of June 22, 1958, thus bringing to an end all electric and passenger operation on the former McKinley system.

Looking from the front window of a Granite City-bound P.C.C., we see Granite City-St. Louis car 472 exiting the truss spans of the McKinley bridge in St. Louis just before we enter, on March 20, 1957. Originally the double tracks were unpaved and vehicular traffic used the roadways outside the spans, but as traffic increased, the tracks were paved. Paul H. Stringham

A pair of St. Louis-bound P.C.C. cars headed by the 450, hustles along Broadway in Venice. The date was June 19, 1958, and the final run was made only a few days later, bringing the electric era to a close on the IT. Paul H. Stringham

The Valley Division

The Illinois Valley Traction Company was incorporated on December 27, 1901 by the McKinley interests to build an electric line between Ottawa and Ladd. On January 14, 1902, the powerhouse and carbarn of the LaSalle-Peru City Electric Company burned, destroying most of the rolling stock and closing down operations. The company had no money to rebuild and shortly thereafter sold out to the Illinois Valley Traction.

Work began immediately on a temporary powerhouse and carbarn; on February 19, two cars arrived from Danville. With the powerhouse back in operation a few days later, the system ran again; in the meantime, the interurban line was to begin construction.

The line of the Chicago Ottawa & Peoria from Morris to Joliet was built to high standards. Car 43 speeds along on a high fill just east of Minooka, Illinois, on July 25, 1912, when the line was brand new.   Illinois Traction, Paul H. Stringham

By mid-April a large crew was grading roadbed between Peru and Spring Valley. A steel viaduct 660' long and 63' high over Spring Creek and the Chicago & North Western Railroad was the largest structure. On October 16, a trial run was made from Peru to the east end of the Spring Valley Viaduct. On December 13, a test run was made across the viaduct, service beginning the same day. On December 20, the first car ran into Ladd, 11.6 miles from LaSalle.

The LaSalle-Ottawa section was built during 1903, and at Ottawa was to connect with the Ottawa, Marseilles and Morris River Railway, also under construction east of Ottawa. The McKinley syndicate gained control of this latter road during the year, together with the partly-graded line of the Illinois River Railway near Marseilles, which was bought for $20,000. This company had also built the piers and abutments for the Fox River bridge in Ottawa and these were included in the sale.

Late in May 1903, tracklaying began west from Ottawa, and was completed east from Ottawa to Marseilles by the end of July. A dispute between the Company and village officials blocked construction inside the village. By November, the track was complete from Ottawa to Utica. The Fox River bridge was also finished, and a construction car made its first trip on November 13. Later in the month a LaSalle city car was shipped to Ottawa via the Burlington Railroad and put on the interurban track. On November 29, a trial run carrying Company officials and reporters made a trip on the line, regular Utica-Marseilles service beginning next day. By December 18, the LaSalle powerhouse was in operation and on the 20th, two of the interurban cars were put into service.

Construction of two sizeable bridges at Split Rock, one over the canal and the eastbound track of the Rock Island Railroad, and the other over the westbound track, slowed the work west from Utica, and it was not until April 24, 1904 that the first car ran as far as the bridges. At the same time, the Marseilles dispute was resolved; on May 12, the first car ran to the Main Street terminal. By May 15, cars were running as far west as Rockwell Siding, 1.25 miles east of LaSalle. Until July 15, one car operated west from Ottawa and one east toward Marseilles. After the County Home siding was complete, through Marseilles-Rockwell service began.

As built, the line crossed Garden City Sand Company property. Litigation ensued, the Sand Company insisting the Traction Company had no right to condemn their land since a traction company wasn't a "railroad" and therefore didn't possess condemnation powers.

On June 28, 1904, therefore, the Illinois Valley Railway Company was organized, taking over both Illinois Valley Traction and the Ottawa, Marseilles and Morris River Railway. At that point, Garden City Sand settled, and cars ran once again to Rockwell Siding.

LaSalle did not grant the IVR a franchise until October 18, 1904. Only 1500 feet of track was involved, but a bridge had to be built across the Little Vermillion River, plus two crossings of railroad spurs. About December 15, 1904, cars began operating to the east bank of the river from Ottawa, while cars from Ladd ran to the west bank, leaving about two hundred feet for passengers to walk from car to car. On January 15, 1905, the bridge was complete; through service began from Ladd to Marseilles, 33.2 miles.

Construction from Marseilles east toward Seneca (5.5 miles) began during mid-July 1905, including a bridge over the I&M canal, not completed until the end of December.

But on December 31, 1905, LaSalle single-truck car 101 (by now known as The Pioneer since it had opened the lines to Utica, Marseilles and Seneca) made the first run to Seneca. Regular service began the next day, with passengers transferring at Marseilles, and on this same day, through Ottawa-Seneca service began.

Surveys for an 18.5 mile line west from Spring Valley to Princeton began about the middle of April 1906. Very heavy grading was needed once construction began. Early in September, a crew was put to work on the grade of the defunct Marquette, Spring Valley & Northwestern Railroad, recently acquired by the McKinley Syndicate. That company had laid 2.1 miles of track and graded another 1.5 miles. The first cars ran the 2.5 miles from Spring Valley to Marquette November 22, and the service was extended to DePue, 6 miles from Spring Valley, on December 24.

Car 55 made the first run into Princeton February 15, 1907 to an enthusiastic local reception; two days later, regular service began. With this line's opening, the old line from Hicks Junction, just west of Spring Valley out to Ladd, became a branch line.

The Chicago, Ottawa & Peoria Railway Company was incorporated on April 19, 1907, and on June 1 leased the Illinois Valley Railway, buying it outright on April 15, 1908. In December of 1908, the CO&P built a steel viaduct over the ravine at the line joining Peru and LaSalle, along the north side of the highway viaduct.

Four large flags adorn the Starved Rock station, between Ottawa and Utica. From the scrap lumber lying around, the station building had probably just been completed. A ferryboat took passengers from here across the Illinois River to Starved Rock State Park. Glenn Sticken Collection

The Chicago Ottawa & Peoria right-of-way and station shelter at Chautauqua Park, just west of Ottawa. This view was probably taken in the company valuation of 1910. Just beyond the shelter, the poles on the left side of the track are painted white; it was the practice in the early days that at sidings and near sharp curves, a car approaching the danger point would first encounter a pole with just a stripe of white. The next pole would have more white paint, until the last pole before the danger point would be white halfway up. This gave the motorman advance warning in foggy weather and at night — headlights in those days were not usually very bright. Illinois Traction, Paul H. Stringham

Express motor 302 was one of the first express cars on the line; it sported a rather odd pilot. The location is unknown, but the photo was made during the 1910 valuation.
Illinois Traction, Paul H. Stringham Collection

Surveys for a 10.3-mile extension from Seneca to Morris began March, 1909. Though track gangs were within three miles of Morris by December, severe weather then impeded progress. Not until February 2, 1910, did the first car run from Seneca to Morris, with regular service beginning February 5.

The Peoria, Streator & Ottawa Railway Company was incorporated March 1, 1906, and sold its rights and franchises to the CO&P on September 30, 1907. At the time the Morris extension was built, a 17.01-mile Ottawa-Streator line was also under construction. By the end of May, 1909, several miles of track had been laid north of Streator, but the Illinois Railroad and Warehouse Commission refused to allow the interurban the use of Streator's Main Street since there were several steam railroad crossings.

The Commission issued a ruling that the CO&P build south on Illinois Street to the Santa Fe Railway, southwest on private right-of-way along the Santa Fe a block-and-a-half to Bridge Street, then west on Bridge a block to Everett, then north a block to Main Street, west on Main two blocks to Sterling, north a block to Hickory and then west to Bloomington Street where the station was located. The line alongside the Santa Fe permitted the interurban to come under the protection of the interlocking plant where the Santa Fe crossed the New York Central and Chicago & Alton Railroads.

In mid-June, grading began north from Grand Ridge, while in the meantime, the line from Streator to Grand Ridge was nearly complete. On August 14, a trial run was made on the eight miles between Streator and Grand Ridge, with regular service beginning three days later, using cars hired from the Illinois Light & Traction Company, operators of Streator's city lines. They were replaced on September 1, when the first interurbans were put on the line. Service began from South Ottawa to Streator on December 29, 1909, passengers transferring to Northern Illinois Light & Traction Company city cars at South Ottawa. At the south end of the Illinois River Bridge, then under construction, passengers walked two blocks to the Burlington Railroad, which ran a shuttle train to take them to downtown Ottawa.

A work train on the CO&P waits in the clear at Rock Run siding, 6.4 miles west of Joliet, shortly after the completion of the Joliet extension. Illinois Traction, Paul H. Stringham Collection

The city bridge was completed in April 1910; on the 6th, the first city car crossed the river, but it was not until July 4, 1912 that the first interurban crossed the bridge, after the company agreed to pay $150 a month for the privilege. All the same, the City of Ottawa insisted the CO&P operate city service along their line, so on January 13, 1909, local service began from the east to west city limits, with transfers being issued to the NIL&T cars. The service was not used at all and soon disappeared.

Early in April 1911, eight large new interurban cars arrived from the Danville Car Company. On April 26, car 265 made its first run, carrying a group of newspapermen over the entire line from Princeton to Morris. They could not have helped noticing that a 21.8 mile extension from Morris to Joliet was under way, and had been since February.

The Morris-Joliet section was the best-constructed line on the entire C&OP, with no sharp curves at all, except in Joliet. East of Minooka was a cut where 90,000 cubic yards of earth were moved, most of it used to construct a nearby fill about a mile long, from seven to thirty-three feet high. There were three steel bridges, two being plate girder structures over the Aux Sable and DuPage Rivers respectively, the third being the McDonough Street Bridge, a three-span truss over the Des Plaines River in Joliet.

The first car left Morris for Joliet on December 17, 1911, and regular service began.

For a few weeks, the service was Ottawa-Morris and Morris-Joliet, but through service followed soon after. A 1911 relocation saw a mile of track built around the south side of Utica to take the interurban off city streets; a new station opened at the same time. Power for the Joliet extension came from a new hydro-electric plant at Marseilles. At the same time, the LaSalle power plant was enlarged, and the older section's high-tension lines were upped from 15,000 to 33,000 volts.

With the Joliet extension, the CO&P reached its peak. Though 76 of its 106 miles of line ran practically alongside the Rock Island Railroad's mainline, business was good.

The interurban had frequent service, and many stops were made between towns.

Consequently, all short-distance riders rode the interurbans, while longer-distance travelers used the steam trains. The greatest part of the CO&P's business was passengers, with only a limited amount of freight service.

After World War I, the State of Illinois began a highway paving program. Automobiles were becoming common and the clamor for all-weather roads was incessant. Each new automobile meant less riders for the interurban; gradually, ridership began to decline. Finally, runs had to be dropped due to lack of business. As each run was cut, even more passengers left the line. It was a vicious circle.

The first abandonment was the Hicks Junction-Ladd Branch. There was almost no freight service on the line, and after the highway was built along the track, there were few passengers. In September 1923, authority to abandon was granted by the Illinois Commerce Commission, some four months after the May 1923 reorganization by which the Illinois Power & Light Corporation took over all McKinley System lines. The CO&P became the Illinois Traction Inc. (Valley Division) under this arrangement.

Ottawa began construction of a new Main Street bridge over the Fox River late in 1923. The old bridge was a spindly structure, too light for the interurbans, and when the line was built, the Company built its bridge right alongside the city bridge. The Valley Division shared the expense with the city, and a heavy bridge was opened in February 1924 with the track in the center.

In 1923, the Valley Division ordered seventeen lightweight cars from the St. Louis Car Company. Weighing 18 tons, they were half the weight of the 260 class cars they replaced. They were delivered in the summer of 1924; after break-in runs to teach crews the art of one-man, operation, they were placed in service on August 3, 1924.

A former employee described one test. A number of officials were on a car driven by a long-time employee. He was getting the feel of the new car, but still tended to slow down too much at curves. One of the officials told him that they now wanted to test how the car handled, and if they wanted him to slow down, they would tell him. He took them literally, breezed along past Utica and up the long incline to the Split Rock bridges. The officials were visiting among themselves by this time, not keeping an eye on the right-of-way. At the top of the incline was a sharp curve, which on this trip was taken at full speed. The car held the rails, but most of the officials landed in a heap on the floor. They took it good-naturedly, since the operator was only obeying orders.

With inauguration of one-man cars, schedules were doubled, with a car every hour instead of every two hours. The new service lasted only five days, however, when the line west of Spring Valley was devastated by a storm. Several bridges between Princeton and Bureau were washed away, and a fill 200 feet long and 30 feet high near Hicks Junction was washed out. Full service resumed on December 3, 1924.

With abandonment of the Illinois Light & Traction Co. streetcar lines in Streator, the Valley Division asked authority from the Illinois Commerce Commission to buy the old Hickory Street track and reroute their cars. Authority was granted April 15, 1925. Once the connections were put in, the roundabout route in Streator ceased.

In an effort to make its service more attractive, the Valley Division arranged with the Chicago & Joliet Electric to install connecting tracks, and run cars via the C&JE lines into the Archer and Cicero Street terminal in Chicago. Several cars were sent through the shop, equipped with wicker chairs, and painted orange below the belt rail and cream above. They were named *Chicago and Illinois Valley Limiteds* and began through Chicago service in May of 1927. Unhappily, this was an ill-starred venture. As previously noted, Chicago-bound travelers preferred the Rock Island, which paralleled both the CO&P and the C&JE from Bureau to Joliet and on into Chicago, making the run in much less time.

Streator line ridership was now poor, and there was little freight. Ottawa wanted track off Courtney Street Hill so the street could be repaved. With Courtney Hill trackage out of commission, there was no way to run cars to Streator; the Valley Division preferred to abandon car service altogether. City pressure, however, made discontinuance temporary from August 25, 1928. Buses took over the next day, and track lifting began. However, no cars ever ran to Streator again; on January 9, 1929, the temporary closure was authorized to become permanent.

The Princeton-DePue section was also in trouble, with plummeting ridership, and authority to abandon that stretch was sought in March 1929. Nature, however, took a hand: on July 8, 1929, a severe storm

It's quitting time at the Westclox factory in Peru, Illinois, and an interurban motor and trailer, plus three LaSalle-Peru city cars, are loading up. Motor 56 came to the line when the CO&P was only a couple years old, and it was still on the property when the line was abandoned. Westclox Collection

Westbound car 64 rumbles across the long viaduct over the Chicago & North Western tracks and Spring Creek, just east of Spring Valley, in January 1934. Back prior even to the coming of the 260-class interurbans in 1911, a runaway car, No. 42, left the track just to the left of the signal and rolled down the embankment, completely destroying the car. Paul H. Stringham

A portion of the devastation caused by a severe storm in 1929, about six miles east of Princeton. The Princeton-DePue section of the line was abandoned after the final straw.

Paul H. Stringham Collection

struck the area. Ten trestles were destroyed and long stretches of grade and track were washed out. Cars stranded in Princeton by the washout were by July 23 loaded onto Burlington route flatcars and taken to Ottawa.

The next day, authority was received to permanently abandon and dismantle the 13.5 miles of line.

With steady decline in ridership throughout the 1920s, the road explored expanding freight service. Originally, Valley Division freight had been short-haul. Sharp curves in cities such as Spring Valley, LaSalle, Ottawa and Joliet blocked movement of standard railroad cars. Most shipments were from a plant or elevator to the nearest steam railroad connection.

Construction of several dams along the Illinois River, to establish a deepwater channel gave the Company a chance to move some of the construction materials. West of Ottawa were large sand and gravel pits. To move such material past Ottawa would mean a new route of some sort. After several studies, a route for a 3.2-mile belt line (mostly on the towpath of the old Illinois and Michigan Canal) was selected. Work began in 1930, and it was opened October 20. Passenger cars, however, continued to use the streets through Ottawa's business section.

As Illinois River dam construction got under way, more freight cars were added to the Valley Division. In 1926/27, fifty flat-bottom gondolas came from the St. Louis Troy & Eastern, but lasted only until 1929. Twenty-five more came from the same source in 1927, plus several side-dump cars. In 1932, twenty more flat-bottom gondolas were provided, by the ITS. Most were still in service when the line was abandoned in 1934.

A connection with the Illinois Central at LaSalle was placed in service on June 10, 1931, but this came too late to be of much help. At Marseilles, the huge Certain-Teed plant was served by the Valley Division, but most freight from that plant was turned over to a steam road after only a few miles.

By now, there were connections with the Rock Island at DePue, LaSalle, Utica, Ottawa, Marseilles and Morris. At DePue there was also a connection with the Chicago Indiana & Southern division of the New York Central, while at Hicks Junction a connection was made with the Chicago & North Western. There was a connection with the Elgin Joliet & Eastern at Minooka.

As late as June 1931, two-hour service was maintained from Joliet to DePue, but as the Depression deepened, ridership dropped alarmingly, and nothing could turn it around.

Bill Janssen hustles across the front of the Ottawa shops in January 1934, the final days for operation of the line. Four months later, the line was history. The shop site today is a deep stone quarry.   Paul H. Stringham

By December 3, 1933, there were but four Joliet-LaSalle round trips, plus a few shorter runs. West of LaSalle only three round trips survived, and overall there was insufficient revenue to pay expenses. Track was in deplorable shape, and with the winding down of activity on the Illinois Waterway, the brief freight boom was over.

Abandonment was, therefore, inevitable; on May 14, 1934, the last car pulled into the barn.

The Illini trail, as the Valley Division was often called, did not come up to the standards of its ITS parent. It was built through an entirely different territory, with a number of fairly large cities, not very far apart. It followed the Illinois River Valley most of

Dale Jenkins Collection

THE VALLEY DIVISION • 81

the way, but, although most of the eastern section was through relatively level country, the western thirty miles was liberally endowed with steep grades and sharp curves. Since distances were short, no attempt was made to build a high-speed line. It was built to serve the needs of the area.

The western terminal was near the Burlington Railroad station at the north end of Princeton. The track ran south through the town, then curved southeast to run across flatlands for a few miles until dipping into the Illinois River Valley near Bureau. Just east of DePue, a long climb brought the line to Hicks Junction (18.6 miles) where the Ladd line joined. The 3.9 mile branch left the terminal in downtown Ladd and followed the west side of the highway to Hicks Junction.

From Hicks Junction tracks entered Dakota Street in Spring Valley, which they followed to Greenwood (19.1 miles), then turned south down a long grade to a one-story frame station. Leaving the station, the tracks continued down Greenwood Street hill, curving sharply east near the bottom to cross a long, high steel trestle over Spring Creek and the Chicago & North Western. Just east of Spring Creek, a smaller steel bridge carried the line over the Burlington Railroad.

At Webster Park (21.34 miles) the line turned due north to Gunthers Crossing, where it made another right-angled turn onto the north shoulder of what is now US Highway 6, running on the road edge to Peru's west limits and the city streets. Peru Station (24.34 miles) was a one-story frame building at Fourth and Grant.

At the Peru/LaSalle city line was a deep ravine, where the track turned off to the north side of the street and crossed a steel viaduct built by the interurban. At the east end of the bridge the track curved back into the center of the street, the carbarn and freight house being also at this point. Street running continued to LaSalle station (26.07 miles), a store front on First Street. Just before reaching the Illinois Central Railroad, the track turned south a block, crossed the IC wye at grade, then dipped sharply down to go under the IC bridge over the Illinois River.

At the bottom of the dip, the little Vermillion River was crossed, and a long gradual rise began, peaking at the Split Rock bridges, where at each end of the bridge were very sharp curves. Beyond Split Rock, the line descended to the valley floor and continued for many miles without appreciable grades, going past Utica (30.85 miles), and Starved Rock (32.05 miles) to reach Ottawa via Madison Street, and a station across from the courthouse (40.41 miles). At Columbus Street the track went south one block to Main, then east on Main to the east limits, where private right-of-way began again.

East of Ottawa (and its extensive street running), the line was mostly level to a short distance east of Minooka (74.33 miles), where a deep cut and high fill brought the line into the Aux Sable River Valley. There was some street running in Morris (63.52 miles), three blocks being shared with the Fox & Illinois Union from Yorkville.

That line had but two cars, making five round trips daily, yet survived under wire until February 1931, and as a freight line until October, 1938. In Morris, Valley division tracks used the center of the street, while the Fox & Illinois Union ran along the south side. After crossing the Aux Sable and DuPage Rivers, the line stayed level until reaching Joliet. There, more street running with sharp curves was encountered and it shared the Joliet & Southern Traction's Joliet Station (originally Aurora Plainfield & Joliet) 85.48 miles from Princeton.

Streator branch cars looped in Ottawa via LaSalle, Madison, Columbus and Main Street, crossed the Illinois River bridge and ran up Courtney Street Hill, then south to Van Buren, east to Second, south to Center, and east to a point about a hundred feet beyond Fifth Street, where the private right-of-way began. After climbing a long grade, the track ran due south to Illini Beach Park (4.25 miles) and Grand Ridge (8.28 miles).

Streator's circuitous route was described earlier, but once the local car line closed down, the Valley Division used its tracks to run directly to Hickory and Bloomington Street and the two story brick station (17.20 miles).

Although the Ottawa-Streator branch was abandoned in 1928, the station at Grand Ridge was still in fairly good condition 20 years later, when this view was made. Several of this type station were located along the Valley line. Paul H. Stringham

Illinois Traction System

WARNING
POISONOUS FUMES
HEATED CAR

This Car, Initials_____ Number_____

contains heaters using_____as fuel,
_(STATE KIND OF FUEL)

and they are located in the_____
_(STATE WHETHER IN BODY OR BUNKERS)

When cars are equipped with heaters using either charcoal or charkets, ALL PERSONS ARE WARNED against remaining in such cars WITH DOORS AND HATCHES closed. Doors or hatches must be left open for a few minutes before entering.

Must not be placed next to cars placarded
"Explosives" or "Inflammable"

ONE OF THESE CARDS MUST BE APPLIED TO DOOR ON EACH SIDE OF EVERY CAR EQUIPPED WITH HEATERS
Form 395

Dale Jenkins Collection

The Alton Line

The line via Granite City and Wood River to Alton did not become a part of the Illinois Terminal Railroad's electric operations until July 1, 1930, when the existing property was leased to the IT, but it had played a vital part in the area's transit services since shortly after the turn of the century. Under Illinois Terminal control, the Alton line was destined to do so for nearly a quarter-century more. However, since the line was always operationally distinct from the IT main line services, its history is more conveniently dealt with in a separate, self-contained chapter.

The tri-cities of Venice, Madison & Granite City, located on the Mississippi River's east bank opposite St. Louis, were little more than villages in 1895, when on April 4th, the Venice Madison & Granite City Railway was incorporated by Fred Allen, C. H. Sharmon and E. J. Spencer. They were villages destined

An Alton-to-St. Louis train rolls down Madison Avenue in Granite City, in 1940. The steel towers for the high-tension line were unusual along the Illinois Terminal. Bob Mehlenbeck

to grow fast, and the new street railway enterprise was expected to give that growth a mighty push.

Track laying began May 17, 1895, and was finished by July 1.

The new cars were delivered on July 30; trial runs were made and on August 15, regular service began.

Although opened in August, the new Company continued to experience difficulty in crossing some of the steam railroads in Venice, but by the end of the month, the track was complete practically to the Venice Ferry landing. This passenger ferry linked Venice with North Market Street in St. Louis. Unhappily, in the two blocks between the trolley terminal and the ferry landing were no less than six Chicago & Alton Railroad tracks, which that railroad adamantly refused to have disturbed.

It's not certain if that crossing was ever put in, or if passengers had to walk those two blocks between the ferry and the car line. From that point, however, the track ran from Ferry Street on Main Street to Broadway, east to Madison and northeast on Madison Street to Granite City Village Hall.

On October 24, 1899, the Granite City Venice & East St. Louis Railway Company was incorporated, and on November 10, the Venice City Council gave it a franchise to begin building from the dividing line between Granite City and Madison to Brooklyn and the East St. Louis city limits at Black Bridge. Construction was rapid, beginning in November 1899, and the new line opened on July 2, 1900, running via St. Clair Avenue, a short stretch of private right-of-way, Fourth and Fifth Streets (one way on each street) to Short Street, then on Fourth, Klein, Bissell and Meridian Streets to the Madison-Granite City line.

In May 1901 a line was begun from Granite City to Horseshoe Lake, and completed on June 15; the event was celebrated with a big excursion from the tri-cities to the lake.

The Granite City & St. Louis Railway Company was chartered in 1902 and thereupon acquired the property of the Venice Madison & Granite City Railway, following up in 1903 by acquiring the Granite City Venice & East St. Louis. During 1902 a two-mile loop line had been built in Granite City.

Early in 1904 construction began on a new line from Granite City to East Alton where connections would be made with the Alton Light & Traction Company cars. By April the line was operating to Nameoki (2.5 miles) and on June 4 the first car ran to Mitchell (4.5 miles).

Meanwhile the Alton Light & Traction had its line from Alton to East Alton under construction, and J. F. Porter (President) tried to arrange purchase of the Granite City & St. Louis. Fred Allen would not sell, but in May 1904, the two agreed to consolidate their lines under the name Alton, Granite & St. Louis Traction Company with J. F. Porter as President and Fred Allen as Vice President.

By July 1 a steel viaduct was being built over the Chicago & Alton and Big Four railroads at the east limits of Alton, along with a steel bridge over Wood River at the town of the same name. A carbarn was built at Yager Park in Alton for the interurban cars which were still only to run to Alton's eastern limits, since at the time they had a 4'10" gauge common to the area (both east and west banks: St. Louis originated the odd gauge in 1859) but the Alton city cars were of standard gauge.

On February 26, 1905, a trial run was made; on March 1, the line opened from Alton's eastern city limits to Granite City. From Granite City to the Mississippi River Ferry, the city cars were used through Madison and Venice. East St. Louis passengers transferred in Venice to the Black Bridge line.

On January 10, 1905, the Edwardsville Alton & St. Louis Railway was organized, with Fred Allen again as President. This line was to connect with the Alton Granite & St. Louis at Mitchell and was 8.9 miles long. Grading began on April 1. A large steel viaduct over the Illinois Terminal Railroad (the steam line, not the McKinley interurbans) just west of Edwardsville was necessary, since the railroad tracks it crossed were in a deep valley. The finished structure was 1100 feet long and up to sixty feet high. The first car ran November 6 as far as Edwardsville's western edge, full service into Edwardsville beginning November 26. At Mitchell, the cars connected with the Alton Granite & St. Louis Traction, then still a separate company. Not for long, though! On January 24, 1907, the Edwardsville Alton & St. Louis was purchased by the Alton Granite & St. Louis.

Also built in 1905 was the line from Madison to East St. Louis.

Two large steel viaducts were needed, one at Willows spanning nine railroad tracks with one 112 feet 6 inches long truss span and one steel truss span 237 feet long, plus steel approaches 930 feet long.

The Madison viaduct was no pygmy either, being 1009' long, 30' high and possessed of three steel truss spans plus approaches. The aggregate length of viaducts between Alton and East St. Louis was 4440 feet; the heavy concentration of steam railroads approaching St. Louis, then (and now) the second largest rail center in the country, made them necessary. Construction began in February 1905.

The approach of the standard-gauge McKinley system lines from the northeast, and the relinquishing of control over the East St. Louis lines by St. Louis traction interests some years before spelled the end for the need to maintain 4'10" gauge tracks on the east side. As a result, 1905 saw a gauge change on the east side. The Alton Granite & St. Louis was converted between June 15th and 17th. During the work, a standard-gauge car ran on the track which had been changed, and a wide-gauge car ran on the unchanged track.

Through service to downtown Alton did not begin immediately, however, since the track was single and traffic would have overwhelmed it. On the other end, the line was open from Madison through to the Louisville & Nashville Railroad crossing in East St. Louis. There, things bogged down for many months.

Late in January 1906 work began on a line from Second and McCambridge Streets in Madison to 20th and Madison in Granite City, about 10,000 feet of track. While the new line ran parallel to the original line on Madison Street, it was several blocks to the southeast, and except for a short stretch on 20th Street in Granite City it was all on private right-of-way for high speed operation.

Service began on the new line October 1 and since by that time the Alton city car line had been double tracked, the Alton Granite & St. Louis Traction could now offer through service from Alton City Hall all the way to the Louisville & Nashville crossing in East St. Louis via the new high-speed route, bypassing Madison and part of Granite City.

The Louisville & Nashville crossing itself, after months of litigation, was installed November 13 and on November 16, the first cars ran through from Alton to Third and Broadway in East St. Louis. It was hoped then to get across the Eads Bridge and terminate at Third and Washington in downtown St. Louis, but the Terminal Railroad Association, then (and now) the owners of the Eads Bridge, claimed the interurban cars were too heavy to cross and so they remained in East St. Louis, passengers having to transfer to the Bridge cars to get into St. Louis proper.

For the first few months the largest four-motor cars of the Granite City & St. Louis Railway were used on the Alton line, but soon after, eight 52'9" long St. Louis Car-built cars (51-58) were delivered and put into service.

A new south approach to the Willows Viaduct was built late in 1907 to eliminate the sharp curve. After it was completed on December 29, the Company decided to keep the old line via Seventh Street for local service and use the new line for the Limited cars, plus the recently arrived Illinois Traction System cars.

The situation thereafter was uneventful for years, although on March 29, 1913, a new schedule was introduced by which some Alton Granite & St. Louis Traction cars were diverted via the ITS McKinley Bridge into St. Louis. A major schedule acceleration followed in 1915, when the fastest cars were cut from an hour and twenty minutes to fifty-five minutes for the whole twenty-six-mile trip. These speeded-up services were held down by some rebuilt East St. Louis cars (which system by this time had control of the Alton Granite & St. Louis) which sported comfortable furnishings and in some cases observation platforms. Five new cars arrived in 1917, fitted with wicker chairs, linen covers and carpeted aisles to give a parlor car appearance.

Numbered in the 60 series, they were light enough to be allowed across Eads Bridge into St. Louis.

War-induced inflation caught up with the road; on August 12, 1919, it went into receivership, from which it did not emerge until 1926. The most noteworthy occurrence during the receivership was abandonment of the southern approach to Willows Viaduct September 17, 1925, in favor of the Seventh Street route to and from East St. Louis.

On June 16, 1926, the road was sold under foreclosure and bought by a group who organized a St. Louis & Alton Railway Company to operate it. The receiver ran the line until November 30, 1926; the next day the new owners took charge, only to later relinquish operations to the expanded Illinois Terminal system (by this time consisting of the former McKinley lines plus the steam lines) by lease dated June 4, 1930.

The IT took formal responsibility for the Alton line July 1, 1930, and on July 4, the next year diverted all trains (except for one franchise run) away from East St. Louis and onto the McKinley Bridge.

On February 24, 1932, IT was authorized to discontinue operation of the St. Louis & Alton line Mitchell-Edwardsville, the track being in poor condition and ridership almost zero. Dismantling followed some months later.

Bill Janssen totes his traveling bag and box camera as he comes up to join Bob Mehlenbeck, who is photographing this two-car Alton–St. Louis train, headed by car 104, in 1932. The location is the temporary St. Louis station, which was used while the multimillion-dollar terminal was under construction. Bob Mehlenbeck

This 1934 view shows an Alton–St. Louis train leaving Alton. For a number of years, the electric cars used the tracks of the steam line, to avoid street running. Bill Janssen

A two-car Alton–St. Louis train is about to descend into the subway, as Bob Mehlenbeck waits to take his shot a little further down the line.   Bill Janssen

This was the first of the railbuses which replaced the steam train from Alton to Grafton, in 1933. It is seen here at the Alton station; wonder if the operator had any trouble seeing beyond the bell?
Bill Janssen

A two-car train rumbles across Piasa Street as it approaches the Alton Station in the mid-1930s. Behind the flagman is the Alton-Grafton railbus.
Bill Janssen

Further abandonments came at the end of 1935 when on December 31, 2.31 miles of the St. Louis & Alton from McKinley junction in Madison over Willows Viaduct was abandoned. At the same time the lease on 0.48 miles of track from the Viaduct to Seventh Street in East St. Louis plus 1.75 miles of trackage rights over East St. Louis tracks from Seventh Street to the Third and Washington terminal in St. Louis, were given up.

Still more track was abandoned in 1936 when the old main track from Wood River to Cut Street in Alton was closed October 28. This section had been operated by a Birney after the interurbans were rerouted over the old Alton & Eastern Railroad (now a part of Illinois Terminal) some years earlier. The old carbarn at 23rd and Madison in Granite City was retired, and the entire St. Louis & Alton Railway was sold to the Illinois Terminal on December 27, 1940.

Although the nineteen-forties ridership boom benefited the line, by the late 40's, automobile ownership blossomed and St. Louis-Granite City-Alton ridership dwindled. Less revenue meant deferred maintenance, and the last cars ran March 7, 1953.

At its peak, the St. Louis & Alton operated 26.27 miles of line from Cut Street in Alton to Third and Washington in St. Louis, plus the 8.8-mile Mitchell-Edwardsville branch. The carbarn was at 23rd and Madison in Granite City and there were substations at Granite City and Hartford.

The Alton Railway Company operated 15.01 miles of Alton City trackage. On March 1, 1932, it was taken over by Illinois Terminal and operated under the name Illinois Terminal Transportation Company. The last car ran August 27, 1936, arriving at the carbarn at 1:30 a.m. At 5:30 a.m., Citizens' Coach Company buses began their runs.

The main lines of the former St. Louis & Alton and the St. Louis Troy & Eastern over the Wood River, north of Wood River, Illinois, were seen hanging in midair in this August 16, 1946 view, after a severe storm washed out the bridges. A single-track bridge replaced the structure. Illinois Terminal, Dale Jenkins Collection

A three-car train has just arrived at the Alton station on April 30, 1949. As soon as passengers have finished alighting, the train will board a new group of passengers for the southbound trip, change ends, and head back towards St. Louis. Bill Janssen

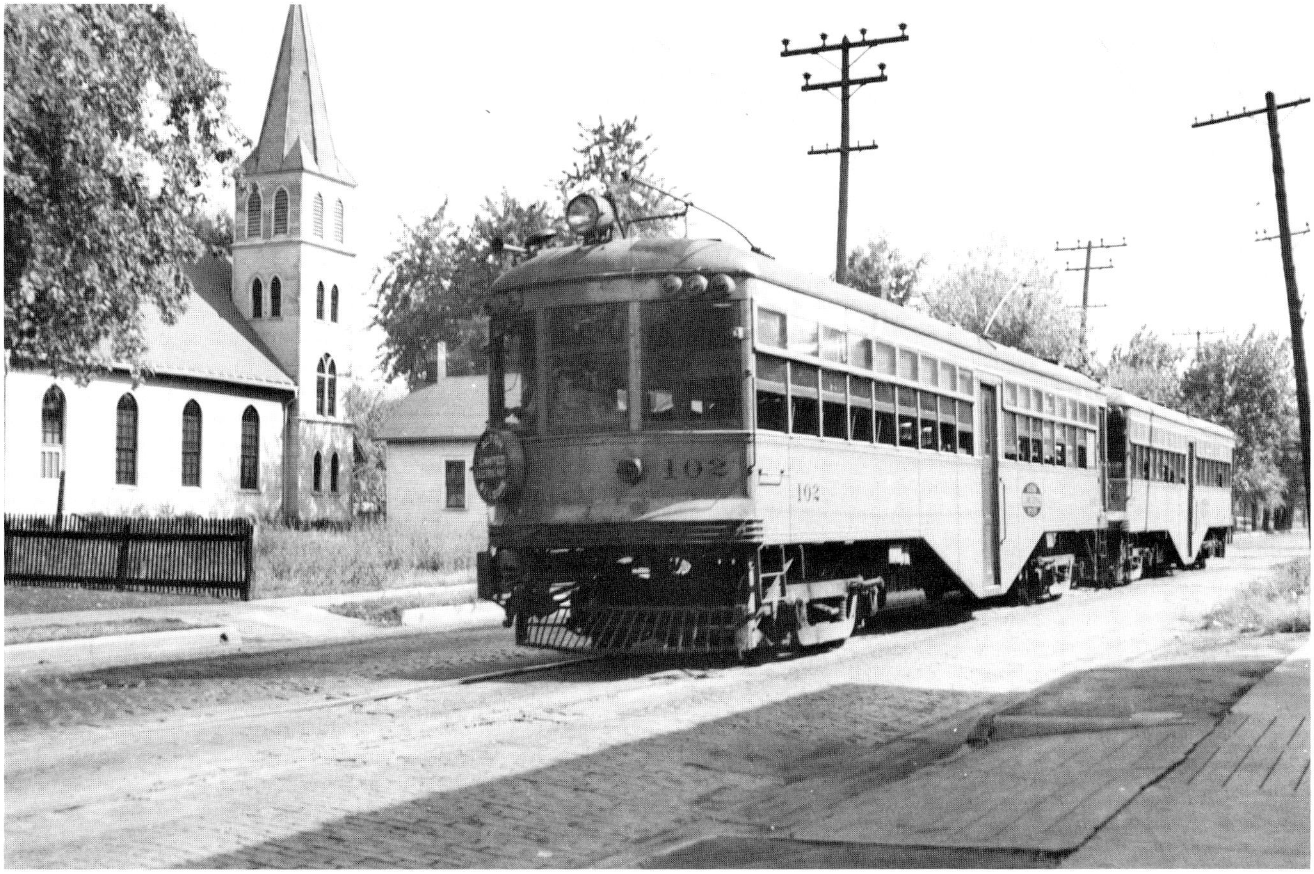

Cars 102 and 100, running as Train (2nd) 94 are headed north on Union Street in Staunton. Normally used on St. Louis-to-Alton runs, the 100s occasionally made runs from St. Louis to Gillespie.
Bill Janssen

ILLINOIS TERMINAL RAILROAD COMPANY

1946-47 No. A

PASS

RAILROAD ILLINOIS TERMINAL COMPANY

BETWEEN ALL STATIONS UNTIL DECEMBER 31ST, 1947
Unless Otherwise Limited Above and Subject to Conditions on Back
NOT GOOD LOCALLY IN SUBURBAN TERRITORY
Valid When Countersigned by MYSELF, W. J. SULLIVAN or C. A. MATZAT

COUNTERSIGNED

A. P. Titus
PRESIDENT AND GENERAL MANAGER

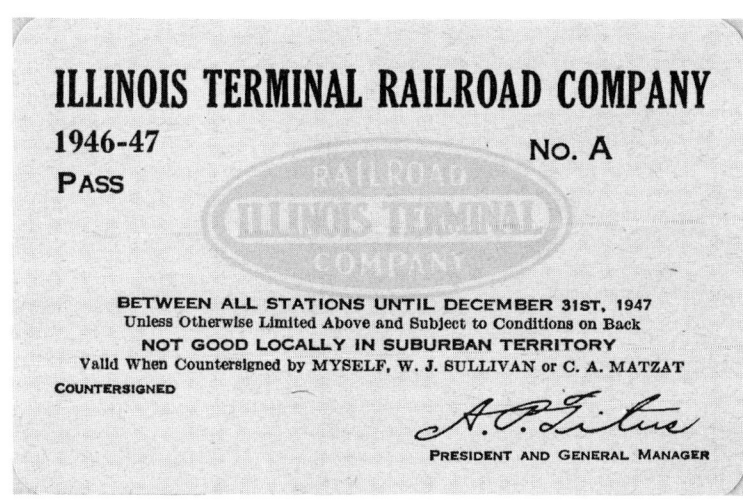

Dale Jenkins Collection

Illinois Terminal Railroad

It was in 1895 that the Illinois Glass Company of Alton decided to build a railroad from its plant near Alton's eastern city limits to Henry Street where connections could be made with the Chicago & Alton, the Burlington Route, the New York Central, the Missouri & Illinois Belt and Bridge and the Missouri Kansas & Texas railroads. On July 8, 1895, the Illinois Terminal Railroad was incorporated and the first 1.35 miles of track were laid in 1896. No equipment was owned; a locomotive plus a crew were rented from the Chicago & Alton.

On April 14, 1899, the Illinois Terminal announced it would extend its line to Edwardsville Crossing (now Hartford), a distance of 4.7 miles. From the crossing to Edwardsville, a Wabash Railroad

Illinois Terminal 31 heads up a mixed freight consisting mostly of tank cars, circa 1930. The location appears to be near the foot of the hill leading up to LeClaire; the train is running from Alton to LeClaire, where there were connections with the IT electric lines, the Litchfield & Madison, and the New York, Chicago & St. Louis (Nickel Plate Road). Number 31 was delivered in 1929; the presence of a pilot dates the photo not long afterwards, as in later years all the Baldwin Mikados such as the 31 had footboards.
Illinois Terminal, George Hadaller Collection

branch would be leased for the sole use of the Illinois Terminal. Construction began early in May and was well along when it was discovered the original charter gave the Company power to build only to Wood River. To legalize their efforts, the Illinois & Mississippi Valley Terminal Railroad was incorporated June 23, 1899, to build or operate a railroad from Wood River to Edwardsville. The new company was merged into the Illinois Terminal September 21, 1899. The first locomotive owned was outshopped from Baldwin the same month; it was an 0-4-0 numbered 1.

The old Wabash branch was in very poor condition and had several sharp curves and heavy grades. Thus while one crew was building the line from Alton's east limits to Edwardsville Crossing, another crew was busy rebuilding the former Wabash branch, lengthening curves and reducing grades. Most of the trackwork was complete by the end of September, but the bridge across Wood River had not been built, and the interlocking plant at the Chicago & Alton crossing was not finished.

Once that work was complete, however, the first train made its journey. This took place November 5, the train being a special carrying a show troupe from Edwardsville to Alton. On November 14, the first freight train ran and on November 26, the first regular passenger services began.

In mid-December a connection from the end of the old Wabash spur to the Chicago Peoria & St. Louis and Clover Leaf railroads at LeClaire (Edwardsville) was begun, being opened for service January 11, 1900.

All the same, the Edwardsville line's curves were still too sharp and the grades too steep for effective operation, so in 1904 surveys began for a new 4.35-mile-long line, to leave the Wabash at Cotters and head due east, then curve southeast to cross the old line. It then followed a valley west of Edwardsville to make a new connection with the Clover Leaf and the Chicago Peoria & St. Louis at LeClaire.

Construction began September 1904 and on May 28, 1905, the first passenger train traversed it.

Another 1904 project was the construction of a five-hundred-car yard, roundhouse and shop at Federal, near the Alton eastern city limits, completed by November 1904.

Once the Illinois Terminal line was in first class shape, the Clover Leaf began to operate some trains over it from Edwardsville to Alton, across the Alton bridge over the Mississippi River into Missouri and a connection with the Missouri Kansas & Texas at West Alton, thus avoiding congested St. Louis, and the Terminal Railroad Association's "Bridge arbitrary." Unhappily, the expense of using the Alton bridge was even greater and the Clover ceased operations on that route in July of 1905.

Just 4.8 miles to the south of LeClaire was the St. Louis Troy & Eastern Railroad's line. This Company was interested in gaining access to LeClaire with its three railroads, and in October 1905, the St. Louis & Illinois Belt Railway (incorporated October 5) began building a 4.8-mile line between those two points. Progress was slow and the line was not ready until August 1909, being immediately leased to the St. Louis Troy & Eastern. Late in 1909 it was extended another 2.8 miles south from Troy Junction to Formosa Junction where a connection was made with the Pennsylvania Railroad.

The St. Louis Troy & Eastern itself had been incorporated August 16, 1899, with grading beginning a few days later near Madison. It was complete from East St. Louis to the Donk Brothers' coal mine (13.12 miles) December 2, 1899, a point near Collinsville at the small hamlet of Donkville. A 6.86-mile extension from near Donkville to Troy was begun in October, 1899 under the aegis of the Collinsville & Troy Railroad (incorporated September 25, 1899), and that was complete February 16, 1900, operating independently until sale to the St. Louis Troy & Eastern October 27, 1902.

On March 21, 1907, the Illinois Terminal was separated from the Illinois Glass Company. The railroad closed down its office at the glassworks and moved to Second and Alby Streets in Alton. By 1910, the IT had agreed with the St. Louis Troy & Eastern that the St. Louis & Illinois Belt would be operated jointly under lease by both roads.

The Federal shop was destroyed by fire May 3, 1912. A 180' x 80' building full of machinery, a box car, coal car, flat car and caboose were burned and a Litchfield & Madison Railroad locomotive under repair was so badly damaged that it had to be scrapped.

The lines were built to move freight, passenger service being marginal to their fiscal health; it came as no great surprise when on March 23, 1913, passenger and mail services were withdrawn. After a series of hearings, however, the Illinois Commerce Commission ordered on November 10, 1913, that service be restored for at least a month.

Competition from the Edwardsville Alton & St. Louis interurban line was too great and the ICC then authorized withdrawal. The last run was January 17, 1914.

Looking east from the switching lead of the former St. Louis Troy & Eastern yards at Federal, near Alton. LeClede Steel is in the left background, IT's Federal Shops are in the right background.
Illinois Terminal, Dale Jenkins Collection

Looking west from the switching lead of the former StLT&E yards at Federal. The yard/dispatch office is at center right.
Illinois Terminal, Dale Jenkins Collection

Operations were uneventful for the next fourteen years, other than the road's name being changed to Illinois Terminal Company on December 22, 1922. But in 1928, after months of negotiation, the Illinois Power & Light Corporation, parent company of the Illinois Traction System, acquired control of the Illinois Terminal. On April 26, 1928, a further move was made in which the newly acquired Illinois Terminal Company then acquired by lease the St. Louis Troy & Eastern (acquired by Illinois Power & Light in March 1925), the St. Louis & Illinois Belt, and the former ITS electric lines, including Illinois Traction, Incorporated (Main Lines) and the St. Louis Electric Terminal Railway.

The lease was backdated to January 1st. Once signed, all rolling stock was lettered Illinois Terminal, replacing the previous Illinois Traction.

This unification of lines gave the Illinois Terminal line haul capability to Peoria and Danville from the St. Louis area, plus a belt line from Alton via Edwardsville, and Troy Junction to Madison, serving a very heavily industrialized region.

In 1928, the Pennsylvania Railroad built a low-grade cut-off on its Indianapolis-St. Louis line, which missed Formosa Junction by two miles, so late in 1928 the IT extended its line south to Pait where a new connection was established, and on further to O'Fallon, being complete in April 1929. At O'Fallon connections were made with the Baltimore & Ohio, Louisville & Nashville and the O'Fallon freight line of the East St. Louis & Suburban.

This last was leased by the IT from the East St. Louis & Suburban in June 1930, being a 9.9 mile segment of the former interurban between East St. Louis and O'Fallon serving the St. Ellen and Pontiac mines.

Two other lines were leased at the same time, the Alton & Eastern Railroad and the St. Louis & Alton Railway, the electric line described elsewhere in this book.

The Alton & Eastern Railroad was incorporated January 8, 1925, to acquire that part of the old Chicago Peoria & St. Louis running 37.91 miles between East St. Louis and Grafton. That line had been sold at bankruptcy November 20, 1924, and the new company began operations April 1, 1925. However, after the President, James Duncan, died in 1926, the line was run by individuals unfamiliar with railroad operations. As a result, the line declined steadily until it was unsafe to run trains. Several industries along the line had no other rail facilities and they persuaded the Illinois Terminal to take it over and run trains.

The history of the line went back to the 1880s. The St. Louis Jerseyville & Springfield built its line between Springfield and Grafton in 1881-1882, including 3.68 miles from Grafton to Elsah. In 1888-89 the St. Louis Alton & Springfield, which had acquired the Springfield-Grafton line, built a line from Alton to Lock Haven, followed in 1889 by a 4.3 mile line from Lock Haven to Elsah which completed the line from Alton to Grafton.

It was subsequently bought by the St. Louis Chicago & St. Paul Railroad at foreclosure on July 9, 1892. This company built a line from Alton to Granite City (not to be confused with the later electric interurban line of the Alton Granite & St. Louis Traction between the same two points) which opened July 1, 1894. On March 1, 1900, this company was consolidated into the Chicago Peoria & St. Louis Railroad and acquired, as we have seen, by the newly formed Alton & Eastern in 1925, after sale in bankruptcy.

On October 18, 1937, the Illinois Terminal Railroad Company was formed by the consolidation of the Illinois Terminal Company, Illinois Traction Inc., St. Louis Troy & Eastern, St. Louis & Illinois Belt Railway Company and the Alton Terminal Railway. Missouri laws forbade the merger of any Missouri company into one in another state, so the Illinois Terminal Railroad bought the St. Louis Electric Terminal Railroad and the McKinley bridge to both complete the merger and stay within the law.

Finally on May 1, 1940, the Illinois Terminal bought from Union Electric Company the lines of the St. Louis & Alton Railway and the East St. Louis & Suburban's O'Fallon freight line for $200,000. The electric lines continued, while all other lines continued as steam operations. This remained the case until 1948, when the first diesel-electric locomotives arrived, six Alco S-2s and three Alco RS-1s.

Dieselization of the steam lines continued apace, and on June 30, 1950, the last steam locomotive, 2-6-0 No. 21, was sold for scrap. New diesels continued to arrive and now began to displace electric locomotives on the former ITS interurban lines, so that once electric

This publicity shot was staged near Edwardsville along the old StLT&E tracks, circa 1935. Note the footboards on the locomotive.
Illinois Terminal, Dale Jenkins Collection

passenger service was discontinued in March 1956, freights were wholly diesel-operated except for the Bridge suburban car service, which continued to run between St. Louis and Granite City until June 21, 1958.

Unhappily, all was not well. The surviving interurban tracks and their routes, though certainly able to handle the big freights, were still largely interurban in engineering and construction. For example, track in many of the smaller cities and towns ran through the streets. While that condition had been locally acceptable with electric passenger service available and relatively quiet electric locomotives hauling freight, that ceased to be the case when diesels took over.

Objections to diesel noise and exhaust arose almost immediately, and moves to get IT freights off street tracks began. These efforts culminated in the Railroad (now owned by a consortium of main-line railroads) acquiring trackage rights over paralleling rail routes.

In theory, trackage rights should have been a change for the better; in practice it was quite another story. Unfortunately, a company with trackage rights over another is hardly likely to get priority treatment for its trains over those of the owner railroad, which was certainly true in the IT's case. Typically, owner lines would not delay their trains to let an IT train over their lines; many times IT trains would be made up and a crew called, only to wait until the crew went off duty, owing to lack of clearance from the owner railroad. Consequently, the approximately twelve-hour East Peoria-St. Louis schedule stretched out so far that it became something of an occasion if it could be completed within 24 hours.

As the years went by, more and more IT tracks (now in very poor shape) were abandoned in favor of trackage rights. The use of eight-wheel diesels of the same power as the sixteen-wheel Class D locomotives was highly destructive to the already-deteriorating track, since both weight and horsepower per axle were doubled. By the the Norfolk and Western takeover in 1981, IT freight services were a pale shadow of their former selves.

The Belt Lines and Freight Services 1906–1981

As originally conceived, McKinley system lines were to have been passenger interurbans. Freight would be handled in the time-honored way: less-than-carload lots or short trains, needing special freight cars of streetcar profile (generally with rounded ends and radial drawbars) in order to negotiate the sharp curves commonly encountered on an interurban route. Not only were such cars non-standard so far as the steam railroads were concerned, many towns and cities en route had strict regulations concerning the movement of freight in their streets. Traditionally, too, interurban operators were unable to negotiate freight interchange agreements with steam roads. It was almost universally true of interurbans east of the Mississippi that interchange freight services were conspicuous by their absence.

Class D locomotive 71 has just topped the grade on Caldwell Hill on August 22, 1954, and is passing the Caldwell substation. A pusher is working at the rear of the train. Often the East Peoria switcher brought a string of cars up the hill and set them out on Caldwell siding, where the regular freights picked them up.
James Barrick

Until paved roads became common, the IT had milk platforms, such as the one shown here, at almost every road crossing. Local cars would stop, pick up the milk, and deliver it to its destination. Later trains running in the opposite direction would return the empty cans to the platforms, where farmers would pick them back up. It was a classic example of the less-than-carload services which the IT offered. This particular scene is at Frankfort stop, just east of Morton, circa 1920. Bill Janssen Collection

McKinley didn't see things that way. For a variety of reasons, the Illinois Traction System as it had evolved by 1906 was unique because of its size and the distances it covered. Its principal long-distance routes, which competed with steam lines on almost all their mileage, were not just competitive, but in many cases the preferred way to travel. Making an effort to develop freight services, therefore, made sense; even more sense if the ITS could handle full-size railroad freight cars in interchange service.

But how was interchange to be accomplished? The system was built initially to interurban standards, which were not greatly different from streetcar standards so far as curves, street running, and side of road operation were concerned. Most urgently needed was some way to get off the streets in the major towns; belt lines were the means to accomplish this.

The first to be incorporated was the Springfield Belt on November 24, 1906. The concept was to take freight trains off Springfield's streets and at the same time allow the ITS to tap a number of hitherto unreachable coal mines. Litigation with the Illinois Railroad and Warehouse Commission regarding railroad crossings held back work for some time. The

A construction view of the Harrison Street subway, under the Illinois Central Railroad, on the Decatur belt line.
Illinois Traction, Paul Glassbrenner Collection

until the line was complete. By June 27, 1911, the eastern section was far enough along to be put into service, although work at the Illinois Central Railroad Freeport line underpass was not finished until July 19. A cut 35 feet deep was made at the deepest point. A large yard was built near Decatur shops where the Belt Line joined the Champaign mainline.

Late in 1912 work began on a connection between the ITS and the Wabash Railroad near Fairview Park, entering service on January 20, 1913. The line was then

Another construction view along the Decatur belt line shows the construction nearly complete for the Wabash trestle over the line.
Illinois Traction, Paul Glassbrenner Collection

final ruling was that a viaduct over the Chicago & Alton at Iles and an underpass under the Illinois Central in south Springfield were needed.

Though the project formally got under way in 1908, it wasn't until the next year that construction really began to move, and it was 1910 before work began on the 2343-foot long 48 span Chicago & Alton viaduct at Iles. Formal inauguration took place on March 20, 1911, together with the opening of a new Springfield yard. From that day, all freight trains were eliminated from the city. Curiously, it was opened later than the Decatur Belt Railway, a project not even formally incorporated until October 16, 1909.

The 5.9-mile Springfield Belt left the main line just south of Springfield, ran due east over the long Chicago & Alton viaduct and under the Illinois Central, curved northeast and finally due north along the city's east side to East Belt, where it connected with the Peoria and Danville main lines.

The Decatur Belt Railway, although incorporated late in 1909, began construction earlier when a short stretch of track was laid from the Chicago Bloomington & Decatur west to the Knights of Pythian property in the north part of Decatur. Another disconnected piece at the west end was built in 1907; in the Fall of 1909, work began on connecting the two segments. Heavy grading was needed, a trestle over the line for the Wabash, and a 3000-foot-long cut leading to the underpass beneath Illinois Central's Peoria line at Harrison Avenue. A Decatur freight house was opened November 28, 1910. The West Belt-North Junction section was opened January 1, 1911.

This Belt Line eliminated freight operation through the Decatur business district, since the original belt line along Garfield Avenue could be used

handling over 1000 cars of grain each season, plus a large amount of coal and other commodities.

From the Springfield line connection, the 5.3-mile long Decatur Belt crossed a corner of Fairview Park, then ran parallel to the Wabash to near Van Dyke Street, where it went under the Wabash to curve due north. A short distance north of the Illinois Central underpass it curved east, crossing the Bloomington line at North Junction, going under the Illinois Central Freeport line with an underpass, then across the IC Champaign line at grade. Just east of that crossing it turned south to connect with the Danville line.

This photo, taken on March 1, 1911, shows the Traction's downtown freight house in Decatur, used prior to the opening of the new Decatur Belt Line.   Illinois Traction, Jack Hass Collection

The "new" freight house in Decatur was located on the Belt Line, just south of the Wabash overpass. Most of the tracks serving it were curved. The main line to Springfield curves to the right to cross Van Dyke Street; the date, August 19, 1953.   Paul H. Stringham

The Edwardsville Belt Railway was incorporated on October 16, 1909 to eliminate city running and sharp curves in that town. Construction began almost at once; an underpass was built under the Clover Leaf Railroad and a viaduct built over Marine Road. The country here was rough; heavy fills and cuts were necessary. Grade crossings were made with the Litchfield & Madison and the Clover Leaf Railroads at the LeClaire interlocking. The 2.9-mile-long line was complete and open August 25, 1911, connecting with the mainline at Bells, just south of Edwardsville, making an east, northeast and north curve to a junction with the mainline just north of Edwardsville.

With this line's opening, all restrictions were lifted on freight trains between St. Louis and Peoria and Champaign.

Not until 1927 could the ITS get the Illinois Central and Wabash Railroads to electrify part of their lines through Champaign and Urbana, but once this

Early in 1905, the Danville Street Railway & Light Company constructed locomotive 100 for the ITS at its local shops. Number 100 was the first of over 50 freight locomotives owned by "The Traction." This view was taken in Danville, circa 1905; at left can be seen the front of one of the earliest express motors, apparently a rebuilt steam railroad baggage car. The motorman definitely was not blessed with picture window visibility on this car!   Charles Gammell Collection

project was complete, any type of freight equipment could be used from Springfield to Danville.

The manner in which the ITS handled freight business evolved to match expansion of its services. Early in 1905, a center-cab sloping-end locomotive was completed at the Danville Street Railway & Light Company shop for use on the Danville Urbana & Champaign. A second locomotive was completed soon thereafter. (There is some speculation a third was built, though there is currently no hard evidence.) At first, the locomotives were used to move coal into the Danville and Champaign powerhouses, and occasionally they would take a carload of coal to St. Joseph for commercial use.

But from October 27, 1906 a nightly coal train was run from Danville to Champaign, scheduled at night to avoid delaying daytime passenger cars.

On the western lines, express motors were used at first to move freight. At times they pulled a single trailer, but if business warranted, they pulled several. Decatur trains originated and terminated at the streetcar barns (then used as freight houses).

Class A freight motor 1550, built in 1907 for the ITS, is seen here at Mackinaw Junction circa 1910. Even though the wooden gondolas look frail, they rated high by interurban standards.
Illinois Traction, Dale Jenkins Collection

A class A freight motor with two wooden hoppers has pulled almost to the boxcar being loaded with grain at the Union elevator. Office car 233 approaches on the main in this 1910 view.
Illinois Traction, Paul H. Stringham Collection

A typical crew was a motorman, conductor and messenger. On reporting for work, they would begin loading the cars. Once the merchandise was loaded, the dispatcher was called, he gave them their train orders, and away they went.

At each station, a stop was made to drop off or pick up freight. Upon reaching their terminus the crew would unload all of the freight and then was free to leave.

Normally their day consisted of 12 to 17 hours of work, which could include runs from Bloomington to Springfield via Decatur, or Springfield to St. Louis.

In January and February 1907, the American Locomotive Company turned out three center-cab locomotives, two for d.c. operation, the other for a.c. operation on the north end. By now the ITS was doing considerable coal business, and it increased again when, in July 1907, the ITS bought 1200 acres of coal land near Worden. Part of this coal was to be used in the company's powerhouses, while some of it was for domestic use.

On September 26, 1907, the first of nine refrigerator cars entered service between East St. Louis and Springfield on the merchandise train. The cars were the same general design as the freight trailers, with rounded ends and passenger car roofs. By 1908, the ITS was handling over a half million tons of freight.

Some of the most fertile agricultural ground in Illinois was traversed by the ITS. Early in 1909, William H. Evans was commissioned to arrange meetings with farm groups along the line. At these meetings he would point out the convenience of having an elevator within two or three miles of the farms and the excellent service the ITS would supply, eliminating a day's journey into town by horse and wagon. Many of these farm groups would then form companies and build grain elevators. By mid-1909, some were already in service.

In May 1909, interchange agreements were made between the ITS and the Chicago, Rock Island & Pacific, the St. Louis & San Francisco and the Chicago & Eastern Illinois Railroads. On July 22, 1909, the first interchange was made, when several carloads of grain were turned over to the Chicago & Eastern Illinois at Bronson. Further agreements were completed in November, 1909, when connections were made with steam railroads at Girard, Virden and Springfield. In January, 1910, Mr. Evans was appointed Industrial Agent. In addition to interesting farmers in forming elevator companies, he would oversee their construction and convince other industries to locate on-line.

All this time, the ITS had been running freight trains without a caboose; indeed, in 1910, it owned only four. In July of that year, the Illinois Railroad and Warehouse Commission ordered that, in the future, all ITS freights must have cabooses attached.

In 1912 another nine cabooses were purchased.

On August 28, 1910, the first of six Class B locomotives then under construction was released for service. Far more powerful than the earlier locomotives, these locomotives were urgently needed, since the Company had two large coal pits under construction at Riverton and Mackinaw Junction; both pits were operating by December, 1910. The latter was 300' x 60' x 30' deep with a capacity of 250,000 tons, the former pit's capacity being 150,000 tons. (A trestle ran across the center of each pit; the coal was dumped directly into the pits, allowing the ITS to buy large amounts of coal in the summer when the price was down. Once in the pit, the coal was covered with water to slow deterioration.) In addition to coal traffic, Class B locomotives were also used on merchandise trains.

On November 22, 1910, a new cutoff was put in service at Chatham, eliminating two sharp curves and street running in the village.

Along with its campaign to attract more passengers, the ITS also advertised its freight services (even though someone should have gone to spelling school before learning to paint billboards!), as evidenced by this billboard, located at 12th and Broad in St. Louis, seen here on July 21, 1913.
   Illinois Traction, John Hubbard Collection

The downtown St. Louis express terminal, at Eleventh and Lucas, was adjacent to the passenger terminal. In this view, an express motor and two trailers wait at the loading dock on May 11, 1911, as another trailer on the adjacent track is unloaded.
Illinois Traction, John Hubbard Collection

On March 17, 1911, the Terminal Railroad Association of St. Louis signed an agreement to interchange freight cars with the ITS. In that same month, two fast freight runs were inaugurated in conjunction with the completion of belt lines in Edwardsville, Springfield and Decatur. One was from St. Louis to Peoria, the other, St. Louis to Danville. By eliminating the need to split up the trains to negotiate street running in the larger cities, a great deal of time and money was saved. At about the same time, a long spur was constructed in Urbana so the ITS could deliver shale to the Sheldon Brick Company. At Danville a spur was built into the Western Brick Company to haul finished brick from the plant. A commercial track to the Sharon Mine near Georgetown was laid in March, 1911. Late in September 1911 a 2500-foot spur track to the Black Diamond mine at Solomon Siding, south of Auburn, was built.

In April 1911 the ITS was admitted to the American Railroad Association, expediting interchange of freight cars with all steam roads.

Until 1914, the Peoria & Pekin Union (a terminal switching line) would not accept interchange freight from the ITS. They claimed ITS did not use their terminal facilities, so they had no obligation to interchange freight. The Interstate Commerce Commission didn't agree; on September 26, 1914 it ordered that the P&PU must interchange with the

A typical Illinois Traction express trailer, No. 1034, at Decatur. Note the rounded ends, the radial drawbar for rounding sharp curves, and the deck roof.
Illinois Traction, Dale Jenkins Collection

The original ITS freight house at Peoria, located at the foot of the ramp to the Illinois River bridge. Photographed on August 19, 1911, this view looks on from Walnut Street.
Illinois Traction, John Hubbard Collection

This 1911 view shows the Bloomington freight house, at East Adams and Ninth, with two express trailers, a standard railroad boxcar, and an express motor all in evidence. Illinois Traction, Paul H. Stringham

Illinois Traction. On November 18, 1914, an agreement was signed between the two companies. By that time, the ITS had freight interchange with the Chicago & Eastern Illinois at Glover, the Terminal Railroad Association at Granite City, the Southern Railroad at Venice, the Wabash at Decatur and Springfield, and the Peoria Railway Terminal at Peoria.

In the first years of McKinley Bridge access to St. Louis, it was quite difficult to get freight cars into and out of the city. The franchise restricted the St. Louis Electric Terminal Railway to hauling not more than one trailer during the day and two trailers during the night. This meant a southbound freight train could come only as far as the east approach to the McKinley Bridge, where a siding allowed setting out freight cars. At night, the express motor and two trailers would cross the bridge and use the street tracks into the downtown St. Louis terminal. Other express motors and even passenger motors were used to haul the remaining cars into St. Louis.

When cars for northbound trains were loaded, they were moved, one or two cars at a time, into Venice where they would be assembled into a train. At Lucas and Eleventh in St. Louis (adjacent to the passenger station) was an 88′ x 208′ freight house, served by three tracks. Here the freight was transferred from the ITS to drays and trucks (and vice versa).

The Springfield freight house, seen here on July 23, 1913, was located at Ninth and Monroe.
Illinois Traction, Dale Jenkins Collection

It was not until 1925 that the ITS could get the St. Louis franchise modified so more cars could be handled to the downtown terminal. Additionally, standard freight cars were now allowed on the St. Louis section, which enabled the Company to build a number of sidings to serve customers on Twelfth Street, as well as the main freight terminal.

By 1915 the ITS had bought many freight cars which could be handled in interchange service with the steam railroads. (Use of the freight trailers diminished; by the early 1930's they had disappeared completely, except for a few used for work equipment.) In that year there were 23 grain elevators, 10 coal mines, 9 paving brick plants and many other varied industries along the line. Increasingly, freight business was creeping upward, while passenger service began to diminish as automobiles became more plentiful.

At Peoria, the freight house and carbarn were located at the west end of the Illinois River bridge. Farm Creek yard was located at the east end of the bridge; it was here that freight trains originated and terminated. The road engines crossed the bridge alone; the trains were made up or broken up by a switch engine. Any cars for Peoria proper were brought across by the switch engine. The interchange freight was taken a half mile east of the yard and turned over to the Peoria & Pekin Union, which then distributed the cars to various lines.

From Mackinaw Junction to the west edge of Bloomington, any type of equipment could be handled. From the freight house in Bloomington to Decatur there were no restrictions.

However, any freight moving through Bloomington had to be handled in special ITS cars, fitted with swivel drawbars and trucks with special side bearings, which could round the streetcar corners in the town.

Danville also restricted freight movements, partly due to heavy grades at the North and Middle Forks of the Vermillion River. Some freight was taken to Gray's Siding, just west of the Middle Fork, and at that point the freight trains were filled out. The belt lines in Springfield, Decatur, Champaign and Edwardsville

The first class C locomotive to be completed, No. 1579, is seen here at Decatur, posed with four boxcars and three officials. The view was probably taken in late 1924.
Illinois Traction, Dale Jenkins Collection

allowed ITS to handle any type of car without complications; as a result freight revenue alone by 1921 was accounting for 35% of the system's total revenues.

On August 31, 1924, the Peoria Railway Terminal discontinued electric operation, including their tracks on South Washington Street in Peoria. There were a number of industries on that street, and after the closure ITS took over the service. However, the double tracks were in poor condition, and ITS wanted to replace them with a good single track. The City of Peoria countered by insisting that double tracks be kept if service were to continue, and the argument lasted nearly a year before Peoria revoked the PRT franchise. That left the ITS no alternative but closure of the tracks in question, which it did on July 9, 1925, the same day as the revocation.

The gradual increase in freight traffic and tonnage handled mandated more powerful locomotives. In November 1924, the first of the Class C units was released from the Decatur shops. 1579 was exhibited over the entire line and thousands turned out to inspect it.

By May, 1925 there were six class C locomotives operational, 52-foot long 80-ton monsters mounted on four trucks flexibly articulated so that tight street-corner curves could be rounded without difficulty. Their eight 125-horsepower motors gave 1000 horsepower per locomotive, allowing longer trains to move at higher speeds.

The Kankakee & Urbana Traction Company discontinued operations on March 26, 1926, leaving several elevators without service. As in the PRT closure, the ITS stepped in to help. Elevators at Ford's Crossing, Thomasboro and Sharps were served, but the elevator companies would not honor their agreements to ship in three- to five-car lots. Most of the grain was shipped out one car at a time with a Class A locomotive.

Since the KUT track was in poor shape, the ITS tried without success to get the elevator company at Ford's Crossing to move to a location along the ITS, but the company turned down an offer of help. As a result, the ITS gave up on the line and the last car of grain left the former KUT on June 17, 1927.

Illinois Traction express truck 7 is seen here at Decatur in April 1929.
Illinois Traction, Dale Jenkins Collection

The Bloomington freight house in May 1929. Note the billboard advertising "Traction Xpress—From Your Door—To Your Door," and the express truck parked behind the two autos.

For the greater part of its existence, the Mechanicsburg branch was used for freight service only. A large coal mine shipped many cars, as did this grain elevator near Mechanicsburg. At left is an LCL freight house. The view was photographed on December 3, 1954.   Paul H. Stringham

The St. Louis Troy & Eastern (controlled by the Illinois Power & Light Corporation, the IT's parent corporation), and the St. Louis Electric Terminal Railway were authorized July 29, 1926 by the Interstate Commerce Commission to construct a new "high line," which would eliminate street running in Venice. Although not termed a Belt line, this in fact is what it was intended to be, since it would allow the re- routing of freight from St. Louis to Illinois points, bypassing street trackage in Venice, Madison, and Granite City. Construction began on March 1, 1927, and was completed a year later.

With the lease of the Illinois Traction properties to the Illinois Terminal in 1928, major changes were made in the St. Louis area. The Illinois Terminal served many large industries in the Alton area; freight destined toward Peoria and Danville was now routed over the interurban. As a result, freight business, already good, was substantially increased, and major changes in its handling resulted.

For example, on June 9, 1929, St Louis freight runs were radically changed.

Instead of northern crews terminating at Staunton, with another crew taking over from Staunton to St. Louis, trains from the north now ran to Edwardsville (LeClaire), where the electric locomotives tied up, and steam locomotives took the train south to Troy Junction and over the old St. Louis Troy & Eastern line to Madison. At Madison the trains were broken up, cars for interchange were turned over to the proper lines, and cars for St. Louis taken over the Venice high line and across the McKinley Bridge.

In more general terms, considerable upgrading of the former ITS properties was seen the first few years after the lease began. Heavier rail was added, sidings were lengthened and bridges were strengthened. In order to get trains off the streets of St. Louis, a contract was let in March of 1930 for construction of over a mile of elevated structure and a half-mile of subway. On July 1, a temporary freight house was opened, and on October 1 a temporary passenger station was placed in service. The old buildings were immediately torn down. The elevated structure was opened on July 4, 1931, and on October 2, 1932 the subway began service. More than fifteen million Depression-era dollars were spent, speeding up both passenger and freight service and lifting all remaining franchise restrictions on freight service.

It was a cold January 3, 1939, when this shot was made of class C locomotive 1580 hauling a train through Goat Hollow, just south of Goat Hollow. The location was named following a derailment caused by a herd of goats, in the early days of the Illinois Traction. Robert Merriman

A northbound freight rumbles up East Jefferson Street in Morton, on a hot July 30, 1939. Caboose 939 was one of the oldest on the line, still equipped with arch bar trucks. The trains were not objectionable to local residents as long as quiet electric locomotives were pulling them, but in later years this would change when diesels were put on the runs. Paul H. Stringham

Class B locomotive 1577 heads south with a local freight, just north of Heyworth, on October 8, 1942 —just two days before this line was to be scrapped by order of the U.S. War Production Board. Fortunately the order was rescinded, and service continued for another 10½ years. Freight business was very light from Mackinaw Junction to Bloomington, but it was fair from Bloomington to Decatur.
Paul H. Stringham

Once the St. Louis project was complete, the 1930s were very quiet so far as freight business was concerned, and the Company's freight agents exercised much ingenuity and persuasiveness to get a share of the traffic. For example, just before World War II, there was a remarkable example of ITS tenacity in diverting freight to its tracks. A large shipment of pipe was routed from Chicago to the southwest for use in oil pipe lines then building. It left Chicago on the Chicago & Eastern Illinois and arrived at Glover, 126 miles away; it was then routed on the ITS from Glover to Springfield (100 miles), then Springfield-Peoria (71 miles). Once at Peoria, it was routed over the Rock Island to Bureau (47 miles) a point only 114 direct miles from Chicago, but 344 miles as shipped, of which the ITS received payment for 171 miles. Scores of cars loaded with oil pipe were routed this roundabout way for weeks, and the ITS reaped full financial benefit.

The line itself was already shedding unprofitable branches; until 1940 business remained static. However, once the U.S. became involved in Lend-Lease and its own rearmament program, freight business began to pick up substantially. As a result, heavier motive power became necessary and in 1940, the first of five class C locomotives was rebuilt as a Class D locomotive. This monster had eight 225 horsepower motors, for a total of 1800 h.p., nearly double that of the Class C.

Once World War Two was in full swing in this hemisphere, the ITS was hard pressed to handle the crush of business. In addition to the interchange business from the steam rail roads, there was the huge Illiopolis munitions plant, and at many points on the line were smaller plants also fully engaged in the war effort.

On September 28, 1942, residents between Mackinaw Junction and Decatur were stunned to hear that the U. S. War Production Board had ordered the IT to scrap 151 miles of track and turn the steel rails over to the War effort; service was to cease on October 10, 1942. Protest groups were immediately organized all along the line; they pointed out that 84 industries were served by the Illinois Terminal and thousands of people rode the cars daily to reach their war work.

The Government disregarded the protests; on October 8 it signed a contract with the Metals Reserve Company to dismantle the line. Two days later, a temporary restraining order was issued; service would continue temporarily. The objectors would not give in, and, finally, on January 9, 1943, President Titus announced that the abandonment would be postponed. On March 13, 1943, the 151 miles of requisitioned track was turned back to the Company.

The local freight from Mackinaw Junction has just arrived in Bloomington, and is plodding down Madison Street, past the Bloomington Pantagraph *building. The boxcar is equipped with special couplers and side bearings to permit it to round the sharp "streetcar" corners. The head brakeman is probably thinking that the photographer is plotting espionage, during these troubled times of WWII.*
Paul H. Stringham

Train 203, headed by class D locomotive 70, rumbles down Jefferson Street at Main, in Morton. The date was July 20, 1947.
Paul H. Stringham

Locomotive 51 pulls a lone boxcar across the viaduct over the Terminal Railroad Association tracks in Venice, in the late 1940s. According to the photographer, the viaduct was shaking so badly that he could hardly hold the camera still for the picture!   Bill Janssen

By 1945, gross freight revenues totalled $7,840,073, while the inflated wartime passenger revenues were a mere $1,873,611. For many years thereafter, freight continued to do well.

A typical early post-war freight day would see two through freights plus a local freight daily between Peoria and St. Louis. There were two similar through freight runs between Springfield and Decatur, and one between Decatur and Danville. A local freight worked between Mackinaw Junction and Decatur via Bloomington. However, as time went by, not all these runs were handled by electric locomotives. The first diesel locomotives arrived in February of 1948, and although assigned initially to the non-electrified steam lines in the Alton-Edwardsville area, they made their presence felt elsewhere.

By the early 1950s, dieselization was indeed in the air. Passenger service was dwindling, and the electric locomotives were wearing out. In 1953, six new EMD GP7 diesels were purchased for service on the through Madison-East Peoria runs. Although the Danville line had by now been cut back to DeLong, the diesels were put on that line too, running Springfield-Delong trains. In fact, by this time the only electric locomotive activity to be seen on the system was on local freights. Once electric passenger service was discontinued in March of 1956, diesel operation of freight trains became universal.

Train 203 is quite long today, but class D locomotive 71 is having no problem hustling it across the Pennsylvania Railroad viaduct, not far west of Morton. Number 71 will finish its run at Edwardsville, where a diesel will take over for the run over the non-electrified St. Louis Troy & Eastern (IT) line to Madison on December 17, 1949.   Paul H. Stringham

Class D locomotive 71 has just brought several cars up Caldwell Hill from East Peoria, and is in the clear at Caldwell Siding to let the northbound passenger car by. The right-hand siding is new; the trolley wire has not yet been hung. The date is April 25, 1953.   Paul H. Stringham

A new face to the IT—diesels! Here, nearly brand-new EMD GP7s 1605 and 1604 are at Henry Siding, just west of Morton, on February 10, 1954. When freight trains were pulled by electric locomotives, they took the sidings at meeting points. The diesels were too heavy, though, for the light rail in the sidings, so instead of the streamliners whizzing by, they had to stop, pull in the siding, let the freight go by, and only then could they pull back onto the main line and proceed. It was another bad omen for the IT. Paul H. Stringham

Class C locomotive 1596 is about to depart on an extra run to Springfield, on February 18, 1954. On the center track, class B 1569, the East Peoria switcher and pusher for Caldwell Hill, awaits its next calling, while class D 71 stands ready for departure on train 203, bound for Edwardsville. Paul H. Stringham

May 4, 1954, finds class C 1593 rolling across a double-arch concrete bridge west of Allentown, under a cloud-studded sky. James Barrick

Class D locomotive 70 waits for a northbound passenger train, on the siding at Union, with a short extra freight. The 70 was painted a light green, in contrast with the orange of most of the class Ds. The date was June 1, 1954. James Barrick

It was a hot July 8, 1954 afternoon when this southbound freight was captured just a short distance south of Auburn, at Ridgely stop. The phone booth about halfway back marks the south end of Solomon siding. Paul H. Stringham

Electric operations were drawing to a close on the IT as class C locomotive 1592 pulled into a spur track at Wyatt Wye, at the south edge of Lincoln, to drop off a couple of cars. It was February 24, 1955, and the 1592 was in charge of the northbound local freight this day. The main track is at the lower left corner of the picture, which was taken from the freight house platform. Paul H. Stringham

EMD GP38-2 2001 heads up a Peoria-Decatur train, crossing the Salt Creek trestle not far from Kenney, Illinois, on March 7, 1981. This line was formerly the Peoria Secondary Line of the Pennsylvania Railroad, acquired by the IT in 1976, after Conrail acquired the Penn Central. A short time after this photo was taken, the Norfolk & Western took over IT operations; this segment of trackage was downgraded to a local service-only branch, and abandoned on February 24, 1988. Freight formerly routed via this line now goes from Peoria east to Gibson City on ex-Nickel Plate trackage, and from Gibson City to Decatur on ex-Wabash trackage. Paul H. Stringham

With the coming of the diesels the old interurban track began to disintegrate, and the Company began a policy of leasing trackage rights over parallel roads, taking up the lighter track and thus saving much money in taxes and maintenance. The disintegration was almost wholly due to greater axle-weight. A Class D electric locomotive, for example, with approximately the same weight and tractive effort as a GP7, had its weight supported by eight axles, as opposed to the GP7's four.

Welded rail was laid from Mont to McKinley Junction in 1969, while in 1971 the shop at McKinley Junction was consolidated into the shop at Federal.

When Conrail acquired Penn Central in 1976, there were many branches it had no interest in operating. One was a former Pennsylvania line 61 miles long, from Farmdale Junction near East Peoria to Maroa.

It was bought by the IT in April 1976. Trackage rights were also acquired over the Norfolk & Western from Farmdale Junction to East Peoria and over the Illinois Central Gulf from Maroa to Decatur, giving the IT back its old link from East Peoria to Decatur, but on a line wholly different from the old electric route.

The State of Illinois wanted to see this line continue in operation, and granted much money to rehabilitate it, a job well under way when the Norfolk & Western takeover loomed. That line, wanting the interchange facilities of the IT in the East St. Louis area, approved a takeover of the IT, a move which became effective December 1, 1981.

Operational merger was deferred until May 8, 1982, when all trackage arrangements and implementing agreements were concluded.

At the time of the transfer, the IT owned track from Granite City to Alton, from Madison via Edwardsville to Alton and from Maroa to Farmdale Junction. Trackage rights over the Illinois Central Gulf from Decatur to Champaign, Wood River to Springfield and Springfield to Kenney were cancelled. So were Chicago & Northwestern trackage rights from Edwardsville to Wilson, though the C&NW bought a small segment of IT track near the Monterey Mine south of Carlinville. Trackage rights over Conrail from Champaign to DeLong were cancelled and Conrail bought short segments to serve elevators at Fulls, Glover and DeLong. The Farmdale Junction-Maroa segment was abandoned by the Norfolk Southern on February 24, 1988.

Accidents

As is the case with any form of transportation, the Illinois Traction system had its share of accidents. Fortunately most of them were of a somewhat minor nature, especially in terms of injuries and deaths. One which happened in 1910 was a major disaster, and in 1925 and 1928 accidents of a serious nature occured as well.

The first fatal accident happened on November 2, 1902. A heavy fog blanketed the area and as car 134 approached the Sylva Street crossing in Danville the headlight went out. In the darkness and fog, the motorman did not realize he was so close to a sharp curve, and the car overturned killing conductor Lashley.

On October 27, 1905 cars 222 and 225 were both badly damaged when they ran head-on into each other in the south part of Girard. There were no serious injuries in the collision.

The Illinois Traction, and later the Illinois Terminal, had its share of misfortune over the years. This undated photograph, circa 1925, shows a freight train derailment near Danville, which unfortunately has managed to knock down a bridge in the process (probably the Little Vermillion River bridge). The big hook, and plenty of onlookers, are at the scene.
Illinois Traction, Dale Jenkins Collection

A Danville-Champaign limited car, number 137, was badly damaged on November 26, 1906 when it was hit by a Big Four train in Vermillion Heights, just west of Danville. The train struck the rear section of the interurban almost demolishing the car. It was six months before the 137 was back in service.

Several passengers were injured just north of Edwardsville on July 12, 1906 when *Corn Belt Limited* car *Missouri* crashed head on into car 220. The *Missouri* ran 9' into car 220. It is likely that the 220 was scrapped at that time; the *Missouri* was sent to the St. Louis Car Company for rebuilding.

On August 19, 1906 ITS car 203 struck a Horse Shoe Lake car of the Alton Granite & St. Louis Traction, at Twenty-third and Washington Streets in Granite City. The Horse Shoe Lake car was overturned and several of its passengers were injured.

Car 302 had its trolley jump the wire while it was crossing the Litchfield & Madison Railroad near Worden. The crew rushed the passengers from the car but there were three who did not make it before the car was hit by a train. Fortunately they were not badly injured. The Traction car was badly damaged, the L&M locomotive and nine cars were derailed. This mishap happened on January 26, 1907.

Early in the evening of May 10, 1907 *Corn Belt Limited* car *Illinois* lost its trolley at Bluff Road crossing, south of Edwardsville. While the crew was on the roof of the car, replacing the pole, locomotive 103 pulling a flat car loaded with heavy timbers crashed into the rear. Several passengers were somewhat injured and the car *Illinois* was badly damaged.

On November 8, 1907 an occurrence just south of Carlinville gave the locality a name which has stayed with it ever since. Locomotive 103 on a work train was descending a heavy grade into the Macoupin Creek Valley when it ran into a herd of goats that had broken through a fence and were out on the right-of-way. The locomotive, a car of rails and two other flat cars of track material were derailed and 42 goats were killed. From that day on, the location has been "Goat Hollow."

At the north edge of Staunton the Traction crossed a spur track of the Wabash Railroad which ran into Mine #14. On June 8, 1908 the chair car *Champaign* made a safety stop at the crossing; the motorman looking toward the east saw the locomotive in the distance, but in the glare of the sun he did not see the string of flats being pushed by the engine. The interurban was almost across when the first flat car struck it, knocking it onto its right side. A man who had been standing in the rear vestibule was killed and several passengers were injured.

A little after a year later, on September 14, 1909, the southbound sleeping car *Decatur* ran into an open switch at the car barn wye just south of Staunton. An express car had just backed into the wye and the crew had forgotten to line the switch for the main line. The motorman was badly injured and several passengers were slightly injured. The car was badly damaged.

About 3 a.m. on May 20, 1910 the sleeping car *Springfield* was destroyed by fire after it collided with a southbound express train just south of Loveless Siding, located between Carlinville and Gillespie. The express motor and two trailers were also destroyed by the fire. The motorman and conductor on the express train were killed, and the brakeman was badly injured. The crew on the sleeper thought that the crew on the express train was asleep as they were some distance beyond the meeting point at Loveless Siding. The motorman of the sleeper, when he saw the other train, had stopped his car, reversed it and managed to back away for about 50 yards before impact. Five passengers and the porter, motorman, and conductor on the sleeper escaped with minor injuries. The express train was loaded with a large whisky shipment, there was no way to fight the fire, and within a couple of hours nothing remained except some twisted steel.

Car 221 took a 50' plunge into a creek near the Hillsboro Chatauqua grounds on May 23, 1910, when a trestle collapsed. The front truck of the car was near the center of the span, the rear truck had just come onto the span, the car stopped at a 45 degree angle along the abutment fill and not a window was broken in it. Four passengers and the motorman and conductor were slightly bruised. A concrete dam on the creek had broken, undermining the trestle.

By far the worst disaster to ever occur on the Illinois Traction took place on October 10, 1910, just north of Staunton when two passenger trains, both well filled, collided head-on. Train No. 14 consisting of car 238 had received orders to meet Train 2nd-73 at Wall Siding, at the north edge of Staunton. Instead of taking the siding train 14 continued on past Wall Siding, and about one mile north, on a curve in a cut, the two cars met at high speed. Car 239, which was on Train No. 2nd-73, took the brunt of the collision; it was telescoped about halfway back. There were 37 passengers killed outright and about 30 others received serious injuries. On October 26, 1910 the Macoupin County Grand Jury found that the crew on Train No. 14 was responsible for the wreck.

A cab-on flat IT locomotive was regauged and dressed up, plugging block signal safety on "The Traction," and toured all the car lines of the wide-gauge St. Louis street railway system circa 1912.   Illinois Traction, John Hubbard Collection

On July 10, 1911, The St. Louis to Peoria sleeper train was derailed by a 6"x3"x10' timber which had been placed on the track about a mile south of Hamel. Motor 1200 was overturned on one side of the track, the trailer overturned on the other side. The sleeping car was derailed but did not overturn. About 300' of track was torn up and 5 poles were knocked down. No serious injuries took place. When the 1200 was put back on the rails it was able to run to Springfield on its own power.

Two persons were badly injured and eight others slightly injured on January 17, 1912 when the Illinois Central *Diamond Special* struck the parlor car of a Danville-Springfield Limited at Nineteenth and Capitol Avenue in Springfield. The motorman had stopped for the crossing, but did not wait for the conductor to flag the crossing; the motor car had barely cleared the crossing when the parlor car was struck.

Another crossing accident occured between a Traction car and an Illinois Central train on January 29, 1918 at Champaign. The trolley shoe left the wire while the car was on the crossing; before it could be replaced the car was struck by the train, knocking it some distance and injuring two passengers.

One of the most serious collisions occured on March 20, 1925. Line car 1513, running as an extra, was working north from Gillespie, and no one in the crew

ACCIDENTS • 127

This head-on view of car 252 shows an IT block signal in excellent detail. The blades on this home signal were painted red, with a white stripe. Illinois Traction, Dale Jenkins Collection

A head-on view of car 354 shows another IT block signal installation, this time in the American Bottoms, between Granite City and Edwardsville, probably taken in the mid-1920s. This signal is a distant signal, painted yellow with a black forked stripe; note the semaphore blade is forked, not pointed. Impedance bonds in the center of the track let the DC current return through, but blocked the low-voltage AC signal circuits from carrying into the next block. John Leisenring Collection

of five remembered that they had not met local train No. 7, southbound. At the north end of a trestle, near Davis Siding the two cars met head-on with a terrific crash. The wreck might not have been so serious if the line car had been running with its cab end forward, but when the collision occured the low end of the line car rode upward and sheared through the front of passenger car 250 and over halfway back, killing 6 persons and injuring several others.

An unusual occurrence happened in the late evening of October 2, 1926, south of Clinton. A terrific rainstorm had taken place earlier in the day and the subway under the Pennsylvania Railroad at Maroa was flooded, so a southbound car had turned on the wye at Clinton and the crew planned to back the car into the subway, where passengers would be transferred past

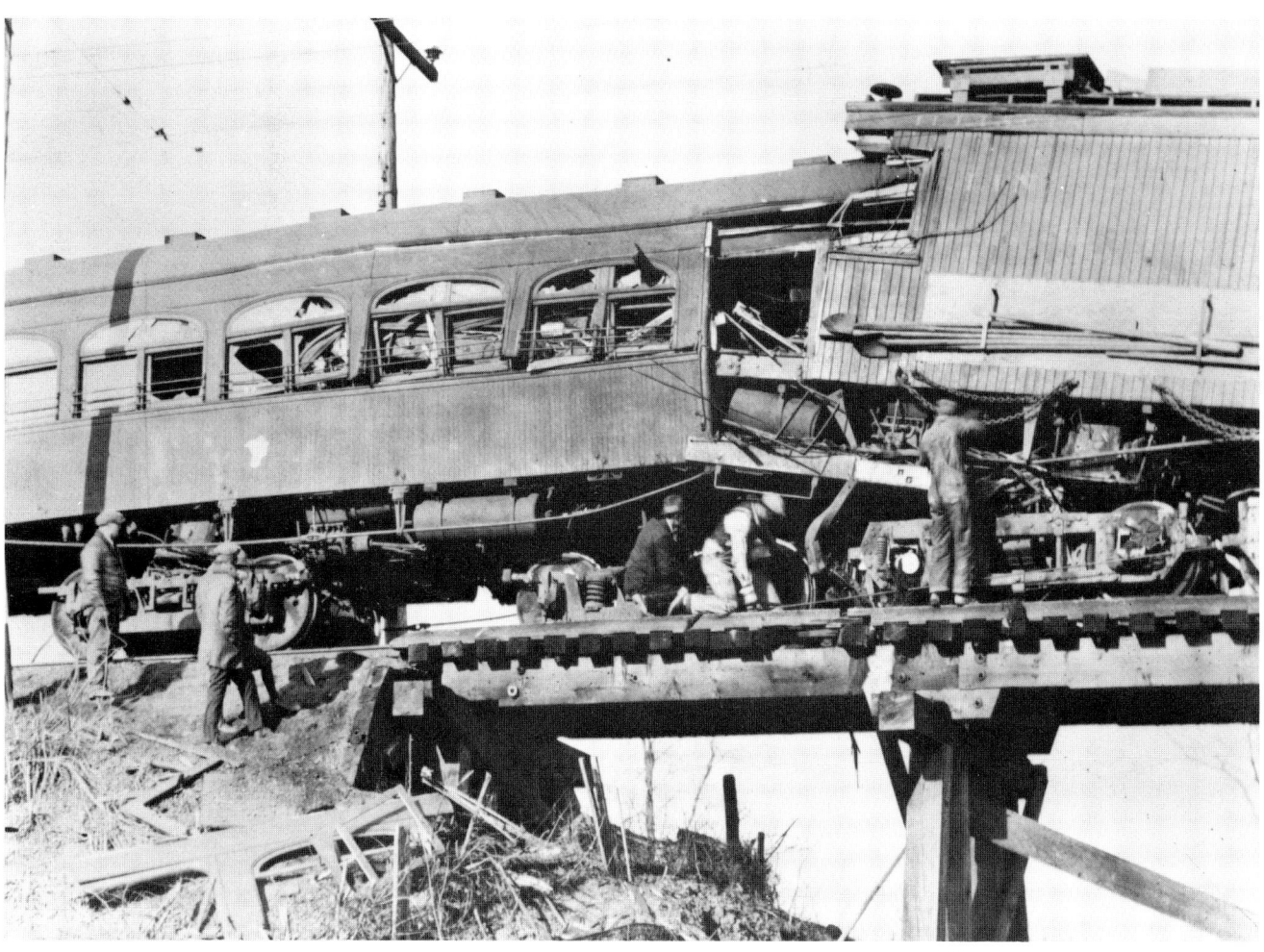

The crew of line car 1513 overlooked their meet with local train 7, consisting of car 250, and the two met on a trestle in Goat Hollow, just south of Carlinville, with these tragic consequences. The floor of the line car penetrated over halfway into car 250, killing six and injuring several others. The date, March 20, 1925. Robert Merriman Collection

the flooded subway and put on a car sent up from Decatur. They had proceeded only a few miles when the car backed into a washout and overturned. Several passengers were injured, none seriously.

At Edwardsville, trains from the south came quite close to the business center of town before they came onto the city streets. On October 1, 1927 a northbound three car train came rolling into town, and when the motorman applied the brakes to slow down, they would not hold. When the curve from Benton St. to St. Louis Avenue was reached, the speed was so great that the motor car and trailer overturned, the motor car knocking down the porch of an Edwardsville hotel. The parlor car was derailed but did not overturn. Several persons were injured.

The last serious collision occured at DeLong Siding, west of Fithian on May 31, 1928. Eastbound limited train No. 74 consisting of car 271 ran past the meeting point at DeLong and a short distance beyond struck Limited train No. 77, consisting of car 259. Car 271 was slightly narrower than car 259, and it telescoped into car 259 almost halfway. Six passengers and the motorman on train No. 74 were killed and 15 passengers were injured. Since the motorman on No. 74 was killed, it was never found why he passed the siding even though his conductor signalled him, and had as a last resort, pulled the emergency cord.

On February 3, 1944, train 91, consisting of car 278 and a Nickel Plate local passenger train, arrived at the unprotected crossing in East Peoria. Both stopped, then both started again, resulting in this unfortunate scene. The Nickel Plate locomotive's tender received a large hole as well, ending the trips of both trains. No one was seriously injured, as fortunately the poles behind the car did not break, keeping the car from rolling into Farm Creek. Peoria Journal-Star

During a heavy snowstorm on March 7, 1931 the southbound *Illmo Limited* derailed about a mile south of Frankfort stop (near Morton). The motor overturned but the parlor car did not derail. The conductor was badly injured and nine passengers recieved minor injuries.

On May 20, 1943 train No. 91, with cars 283 and 513, struck a Nameoki Transit Co. bus at a crossing just east of Granite City. Witnesses said several automobiles were waiting, and the crossing lights were flashing, but the bus driver drove around them, directly in front of the train which was running at 55 miles per hour. Nine of the bus passengers were killed and sixteen were injured. There were no casualties on the interurban train.

Freight train 200, pulled by class D locomotive 72, lacked about a minute of reaching Kings siding, just north of Lincoln, when it met car 275, running as train 95, on August 12, 1948. The passenger car was traveling at about 60 mph, and the freight about 30. Several passengers were injured, a few seriously, but all eventually recovered. As the streamliners were about to be delivered, the 275 was not rebuilt. Lincoln Courier

On February 3, 1944 train No. 91, consisting of car 278, and a Nickel Plate Road passenger train pulled by locomotive 157 collided at a crossing in East Peoria. Both trains had stopped, whistled, and started simultaneously. Although both were moving at slow speed when the collision occured, car 278 was derailed and would have fallen into Farm Creek if the trolley support poles had not held. Car 278 had some front end damage, and Nickel Plate 157 had a big hole punched in the tender. Six persons were injured, none seriously.

Train No. 95, with car 275, and freight train No. 200, with locomotive 72 collided head-on at the U.S. highway 66 overpass just north of Lincoln on August 12, 1948. The two trains met on a curve directly below the overpass, where neither crew had a view of the other train until they were almost together. So great was the impact that the freight train pushed the 275 backward almost a car length. The freight was scheduled to be at Kings Siding for the meet, but it lacked about a minute of reaching the siding. Locomotive 72 was returned to service after being rebuilt, but the 275 was dismantled. Nineteen persons were injured, a few of them seriously, but all of them recovered.

Train No. 85, with cars 278 and 607 arrived at a meeting point at Hurlbut Siding, near Elkhart just a few seconds too late on February 1, 1951. Train 94 consisting of cars 300, 331, and 350 struck car 278 about 16 feet from the rear as it was pulling into the siding. Considerable damage was done to cars 278 and 300 and express trailer 607 was completely demolished.

In addition to the wrecks involving passenger trains, there were many others over the years which involved freight trains, especially in the later years when the heavy diesel-electric locomotives proved to be too much for the interurban track. Actually the diesel electrics were not much heavier than the class D electric locomotives, but the diesels rode on only eight wheels, whereas the class Ds had their weight spread over sixteen wheels.

There were also numerous grade crossing accidents between the Traction cars and automobiles. Many of these happened at crossings protected by warning signals; motorists were too impatient to wait the few seconds for the cars to pass, or they underestimated the speed at which the cars were approaching the crossing.

Considering the millions of passengers who rode the line throughout its existence, all in all it was quite a safe way to travel.

Many accidents happened on the IT at grade crossings, even though many of these crossings were protected by a variety of signal devices. This interesting Hoeschan WigWag signal was located at Broad Street in Carlinville; the view is circa 1925.
Illinois Traction, Dale Jenkins Collection

A Ride over the Line

By Mac Sebree

The ride on the Rock Island's posh *Peoria Rocket* the previous afternoon was nice--very nice, but in this bustling post-World War two year of 1949, nothing special. After all, fancy new mainline streamliners are popping up almost everywhere now. But this young railfan isn't interested in the latest in passenger comfort. The Rock Island line is a mighty fine line, but there's another time to be recaptured.

The Indiana Railroad went out in 1941. This young fan was too young to ride it. The Cincinnati & Lake Erie was gone before that. The three Chicago super-interurbans are too much the big time; the Iowa electrics are just disguised steam roads. But the Illinois Terminal, ah, this is it: the real McCoy! Middle America on rails and under trolley wire, big, yes, but friendly. And it's not only still running, but seemingly set for a long ride into the future.

Up until today, the 18-year-old from New Mexico had only read about the Illinois Terminal, and then not in regular books or magazines, but in the bulletins of

The southbound Capitol Limited *climbs Caldwell Hill, just east of East Peoria, en route to St. Louis on June 19, 1937.*
Bill Janssen

the Central Electric Railfans' Association. The Illinois Terminal was every fantasy interurban rolled up into one. He wanted to ride, had dreamed of riding, had saved up for three years to get to the Midwest, and today, now, he was going to ride.

Up at dawn, quick breakfast, check out of the walk-up hotel and arrive ahead of time at the Illinois Terminal's Peoria station at South Adams and Walnut. The young man noticed the classic architecture of the station; more like a bank, maybe--and he couldn't immediately see the trains. The ticket office is on the street floor, along with the waiting room and lunch counter. The young man has marked his IT timetable; he'll take train 93, leaving at 7:35 a.m. to make the 171 miles to St. Louis in two hundred and seventy-five minutes flat. Boy! Bet that controller handle rides the peg most of the way! Ticket in hand, he takes the steps to the downstairs train level two at a time--must be first in line to get as close to the motorman as possible. He's heard about the streamliners but would rather ride the old orange cars. Train 93 is supposed to be the blue-with-stainless-steel-trim streamliner *Fort Crevecoeur*, but, wonder of wonders, today it consists of 1914 St. Louis-built 284, towing trailer 528 and reserved coach 512, all in traction orange as the Good Lord intended interurban cars to be.

Blue traction cars? Well, the IT has started on that route with the new streamliners, but nobody can accuse them of a lack of variety, since today our intrepid young traveler will see IT cars in orange and blue, plus the green and cream of suburban cars.

The conductor, in his blue serge uniform and brass-buttoned vest, boards his last passenger as departure time arrives. With a quick toot of its whistle, the traction car is carefully nosing out of the station, air compressor thumping to compete with the moan of the gears.

Indianapolis Traction Terminal this isn't. The inside tracks here merge into one, which shoehorns the cars 'round sharp corners and out into the street. The big, lumbering train makes maybe three miles an hour as it follows Walnut Street a half block to Washington, then lurches around the reverse curve to the right and starts up the Illinois River Bridge approach.

To his right, the young man can make out the carbarn, storage tracks and powerhouse. High over Water Street (he checks his Peoria street map to be sure), the train towers over several railroad tracks down below as it approaches the draw span, the only one on the line.

Then it's onto the bridge at a snail's pace as the motorman glances back along the consist to make sure all is well.

With the river beneath, speed begins to pick up, the powerful motors underneath working harder and sending a surging vibration through the floor, the hum of the gears rising in crescendo. Even the smells--a mixture of ozone and brake shoe dust, with just a hint of the musty frowstiness exuded by 35-year-old interurban upholstery thrown in--strike the young man as ambrosia.

The city fades away as the train passes Farm Creek yard where freights are made up alongside the creek's north bank. Soon East Peoria's eastern limits flash by as the cars follow Kerfoot Creek up a long and steep grade, speed dropping.

Caldwell Siding, top of the grade. Now the cars pick up speed, following the single track through rolling country with deep cuts and high fills. Our young man marvels that the right-of-way seems to resemble a mainline railroad in some places and a small-town trolley in others. Always of course, there's the catenary, suspended from bracket arms, the subtle difference that makes all the difference.

Morton's the first town of any size, and the first street running.

Just west of town, the line crosses the Pennsylvania Railroad on a high steel viaduct before entering the street and crossing the Santa Fe at grade. The train soon rolls down the middle of Jefferson Street, those 1947 Fords and Hudsons giving the cars a wide berth. At the station, several passengers get on. The conductor helps load several crates into the baggage compartment, while the motorman tosses off a bundle of newspapers, for the Chicago Daily Tribune has finally arrived in Morton, after two changes of car.

Leaving Morton, the cars rock along, establishing a gently rolling gait. The interurban tracks run alongside the Pennsylvania Railroad; there are several deep valleys, and both steam and electric road tracks curve right and left to keep to the high ground. The curves, however, are long and sweeping, so the speed stays high. At Dodd's a northbound sits in the clear. The timetable says it's train 82, an all-stops local out of St. Louis which began life in the middle of the night and is due into Peoria at 8:30 a.m. Its sole consist is car 277; we slow down, but do not stop.

Allentown is passed in a flash; two miles further on, the tracks drop down into the Mackinaw River valley, crossing the river on a steel truss bridge. Then, there it is: Mackinaw Junction. Our train stops at a two-story brick station resembling an interlocking tower in the vee of the junction: the Decatur line keeps straight ahead, the St. Louis line curves away to the south. There should be a car coming in off the Decatur line, but where is it? Several times a day the timecard shows meets here--convenient, say, for a passenger from Bloomington wanting to go over to Lincoln. Evidently there are none today, for our train doesn't wait, but instead plunges south past Cash Siding and yard. Then it dips through an underpass beneath the Pennsylvania Railroad and then another, under both the Peoria & Eastern Railroad and Illinois Highway 9. Then it's a long, gentle climb out of the valley, past Summit Siding and then the train starts to fly. For miles and miles there are nothing but farms and grain elevators on the flatland, whizzing by the cars at frequent intervals.

The young man checks his timetable. Just before Mindale a viaduct carries the IT over the old Chicago & Alton Railroad and Illinois Highway 122. After Mindale, the cars reach the fastest track on the system, where several Limiteds are allowed only ten minutes for the ten miles to Union, after which comes a downgrade--75 m.p.h. country! The train crosses Sugar Creek, then soon after it's Kickapoo Creek.

A short distance further on, it curves left along the Illinois Central Railroad to Athol Tower in Lincoln. Here the cars curve sharply to the right, cross the Illinois Central and Alton Railroads, make another sharp turn and start rumbling down Lincoln's Chicago Street.

The street trackage isn't what it could be; the brick paving has spread badly along the sides of the rails, and the joints pump badly-- but our young man guesses it is a miracle the Traction is still in business at all. In truth, freight's kept the IT healthy; it's the heavy locomotives which have contributed more than their fair share to the bad city track.

South of Lincoln, the IT follows the east side of the Chicago & Alton tracks; at Broadwell the interurban curves away from the railroad and runs four blocks down Jacob Street. There's street running in Elkhart too. Leaving Williamsville, the train follows the Chicago & Alton almost to Sherman, where it swings almost due south to cross the Sangamon River on a long steel bridge. Just south of there and it's into Ridgeley Junction; soon after that, the train is in the northern suburbs of Springfield, the Illinois state capital.

Fast running ceases for a while because of the numerous grade crossings, including the Illinois Central and Wabash Railroads at Starne Tower (our young passenger sees a headlight in the distance on the Illinois Central--is it the Green Diamond?) Now it's double track and into Springfield station; not downtown but on the outskirts since street running was eliminated in the 1930's with one of the IT's expensive but necessary freight belts.

Five minutes gives our intrepid traveller time only to buy a candy bar in the station. With a new crew the train soon backs out, around a very tight wye and back along the same stretch of track to East Belt.

Another tight curve (scree-e-ch!) and the train passes through the East Belt yards and south along the Belt line, crossing the Decatur line of the Baltimore and Ohio, the B&O's Shawneetown branch, then west along the south side of town, going under the St. Louis line of the Illinois Central and over the C&A's long viaduct (GM&O by 1949).

Finally headed south again, the train passes under the Kansas City line of the Chicago & Alton Railroad, and follows the C&A's St. Louis main along its west side. Another glance at the timetable tells the young man that the northbound streamliner Mound City (train 90) should be met somewhere along here. In fact, it's running a few minutes late and the meet will be just north of Carlinville. We're on flatland again, fast track through former coal mining country. Once the Traction hauled not only the coal, but many of the miners.

Our avid train lover watches carefully as the cars rumble through Chatham, but *around* Auburn (that city never did give the IT a franchise) before a little further south the Chicago & Illinois Midland's Compro branch is crossed. Soon his train passes the spot where a half-mile branch once ran east to the Black Diamond mine.

At Virden, the train uses Dey Street through town; at Girard, the single track threads its way along First Street. At Carlinville, the cars dive under the Chicago & Alton Railroad to follow West Street through town for a delayed meet with the northbound streamliner at Moody Siding. When the meet is made, the young man sees the lead car to be 301, in blue and silver. St. Louis Car Company supplied the first of three streamlined trains late last year, and 301 still looks new and shiny.

Once the streamliners have zipped on by, it's down a long grade to cross Muddy Creek and then the larger Macoupin Creek, which is in a deep ravine. "This is Goat Hollow," the conductor informs our traveller. "We have to climb out of it to get to Gillespie." Then the man in blue serge points out the busy Little

Dog mine to the left, exclusively served by the Illinois Terminal. In addition to the regular siding, there are no less than five mine tracks. Suddenly, the cars make a lurching reverse curve to the left, pass between a Lutheran church and a house and shoot along Macoupin Street in Gillespie.

Two miles south of Gillespie, the train hits Benld and crosses the Chicago & North Western at grade. It's now 10:55 by the young man's Bulova watch--right on the advertised. These old cars sure go! "Here's Dickerson," interjects the conductor, "it's where the Traction had its most disastrous wreck, back in 1910." Our young fan is getting a bit of history with his ride, and soon, Staunton brings another historical comment from the conductor.

"In the early days, they had a dispatcher's office above the station in the center of town, a carbarn and shops for the Litchfield and Hillsboro cars, and some of the mainline freight locomotives," he reminisces. Then, more mournfully," Course, the Traction isn't what it was, with these new streamliners and such.

They're trying to beat the buses, but many of my old passengers are driving new Studebakers and Nashes now. Dunno what's going to happen." Our young voyager looks back along the car. It's only about one-third filled. Still, at every stop passengers are getting on. There's a moderate crowd in the trailer, too.

Now it's southwest along the Wabash to Worden, where the IT dives under the railroad, crosses the Chicago & North Western and finally takes an underpass beneath the New York Central main line. A county road shares the IT right-of-way under the railroad.

Once past the subway, the train picks up speed approaching Hamel, where the tracks cross the intersection of Illinois Route 160 and U.S. 66. The acute angle of the track causes nearly a city block to be taken up by the crossing! Flashers flash, bells ring, horns blast; the road is crossed. Edwardsville. Our young man won't see much of it, for the tracks use the freight belt around the east and south side of town. But the train is nearing metropolitan St. Louis now and the rolling country and farmlands are beginning to give way to industrial drabness and city congestion.

At LeClaire, the cars cross the Chicago & North Western and the Nickel Plate tracks, plus the Illinois Terminal's own steam line. To the left are the LeClaire yards where the electric locomotives end their runs. Steam or diesel locomotives take over for the rest of the trip into Madison via the old St. Louis Troy & Eastern line.

The cars now roll downgrade for several twisting and turning miles before emerging in the Mississippi River's American Bottoms. In Granite City we join the old Alton Granite & St. Louis right-of-way, and the motorman opens it up one final time for a burst of speed. We're due in St. Louis at 12:10 p.m. Apparently our head man thinks he can make it.

With Madison astern, the cars climb onto the "high line" trestle and cross dozens of railroad tracks before finally gaining the Mississippi River and the McKinley Bridge. At the "high line" trestle's west end, the local Granite City line tracks join us, and once we're on the big bridge itself, suburban car 470 lumbers into view.

"Fantastic," thinks our young fan. He's been to Los Angeles and the 470 certainly looks the spitting image of the way Pacific Electric's "Hollywood" cars looked prior to the 1939 upgrading. That afternoon will bring a ride on the Granite City local, and he wonders if the new double-ended PCCs are in service yet. He'll soon find out.

The home stretch. We've crossed the Father of Waters, the Mighty Mississippi, the Big Muddy, and are into Missouri and the City of St. Louis. The double tracks curve from west to south (two tracks lead straight ahead; now, where do they go?) and parallel the river as they descend to ground level through Branch Street yard, only to climb again onto another elevated structure.

Local cars stop at a station above Broadway, where below the young man spies two mountain ash scarlet-and-cream PCC cars of the St. Louis Public Service Company (that system, too, will soon be investigated).

But his train speeds by the Broadway Station only to descend again and run over two blocks of street trackage. There's a general stir inside the car now, passengers are getting up, picking up their belongings, preparing to get off. The train slows as it descends a short subway ramp and almost immediately shudders to a stop at the downtown St. Louis terminal, a short block away from Washington and Twelfth Streets.

Train 84, slated to leave at 12:10 p.m. for Peoria, is on an adjacent track, its three orange cars looming majestically over us in the murk of the subterranean terminal. We arrived on time; it's about to leave. People bustle around; another 470 class car pulls in from Granite City; the crowd from our train, Number 93, disappears into a gargantuan passenger elevator. Our young man's odyssey is over.

Illinois Terminal--alive and well in 1949.

Car 1200, running as train 43, clatters across switches and frogs at Walnut and Washington as it leaves Peoria. Above and to the right of the car is the Peoria station, which the car has just left. The tracks in the left foreground lead to the freight house and carbarn. Paul H. Stringham

An aerial view of Farm Creek Yard in East Peoria, later known as East Peoria Yard. Farm Creek runs along the bottom of the photo. The appearance of this yard changed drastically in later years, when it was decided to build a carbarn and station at the site. Near the lower right-hand corner, a two-car train is bound from Peoria. J. Holling, R.W. Deller Collection

The U.S. Mail Limited, *train 38, with car 249 doing the honors, is arriving at the unprotected Peoria & Pekin Union Railroad crossing in East Peoria, nearing the end of its journey from Decatur to Peoria.* Bill Janssen

Approaching the steepest part of Caldwell Hill, the southbound Capitol Limited *is seen circa 1935.*
Robert V. Mehlenbeck

The northbound Illmo Limited *is a pretty sight, as it approaches Caldwell Siding at about 70 mph on July 4, 1941. Today it consists of motor 277, trailers 528 and 531, and parlor car 512.*
Paul H. Stringham

Less than 15 minutes out of Peoria, train 95, with cars 285 and 528, shoot across the viaduct over the Pennsylvania Railroad, headed for St. Louis. The viaduct in the background is U.S. Highway 150.
Paul H. Stringham

A little snow was on the ground as car 273 zipped along west of Morton, headed for Peoria, on January 31, 1939. Paul H. Stringham

Right on the advertised, the Illmo Limited *makes its way out West Jefferson Street in Morton, on its way to Peoria. It's a beautiful Sunday, July 30, 1939, and motor 284, pulling trailers 530 and 528, and parlor 512, make up the train.* Paul H. Stringham

Under a threatening sky car 284, running as train 95, scoots across a short wooden trestle spanning a county road. Allentown is about a mile ahead; the date, May 9, 1940.
Paul H. Stringham

The southbound Illmo Limited *hustles across a concrete arch culvert not far west of Allentown on November 12, 1931.*
Paul H. Stringham

Car 275 rumbles across the Mackinaw River bridge, ready to curve to the left on its way to St. Louis. Car 1201 waits at right, on the Bloomington line. The scene is at Mackinaw Junction, on May 15, 1938.
Paul H. Stringham

Motor 283 flies over the Alton Railroad just north of Mindale, headed for St. Louis. The steel span at left is over Illinois Highway 122. Paul H. Stringham

With a clatter that can be heard for blocks, car 283, running as train 95, pounds across the double-track main of the Gulf Mobile & Ohio at Athol Tower, in Lincoln. This was a three-way crossing; the Illinois Central is beside the near side of the tower. The date was February 24, 1955.

Paul H. Stringham

Just a few more feet and the northbound Illmo Limited *will be at the station in Lincoln on August 20, 1948. The train is on Chicago Street, crossing Broadway. The Gulf Mobile & Ohio station at Lincoln was shared with the IT.* Paul H. Stringham

Train 95 is only about a mile out of Lincoln and dropping down quite a grade on November 2, 1954. The speed must have been at least 70 mph when it clattered over the Lincoln Sand & Gravel crossing. The interlocking plant was manned by LS&G crews, being lined for the Illinois Terminal except when an LS&G train was crossing. Paul H. Stringham

Lots of railfan "music" is heard as a streamliner clatters across the Illinois Central double track and the Wabash single track at Starne, just north of Springfield. The Danville branch takes off to the left; the date, July 8, 1953. — Paul H. Stringham

W. C. Janssen Collection

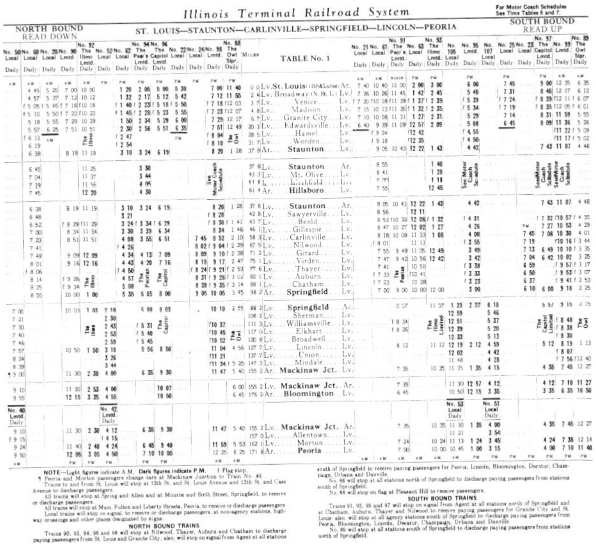

W. C. Janssen Collection

A RIDE OVER THE LINE • 145

The Peorian *pauses for a few minutes at the Springfield station, en route from Peoria to St. Louis during the summer of 1935.* Bill Janssen

Near Girard, the St. Louis line of the Chicago & North Western crossed this long viaduct over Illinois State Highway 4, the Illinois Terminal, and the Gulf Mobile & Ohio. The viaduct is seen here on September 28, 1955. Paul H. Stringham

Train 96, the northbound Capitol Limited, is picking up speed leaving Staunton as it passes Wall siding.   Robert V. Mehlenbeck

Motor 278 leads a trailer down Union Street in Staunton, running limited from Peoria to St. Louis.
Robert V. Mehlenbeck

Approaching the west end of the McKinley Bridge in St. Louis, this view was taken from the front window of a Granite City suburban car on March 20, 1957. The black streak is the rope attached to the front trolley pole.
Paul H. Stringham

A two-car limited is just leaving the subway in St. Louis, bound for Peoria in 1935. Bill Janssen

Car 1203 has just dropped off a passenger and a couple of newspaper bundles at the Riverton station, and is picking up speed as it continues its journey towards Decatur and Danville. The date is July 8, 1953. Paul H. Stringham

The Sangamon River bridge at Riverton originally had five truss spans. After two freight derailments destroyed the two eastern spans, one was replaced with a through girder span and one with a wooden trestle. Here, train 72 heads towards Danville on July 6, 1941. Paul H. Stringham

By the time this photo was taken on March 15, 1955, service on the Springfield-Danville run had been reduced to one train each way daily. Here, train 71 does station work at Illiopolis. Paul H. Stringham

Train 70 rumbles over a bridge in Decatur's Fairview Park, on September 1, 1948.
Paul H. Stringham

Springfield is a little more than an hour away as car 260 scoots across the Lake Decatur bridge on October 27, 1938, just before stopping in Decatur. Paul H. Stringham

Rocking through the corn country of central Illinois, car 263 heads for Danville. The location is near Cerro Gordo, between Decatur and Champaign, the date, July 6, 1941. Paul H. Stringham

There were a lot of milk cans to unload at Monticello on this April 25, 1952. Paul H. Stringham

Car 270 clatters across the Illinois Central main line at Champaign on July 24, 1947. On the far side of the interlocking tower is the main line of the Peoria & Eastern. Paul H. Stringham

About to pass under the Illinois Central main line on University Street in Champaign, car 271 is on a Springfield-to-Danville run, circa 1940. A corner of the Illinois Central station is at right. Bill Janssen

A Danville-Springfield train stands in front of the Champaign station circa 1936. Behind the trailer is the Illinois Central viaduct over University Street, with a crack Pullman train doing station work.
Bill Janssen

Just a couple of blocks back, car 270 swung from side-of-the-road trackage into the center of tree-lined East Main Street in Urbana. Soon it will curve onto the Wabash tracks, to continue through Urbana and into Champaign, on this September 29, 1949.
Paul H. Stringham

Car 271 enters the street in St. Joseph, headed for Springfield, on February 5, 1949.   Bill Janssen

A beautiful spot just west of St. Joseph is the Salt Fork River. Here, the 271 crosses, bound for Danville. The Peoria & Eastern trestle may be seen behind the IT trestle.   Bill Janssen

Bound for Danville, car 284 pauses at the Ogden "station." What appears to be a siding in the background is actually a part of the wye where the Homer branch took off from the Danville line. When the line was cut back to Danville-DeLong, all cars turned on this wye and backed the couple of miles to DeLong.   Bill Janssen

Car 270 rumbles across the Vermillion River bridge at Danville, on a Springfield-Danville run. The bridge was formerly a truss span, but after it was knocked down in a derailment, it was replaced by a deck girder span and a pile trestle. (See chapter on Accidents.)   Bill Janssen

Looking south over the Vermillion River bridge. The tracks make a sharp left turn and head uphill to Main Street.
Illinois Terminal, Dale Jenkins Collection

A Springfield-bound train turns onto Logan Avenue from West Main, in Danville in late April 1952, just before the line was abandoned. Logan Avenue was a steep downgrade to the Vermillion River bridge. Bob Mehlenbeck

Car 270 and a trailer head north, past the Danville powerhouse, in 1948. It will soon turn west onto West Main, and soon be out of town headed for Springfield, in 1948. Bob Mehlenbeck

A RIDE OVER THE LINE • 159

With the beautiful Mackinaw River valley in the background, car 1202 is just leaving the Mackinaw station, headed up a long grade out of the valley. The date is November 3, 1942. Block signals were few on the Mackinaw Junction-Decatur line.　　　　　　　　　　　　　　　　　Paul H. Stringham

Car 1202 makes a graceful entrance into Danvers at the west end of town, where the tracks curved between neat little cottages with their well-manicured lawns, onto the street which it followed through town. The date was October 7, 1942.　　　　　　　　　　　　　　　　　　　　　Paul H. Stringham

Headed for Bloomington and Decatur car 282, running as train 102, lopes slowly down the main drag in Danvers, on June 20, 1947.
Paul H. Stringham

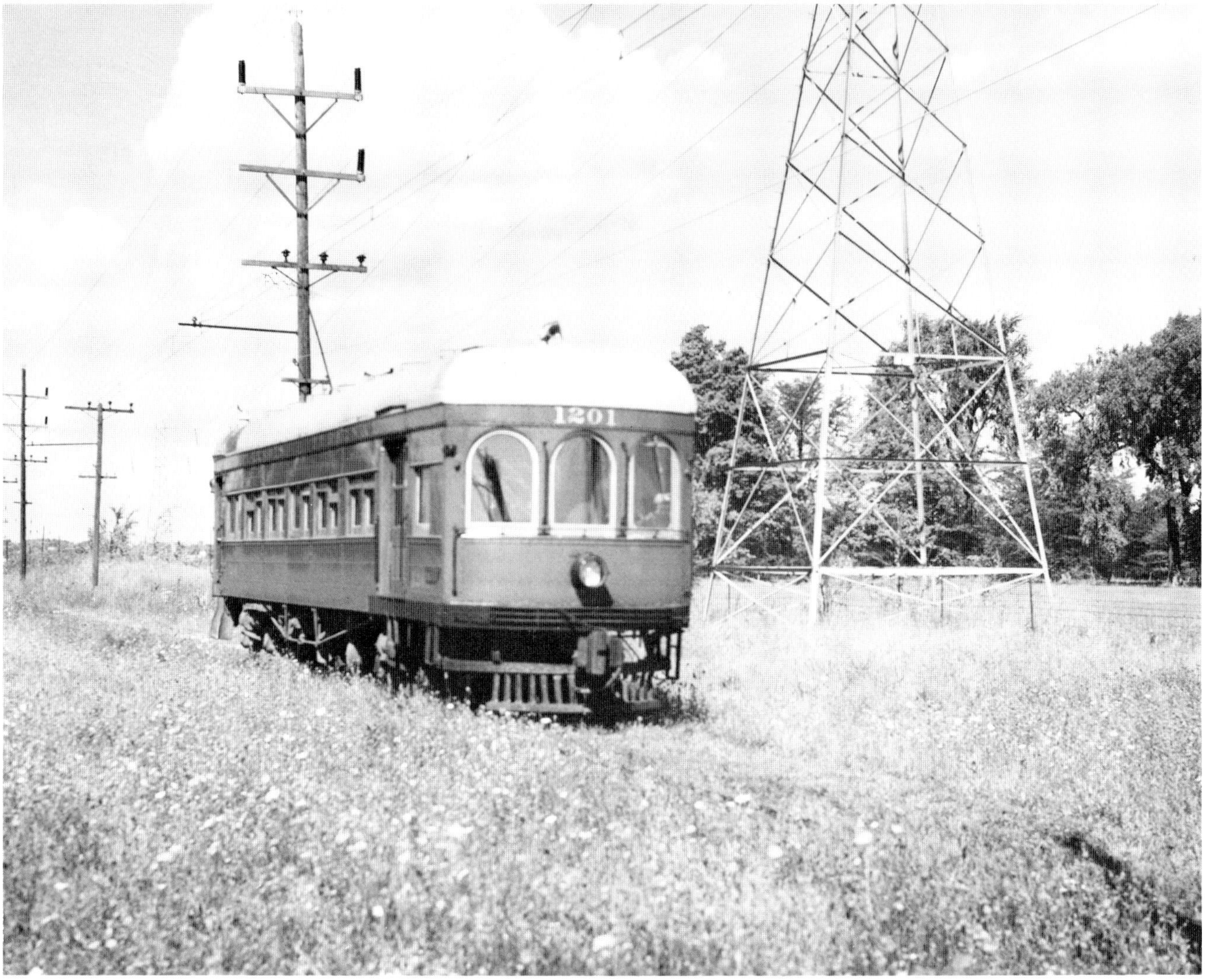

No, it isn't a "trackless trolley"; if you use your imagination you can tell where the rails are. The date was September 23, 1952, at Twin Grove, just west of Bloomington and five months to the day when the Bloomington line was history. With the end so close, the IT was wasting no money on maintenance.

Paul H. Stringham

EXHIBIT "B"

COMPARATIVE STATEMENT OF SUBSIDIARY COMPANIES OF ILLINOIS TRACTION COMPANY SHOWING

RECEIPTS AND EXPENDITURES FOR YEARS 1909 TO 1916

EARNINGS:	1909	1910	1911	1912	1913	1914	1915	1916
Interurban Lines	2,282,439.24	2,793,789.94	3,238,712.90	3,395,634.18	3,604,265.34	3,626,635.54	3,559,028.03	3,993,836.0
City Lines	2,104,911.33	2,675,653.79	2,877,086.58	2,950,562.57	3,072,235.58	3,021,859.55	2,871,035.35	3,110,811.1
Gas	460,469.33	568,174.39	723,983.72	783,679.51	816,911.67	877,982.40	905,702.79	923,642.1
Electric	974,086.17	1,534,320.88	1,835,989.69	2,218,419.13	2,636,713.78	3,002,378.13	3,325,410.62	3,689,851.5
Heat	151,579.33	181,000.47	216,966.17	240,507.15	274,672.16	314,640.22	317,579.84	341,379.5
Water		3,586.31	7,289.40	12,030.68	13,538.77	14,385.69	14,215.86	14,476.2
Miscellaneous	17,673.47	42,142.60	47,087.65	109,644.03	102,760.96	254,972.73	195,022.21	492,450.3
Total Gross Earnings	5,991,158.87	7,798,668.38	8,947,116.11	9,710,477.25	10,521,098.26	11,112,854.26	11,187,994.70	12,566,447.1
Operating Exp. and Taxes	3,472,740.98	4,680,322.77	5,404,622.94	5,775,043.13	6,198,872.65	6,587,462.64	6,657,569.14	7,489,797.3
Net from Operating	2,518,417.89	3,118,345.61	3,542,493.17	3,935,434.12	4,322,225.61	4,525,391.62	4,530,425.56	5,076,649.8
Interest on Bonds	1,644,464.12	2,027,874.77	2,502,173.01	2,672,402.51	2,883,239.52	3,290,786.59	3,268,607.01	3,603,417.3
Available for Depr. Div., etc.	873,953.77	1,090,470.84	1,040,320.16	1,263,031.61	1,438,986.09	1,234,605.03	1,261,818.55	1,473,232.4

ILLINOIS
TRACTION COMPANY
ILLINOIS TRACTION
Thirteenth Annual Report of the Directors
to the Shareholders
1916

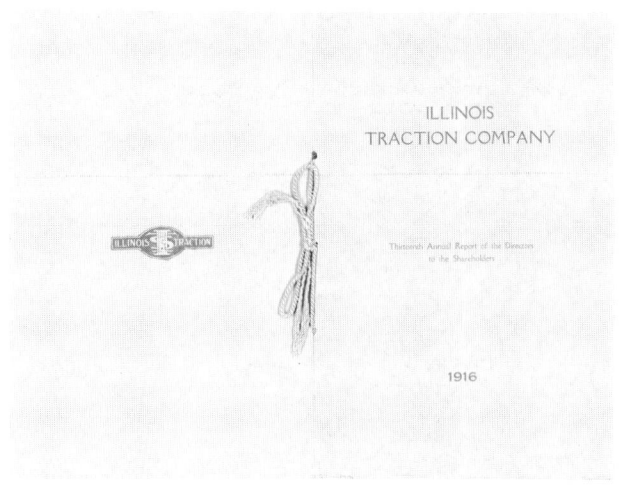

W. C. Janssen Collection

Just four days before the Bloomington line was to be abandoned, the Mackinaw Junction-Bloomington local freight is "in the hole" at Woodruff siding while car 1200 thunders westward towards Peoria. It was October 6, 1942, and fortunately the abandonment order was lifted and the Bloomington line ran for another 10½ years. Paul H. Stringham

Car 281 rumbles down Madison Street at Washington, headed for the Bloomington station on October 16, 1950. Note the curious placement of the overhead support poles in the street along the curb, instead of in the sidewalk. Paul H. Stringham

L.K. McCrillis watches from the cab of car 278 as his train, No. 41, is photographed in front of the Heyworth station on February 19, 1953.   Paul H. Stringham

The white flags mounted on car 273 give away the fact that the car is motionless. This special run was made for a group of railfans on May 15, 1938, running from Peoria-Springfield-Decatur-Bloomington-Peoria. Here, the special has backed onto the Salt Creek bridge, just south of Clinton, for its portrait.
Paul H. Stringham

Three days before the Mackinaw Junction-Decatur line was closed, car 278 was photographed trundling along U.S. Highway 51, in Maroa, on February 19, 1953. The tracks curved onto the street from the east, and left the street toward the east, so northbound automobile traffic crossed the tracks twice and southbound traffic, not at all. The "Trolley Stop" sign at right protected the Maroa station.
Paul H. Stringham

For the first few weeks after the abandonment of the Mackinaw Junction-Forsythe line, the IT maintained service from Decatur to Forsythe. Since there was no way to turn cars at Forsythe, double-ender 404 was brought north to handle these runs. Here she rumbles across a small trestle not far north of North Junction, Decatur, on April 16, 1953.
Paul H. Stringham

Illinois Traction System Stations

Over the years, the Illinois Traction System boasted a variety of stations, ranging from 7 foot by 7 foot "pagodas" found at many of the country crossings, up to the fine urban station buildings found in the larger cities such as St. Louis, Springfield, Peoria and Danville. Generally there were four basic types of structure, each with variations. Many were built when the line was constructed, many of those lasted until abandonment, and some still stand, being used for other purposes.

Of the smaller town stations, the best was the combination station-substation.

A 1200-class interurban is just leaving the Mackinaw station, headed for Peoria in October 1942. Built in 1909, this combination station-substation was of classic ITS design, dreamed up by Mr. H.F. Chubbuck (McKinley's right-hand man). This particular station has been given Federal Landmark status, and is slowly being restored to its former glory. Bob Mehlenbeck

From 1907 until 1923, the IT used most of the main floor of the building at Adams and Hamilton Streets in Peoria. The awning at the lower right corner of the building is lettered "Illinois Traction System." For the first few months of operation into Peoria, the ITS used the Peoria & Pekin Terminal, which was on the main floor of the three-story addition at left (where the men are standing). The photo was taken in the very early 1920s. Lee Roten Studio

The Peoria freight house, at Walnut and Washington Streets, is a busy place in this August 19, 1911 view. A small waiting room and ticket office were located here, the door to which can be seen to the right of express motor 1066. Illinois Traction, John Hubbard Collection

What might have been. This attractive station and office building was designed as the Peoria station in 1912; it was to have been built at the corner of Hamilton and Jefferson Streets, across from the courthouse. The contracts were let and foundations started when World War I broke out, and all work stopped and was never resumed.   Lee Roten

These were one-story buildings with a three foot base of large red rough-faced brick, the rest of the walls being in buff brick. Some of these had a two-story "tower" near the center, others had a "tower" at one end of the building. All had a red tile roof. Another variant was similar, except for the substation and hence did not need the "tower." Many of the older brick stations had flat roofs, a few had hip roofs, while the fourth and last type were hip-roofed frame buildings.

1). Peoria-St. Louis line.

Peoria (mile zero) . When the line first reached Peoria, it shared the Peoria Railway terminal on Hamilton Street, in a small annex to the Meyer building. This building later became the Pascal Hotel. On January 1, 1908, ITS established its own station in the Hamilton and Adams Street corner of the Meyer Building. In May, 1912, Illinois Traction bought the site of the National Hotel at Hamilton and Jefferson, and plans were made for a fine seven-story station and company office building.

Station tracks would have been off-street, with a train shed to protect passengers from the weather. Construction was begun. Only the foundations were complete when World War One broke out in Europe during 1914. By this time, ITS was controlled by the Sun Life Insurance Company of Canada, which was already in the war.

The work was closed down and never resumed.

In 1923, there was a general rerouting of the Peoria streetcars, one of which brought cars of the Heights line around the courthouse. The interurban cars standing on Hamilton Street now interfered with the city cars, so on September 1, the ITS moved its station one half-block to 211 Hamilton Street, thus clearing a way for the city cars. The new location was an unattractive store-front building, but had to serve while studies were made for a more attractive building. Finally, early in 1930, construction began on a fine two-story stone station at Walnut and Adams Streets.

The last train left the old Hamilton Street station late on September 30, 1930, and early on the morning of October 1, the first train arrived at the new station. The tracks were under the waiting room, since the ground had a steep slope. Out of use as a station since 1950, the building is currently the City of Peoria's Police Station. There was also a small waiting room and ticket office in the freight house at Walnut and Washington Streets, where all trains stopped. This was discontinued in October, 1930, when the new station (only a block away) was opened.

East Peoria (0.5 miles). For many years there was no station at all in East Peoria, save for "pagodas" at North Main Street and East Washington Streets.

However once the tracks over the Peoria bridge were abandoned in 1950, two small metal buildings were set up to serve as a waiting room and baggage room. These were used while an attractive buff brick one-story station and freight house was built, and this was complete in November, 1951.

Morton (9.7 miles). One-story red brick flat-roof station, with slightly raised section at the back for the substation. This dated from 1906-7, the time of the line's construction.

Mackinaw Junction (16.6 miles). A two-story frame station was built in the center of the wye in 1908. Since all three tracks of the wye were on high fills, this was a less-than-satisfactory arrangement, and on March 10, 1909, the station was moved westwards to the point where the Bloomington and Springfield lines joined. At the same time, the station was raised to track level with the waiting room on the first floor, and the dispatcher's office upstairs. The building was destroyed by fire January 8, 1925, and was replaced in January, 1926, by a two-story buff-brick station. In the interim, two old interurban car bodies served as temporary station and baggage room.

Mindale (24.5 miles). Combination station-substation, built 1909.

Union (34.1 miles). Combination station-substation, built 1909.

Lincoln (44.1 miles). Two-story concrete block building built in 1907, with station at the front, freight house at the rear, and a spur track alongside. Station closed 1929, when the ITS began joint use of the Chicago & Alton Station.

Broadwell (51.0 miles). One-story frame store building.

Elkhart (54.8 miles). Buff brick combination station-substation, built 1909.

Williamsville (60.5 miles). An old one-story residence, converted to station use.

Ridgeley Junction (67.8 miles). Buff brick combination station-substation.

Springfield (73.6 miles). Originally a store-front at 520 East Monroe, established in 1904. In 1906, a move was made to a two-story brick building at Eighth and Monroe.

The Peoria passenger terminal was an attractive limestone structure, opened in 1930. This photo of the terminal was taken on June 19, 1949.   Paul H. Stringham

The original Mackinaw Junction station burned in 1925, and was replaced in 1926 by this two-story buff brick station. It is shown here in June 1929.   Illinois Traction, Dale Jenkins Collection

This building had room alongside for storage tracks, but was soon outgrown. In 1908, the old streetcar barn on Monroe (near Ninth) was bought and remodelled into a station, opening August 17. It was the original intention to load and unload all cars on the off-street tracks, since all cars either began or ended their runs at Springfield. However, when through Peoria-St. Louis service began, these cars loaded and unloaded on the Monroe Street tracks in front of the station. In the rear was a two-track train shed, plus a two-track repair facility, both under cover. In 1932, a buff brick two-story station was built on Clear Lake Road, Springfield. The waiting room, ticket office, lunch room etc., were on the ground floor, with company offices on the second floor. This station opened February 26, 1933.

When combination station-substations of ITS common design were built in towns, they were usually placed endwise to the track, with the entrance door in the end of the building. Here at Elkhart, on May 12, 1950, this was the case; the track along the near side of the building is the wye, the main track being in the street at left, out of view.   Paul H. Stringham

The Springfield station was located on Clear Lake Road, some distance from downtown. Company offices occupied the second floor while the ticket office, waiting room, and lunch counter were on the ground floor. All trains headed into the station, then backed around the wye on departure.
Paul H. Stringham

As small-town stations went, Girard was among the best on the IT. Monticello and Wapella had similar stations. This was one of the few locations to have a train order signal. The interlocking tower in the distance protected the crossing of the Burlington and Gulf Mobile & Ohio railroads; to the right of the station, the track ran down the street for several blocks. Paul H. Stringham

Chatham (83.7 miles). Small one-story frame station.

Auburn (89.7 miles). One-story frame station.

Thayer (94.2 miles). Three-sided pagoda, open side towards the track. There may have been a larger station here at one time.

Virden (96.7 miles). One-story red brick and stone station, built with the line. Its hip roof was unusual; most of the older stations had flat roofs.

Girard (100.6 miles). One-story buff brick station with red tile roof, built 1910.

Nilwood (104.3 miles). One-story frame residence, rebuilt into a station after the original station burned.

Carlinville (113.5 miles). One-story red brick and stone station, with hip roof. A wye and storage track was alongside.

Gillespie (125.7 miles). Large one-story brick station with flat roof.

Benld (128.1 miles). Large one-story frame station, with hip roof.

Staunton (134.0 miles). This was a one-of-a-kind brick structure, with waiting room and ticket office on the ground floor, and the dispatchers office on the second floor.

Worden (140.1 miles). Small frame station.

Hamel (143.3 miles). Small brick station.

Edwardsville (151.5 miles). First station a store front on Hillsboro Avenue. In 1931, new store-front station opened on St. Louis Avenue, serving until December 18, 1937, when a one-story brick station was opened on the Edwardsville Belt line.

Granite City (165.1 miles). First station at Niedringhaus Avenue at the Terminal Railroad Association crossing was a small frame building. When through East St. Louis-Springfield service began, the building was moved to Niedringhaus and Madison Avenues, not being replaced until 1927, when a new two-story brick building opened. Both main line and St. Louis & Alton trains used this station, which remained in service until the coming of the streamliners in 1949. They could not negotiate the sharp curves in Granite City, so a small metal shed was placed along the Granite City belt line, used until service was finally abandoned.

Car 101, running on the Alton line, rounds the loop at the temporary station at Twelfth and Franklin in St. Louis, in 1930. This station was in use during the construction of the subway and Midwest Terminal Building.　　　　　　　　　　　　　　　　　　　　　　　Robert V. Mehlenbeck

Construction of the St. Louis subway is under way in this January 10, 1932 view looking north, from south of Franklin.　　　　　　　　　　　　　　　　　　Illinois Terminal, Dale Jenkins Collection

Another construction view of the subway looks south at the intersection of Franklin Avenue, on December 20, 1931.
Illinois Terminal, Dale Jenkins Collection

St. Louis, Broadway (169.2 miles). A large station was built under the west approach to the McKinley Bridge. A stairway led up to the tracks and a shelter built alongside the tracks. This was used until the subway-elevated line was opened in 1931, being replaced by an open shelter on the latter line, also at Broadway.

St. Louis, Twelfth Street (171.8 miles). One and two-story brick and stucco building, built 1910. A loop with storage tracks for passenger cars was adjacent and a large freight house to the east. The Midwest Terminal Building was opened in 1932, housing many offices including those of the Illinois Terminal. The waiting room, ticket offices, lunch room etc., were at street level and the trains loaded and unloaded in the subway underneath, the two floors connected by elevator.

2). Peoria-Decatur line.

Trains on this run used the same track to Mackinaw Junction (16.6 miles) before branching off onto their own line.

Mackinaw (17.4 miles). Buff brick station-substation, built 1909. This building has been restored as a National Landmark.

Danvers (27.0 miles). Similar to Morton (9.7 miles), one-story red brick station with raised section at the rear for a substation. Most recently the station was being used as a laundromat.

This July 19, 1931 view of the construction of the Midwest Terminal Building looks northwest from Lucas Avenue.
Illinois Terminal, Dale Jenkins Collection

Looking south from Morgan Street at the east side of the Terminal Building, on February 7, 1932.
Illinois Terminal, Dale Jenkins Collection

The main entrance to the St. Louis terminal. The waiting room, ticket offices, and lunch room were to the left. A huge elevator transported passengers to and from the lower level, where the trains arrived and departed. The photo was taken on March 20, 1957.   Paul H. Stringham

This June 24, 1953 view shows the Twin Grove waiting shelter shortly after the rails and overhead wire had been removed. Before long, the poles and ties will be gone too. The elevator at right was served by the Peoria & Eastern, which was dismantled in 1986. (Twin Grove was just west of Bloomington.)
Paul H. Stringham

The second Bloomington station was remodeled from a former freight house and carbarn. Peoria-bound trains, such as car 1201, backed into the station while Decatur-bound trains loaded and unloaded in the street, near where the Railway Express Agency truck is waiting. The view was taken on June 1, 1948.
                                                                                                    Paul H. Stringham

This small one-story brick station and wooden addition, seen here in June 1929, were located at Heyworth.
        Illinois Traction, Dale Jenkins Collection

Clinton had this brick station-substation, seen here in June 1929. Note the wye tracks, and loading docks at the side of the building.
        Illinois Traction, Dale Jenkins Collection

ILLINOIS TRACTION SYSTEM STATIONS • 179

This early view shows the Decatur station, which served from 1908 until 1931, at the corner of Wood and South Water Streets.
Illinois Traction, Dale Jenkins Collection

Bloomington (37.6 miles). The first station was a downtown store front at Jefferson and Madison Streets. In 1942, the old freight house on Madison, at the Nickel Plate Railroad crossing, was remodelled into a combined station and freight house. It was a brick structure and tracks were arranged for off-street loading and unloading.

Heyworth (49.7 miles). Small one-story brick station, probably built with the line.

Wapella (56.2 miles). Buff brick station, built 1910, still in place 1988.

Clinton (61.0 miles). Large one-story brick station with substation at the rear and a freight room along the south side. A wye was at the building's south side.

Maroa (69.2 miles). Small frame station.

Emery (73.3 miles). Combination station-substation of buff brick with a red tile roof.

Forsythe (76.5 miles). Small frame station.

Decatur (83.1 miles). See Springfield-Danville section.

3). Springfield-Danville line.

Springfield (mile zero). See Peoria-St. Louis line.

Riverton (7.0 miles). Small frame store building with a canopy across the front.

Dawson (11.8 miles). Medium-size frame station when mine was open. Replaced with small frame shed, mostly open on the track side, when the mine closed.

Buffalo (14.4 miles). Combination buff brick, red tile-roofed station-substation.

Mechanicsburg Junction (15.5 miles). No data-- possibly a roofed-over platform, which would have sufficed, since its only use was for passengers transferring between the Mechanicsburg branch and the main line.

Lanesville (17.8 miles). Small frame station with hip roof.

Illiopolis (23.2 miles). One story combination station-substation, with frame freight house adjoining the west side.

Donovan (25.6 miles). Probably the most deluxe of all crossing shelters. Buff brick construction with hip roof, concrete platform, plus a seat along a rear wall.

The interior of the Decatur station, circa 1910. Illinois Traction, Dale Jenkins Collection

The downtown Decatur station was replaced in 1931 by this one-story brick building, located some distance from downtown along the belt line. On this September 1, 1948, car 281 will soon depart for Peoria; the baggage man awaits the arrival of a car from Springfield. Paul H. Stringham

The Champaign station, opened in 1914, had a waiting room and ticket offices on the main floor, and offices on the second and third floors. Two spur tracks ran along the right side of the building. This photo was taken sometime around 1925.
Illinois Traction, Paul H. Stringham Collection

Niantic (27.2 miles). One-story frame station with hip roof.

Harristown (31.7 miles). Small frame station with hip roof. Replaced 1910 by buff brick combination station-substation.

Decatur (39.0 miles). The original station was the street railways transfer house in Lincoln Square, which in addition to the interurban cars, hosted nearly all of Decatur's city streetcars. Late in 1907, the Advance Thresher Company building at Wood and South Water Streets was acquired. It was a one-story brick structure, with ticket office, baggage room and waiting room, plus three tracks under cover, and opened March 10, 1908. It was replaced March 24, 1931, when an attractive one-story brick structure was opened on the Belt Line at Van Dyke and Packard Streets.

Oakley (48.5 miles). Small red brick substation with a waiting room in one corner.

Cerro Gordo (52.6 miles). Large one-story frame station, with a wye on the east side.

Milmine (56.9 miles). Ground floor of two-story brick Odd fellows Hall. A canopy across the front gave weather protection.

Bement (60 miles). Red brick combination station-substation with flat roof.

Monticello (68.3 miles). One-story buff brick station with red tile roof, on the long curve between Market and Livingston Streets. Cars were close enough to the sidewalk (on the inside of the curve) that it could be used as a station platform.

The Wabash depot in Urbana was used after 1937, when cars were rerouted via the Wabash tracks through town. Car 271 loads passengers, bound for Danville.
Bill Janssen

White Heath (74.1 miles). One-story red brick station-substation with flat roof.

Bondville (82.2 miles). Buff brick red tile roof station-substation.

Champaign (89.5 miles). No details on original station. On January 14, 1914, a three- story brick structure opened. Ticket office, waiting room and baggage room were on the first floor, with company offices on the upper floors. A wye and storage tracks were along the west side of the building. In 1937, when the IT ceased to use Champaign and Urbana street trackage, the Wabash Railroad Station was used instead, a one-story frame building, very plain and probably more at home in a smaller town.

Urbana (91.6 miles). Original station opened 1907, on the ground floor of a four-story brick structure owned by the power company. When cars were rerouted in 1937 via the Wabash Railroad, the Wabash frame station was used instead.

St. Joseph (100.4 miles). On ground floor of two-story brick structure. Waiting room and ticket office in front, substation at rear. A canopy covered the sidewalk in front of the building.

Ogden (104.9 miles). One-story frame building with hip roof. Replaced in later years by a very small structure with small freight room at one end, passenger room open to the track, similar to many "pagoda" type shelters at country crossings.

Fithian (109.3 miles). Buff brick red tile roof station-substation. Here, the IT track ran along the north side of U.S. route 150 and the station was on the south side. There was quite a walk from the station to the cars.

Muncie (110.8 miles). Small frame station.

Bronson (112.8 miles). Small frame station with tile roof at the Chicago & Eastern Illinois Railroad crossing, used by both lines. Since the station had the appearance of many C&EI stations, it was probably built by that company.

Oakwood (114.4 miles). Small waiting room. Tickets sold in a store.

This July 1929 view shows the Ogden station.   Illinois Traction, Dale Jenkins Collection

Located within a half block of the heart of the city, the Danville station was this attractive two-story structure, seen here circa 1925. Ticket offices and a waiting room were located on the main floor, with company offices of the Illinois Power & Light Corporation located on the second floor. The freight house was along the south side, next to the two storage tracks.
Illinois Traction, Paul H. Stringham Collection

184 • ILLINOIS TERMINAL

Perhaps the most unique of all IT stations was this two-story brick building in Georgetown, located right smack in the middle of the town square, in the middle of the intersection of Main and West streets. All wagon and auto traffic had to keep to the right, while IT cars rolled right through it. Here, on July 15, 1929, southbound car 302 has arrived and express is being unloaded. Looking south, one can see the waiting room to the left, the freight room to the right, and the open-air bandstand above the arch.
Illinois Traction, Dale Jenkins Collection

Looking west at the freight room side of the Georgetown station, also on July 15, 1929. Illinois Traction, Dale Jenkins Collection

Danville (123.0 miles). Details of original station not known. New station opened December, 1923, a brick structure with two-stories high lobby, plus a floor above. Rear of station three stories high. Ground floor had waiting room, ticket office and baggage room, with freight room on south side. Offices were on the two upper floors. Two tracks ran along the south side.

4. Danville-Ridge Farm line.

Danville (mile zero). See Springfield-Danville line.

Westville (5.9 miles). Frame station, with wye along the north side.

Georgetown (10.6 miles). A unique brick station in the center of the town square. Cars passed through an arch in the center of the building, and in early years there was a bandstand on the building's roof.

Ridge Farm (16.3 miles). Small brick station with wye alongside.

5. Danville-Catlin line.

Danville (mile zero). See Springfield-Danville line
Tilton (2.1 miles). Station in the village hall.

6. Homer-Ogden line. Danville (mile zero). See Springfield-Danville line.

Homer (5.5 miles). Brick station, with a wye track leading inside the station.

7. Staunton-Litchfield-Hillsboro line.

Staunton (mile zero). See Peoria-St. Louis line.

Litchfield (14.0 miles). Original station details unknown, but replaced in 1925 by a one-story brick building.

Hillsboro (23.2 miles). Originally downtown, but no details have been found. The frame station used later was built in 1920.

The Danville Powerhouse, also showing part of the substation at left. A class A electric locomotive switches a gondola and a hopper car, while other similar cars rest on the curved sidings. The photo was taken circa 1915. Paul H. Stringham Collection

POWER SUPPLY

The principal powerhouses when the line was opened were at Danville, Riverton, Peoria and Edwardsville. The system's largest powerhouse was opened in 1910 at Venice right by the east end of the McKinley bridge. Power was also supplied by street railway powerhouses in Champaign, Decatur and Bloomington. All were steam-powered. In July, 1927, the powerhouses at Peoria, LaSalle and Riverton were sold to the Illinois Power & Light Corporation for $82,141,500. The Danville powerhouse was later sold to the IP&L, and the large unit at Venice was sold to the Union Electric Company. From that point power was bought from outside sources. Most substations, including portable units 056, 075 and 076, were also sold to IP&L during the 1930s, the final recorded sale being in 1938. Power was transmitted from the powerhouses at 33,000 volts, reduced to 650 volts before being fed into the trolley wire. When the line opened, substations were about 10 miles apart. On Mackinaw Junction-Decatur and Decatur-Danville, they remained largely unaltered, but the Peoria-St. Louis

The Peoria powerhouse was located at the west end of the Illinois River bridge. It supplied power not only to the interurban line, but also to the Peoria streetcar system as well. This view was made looking south, probably around 1915. The carbarn is at extreme right, with a blurred car pulling in.
Peoria Public Library

Fithian station-substation was of standard IT design. This view looks east, in July 1929.
Illinois Traction, Dale Jenkins Collection

The interior of the substation at Fithian.
Al Spearman Collection

and Springfield-Decatur lines had new substations added from time to time as freight business became heavier and larger freight locomotives were put into service. At the time electrification was discontinued in 1956, substations were about five miles apart on these two latter lines.

SUBSTATIONS: Peoria-St. Louis line

Location	Mile	Type	Owner	Amps
Peoria	0	Powerhouse	IP&L	2500 (A)
East Peoria	0.5	Metal Shed	IP&L	3500 (A)
Caldwell	5	Red Brick	IP&L	3800 (A)
Morton	9	Red Brick (S-S)	IP&L	2000 (M)
Robinson	13	Concrete Block	ITC	2000 (A)
Mackinaw	16	Buff Brick (S-S)	IP&L	3000 (M)
Summit	19	Metal Shed	IP&L	2000 (A)
Mindale	24	Buff Brick (S-S)	IP&L	2000 (M)
Richmond	28	Portable	IP&L	2000 (A)
Union	33	Buff Brick (S-S)	IP&L	3000 (M)
Wilmert	37	Metal Shed	IP&L	2000 (A)
Lincoln	43	Red Brick	IP&L	2000 (M)
Fogarty	48	Concrete Block	ITC	2000 (A)
Elkhart	54	Buff Brick (S-S)	IP&L	2000 (M)
Merriam	61	Red Brick	IP&L	2000 (A)
Ridgeley	67	Buff Brick (S-S)	IP&L	2000 (A)
B&O	74	Buff Brick (Tower)	IP&L	2500 (A)
Iles	81	Red Brick	IP&L	3000 (M)
Chatham	84	Red Brick	IP&L	2000 (A)
C&IM	92	Buff Brick	ITC	3000 (S)
Virden	98	Red Brick	IP&L	2000 (M)
Nilwood	104	Red Brick	IP&L	2000 (A)
Anderson	109	Red Brick	IP&L	2000 (M)
Moody	114	Buff Brick	IP&L	2000 (A)
Hill	116	Concrete Block	ITC	2000 (S)
Loveless	120	Buff Brick	IP&L	2000 (A)
Gillespie	126	Red Brick (S-S)	ITC	2000 (A)
Smutzlar	131	Metal Building	IP&L	2500 (A)
Spring Street (a)	135	Metal Shed	IP&L	3200 (M)
Worden	140	Buff Brick	IP&L	3000 (A)
Cornstalk	147	Buff Brick	IP&L	3000 (A)
Bells	153	Metal Shed	IP&L	3000 (A)
Chemical	160	Red Brick	IP&L	2000 (A)
Sulphur (b)	165	Buff Brick	IP&L	1000 (A)
Chambers (c)	170	Bluff Brick	IP&L	1000 (S)

SUBSTATIONS: Peoria-Decatur line

Location	Mile	Type	Owner	Amps
Peoria	0	Powerhouse	IP&L	2500
Mackinaw	16	Buff Brick (S-S)	IP&L	3000 (M)
Danvers	26	Red Brick	IP&L	1250 (M)
Bloomington	37	Powerhouse	IP&L	2000
Heyworth	49	Red Brick (S-S)	IP&L	2000 (M)
Clinton	60	Red Brick (S-S)	IP&L	1250 (S)
Emery	72	Buff Brick (S-S)	IP&L	1500 (S)
North Decatur	80	Brown Brick	IP&L	2000 (A)

SUBSTATIONS: Springfield-Danville line

Location	Miles	Type	Owner	Amps
Springfield	0	-	-	
Riverton	6	Power House	IP&L	2000 (M)
Rents	11	Metal Building	ITC	2000 (S)
Buffalo	13	Buff Brick (S-S)	IP&L	2000 (M)
Haynes	20	Concrete Block	ITC	2000 (S)
Illiopolis	22	Red Brick (S-S)	IP&L	2000 (M)
Harristown	31	Buff Brick (S-S)	IP&L	2000 (S)
Fairview	35	Metal Building	IP&L	2000 (S)
North Decatur	39	Brown Brick	IP&L	2000 (A)
Oakley	48	Red Brick (S-S)	IP&L	2000 (S)
Bement	60	Red Brick (S-S)	IP&L	2000 (M)
Monticello	67	Open Air	IP&L	2000 (A)
White Heath	73	Red Brick (S-S)	IP&L	2000 (S)
Bondville	81	Buff brick (S-S)	IP&L	2000 (S)
Champaign	88	Powerhouse	IP&L	1500
Urbana	90	Portable	IP&L	2000 (S)
St. Joseph	99	Red Brick (S-S)	IP&L	2000 (M)
Fithian	108	Buff Brick (S-S)	IP&L	2000 (M)
Danville	122	Powerhouse	IP&L	2500

Notes: (a) Staunton (b) Granite City (c) St. Louis (A) Automatic, (S) Semi-Automatic, (M) Manual, (S-S) Combination station and substation. IP&L Illinois Power and Light Corporation, ITC Illinois Terminal Company.

Summit substation was located a few miles south of Mackinaw Junction. The view was taken on August 18, 1954.　　　　　　　　　　　　　　　　　　　　　　　　　Paul H. Stringham Collection

Looking north along the Peoria-St. Louis line at Merriam substation. Seen here on March 15, 1955, the town of Williamsville is in the background.　　　　　　　　　　　Paul H. Stringham

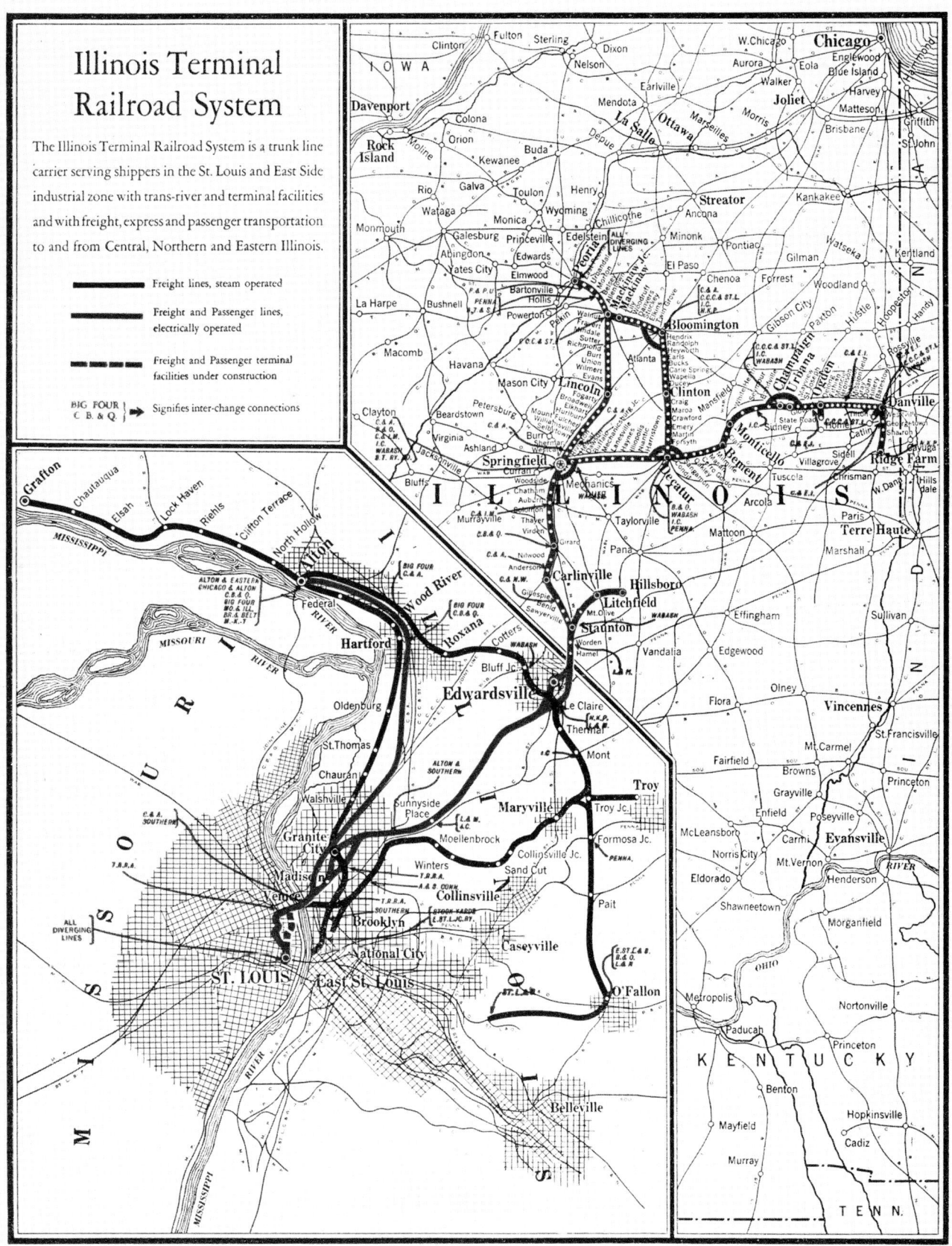

Bill Janssen

Shops and Carbarns

In the first years, ITS cars needing repair were handled either at the ITS carbarn in Riverton or at the street railway carbarns in Decatur, Champaign or Danville. By 1907 the line had grown so large it was decided to build a shop solely for ITS equipment.

The first site chosen was South Madison Street in Bloomington and early in 1907 work began, completed by June. The building had six tracks together with an adjacent powerhouse. However it was intended only as a stopgap, for in March, 1907, forty acres of ground were acquired in Decatur for $18,000. A storeroom was the first building put up on that plot.

The Decatur shops were a very busy place in 1923, when this photo was taken. Truck inspection and repair seems to be the main activity for this group of men; also note the wheelsets in the foreground, with various inspection marks on them. The old ITS herald on the 275 dates the photo. The truck at left has a pilot attached; it is from the express motor at left. The other trucks are devoid of pilots, as the passenger motors seen here had their pilots attached to the car body.

Illinois Traction, Jack R. Harry Collection

This early view looks northwest at the Decatur shops. Apparently, things were still under construction at this time, hence piles of building materials are scattered around the yard, and next to the 1200-class express-passenger motor. The slogan on the roof sign further helps identify this photo as circa 1910.
Illinois Traction, Dale Jenkins Collection

Another view of the Decatur shops, looking west. In evidence is a class B locomotive, dating this photo as sometime after 1910; more likely, it is circa 1915-1920. The wonderful roof sign on the building is a fake, unfortunately; it has been inked in on the original photo, apparently for publicity purposes.
Illinois Traction, Dale Jenkins Collection

An early interior view shows workers testing and fixing components at their workbenches, while others in the background look over the endsill on an interurban car and still more work on an assembly project at right. An interesting electrical test rack is at left.
Illinois Traction, Dale Jenkins Collection

On May 12, 1907, details were released. The main shop was to be 252' x 300', the permanent store room was to be 125' x 200', and the temporary store room already up 125' x 200'. It was intended the temporary storeroom could be used as a carbarn once the permanent storeroom was built. A lumber house 40' x 100', an oil house 50' x 50' and a heating building 60' x 43' would complete the complex. The paint shop was moved from Bloomington to Decatur early in January, 1908, and in February the first shipment of machinery was en route to Decatur. By July 1909 over 100 men were working in the new brick and steel shops.

The shops did not long remain pristine. On October 22, 1909, they were badly damaged by a tornado, which knocked down the west wall, tore off a third of the roof, killed one man and injured eight. Repairs were speedy and things were soon back to normal, indeed were expanded, since by the end of the year the carpenter and cabinet shop, the blacksmith shop, dry kiln and lumber sheds, the oil house and car storage barn were all completed, followed next month by the wood shop. This latter was 48' x 800' with two tracks, adjacent to the main shop. Nineteen woodworking machines were installed immediately. By August 1910 the carpenter and mill shop followed. These additions nearly doubled the workforce, now 170.

The new Decatur shop could carry out any kind of work. Worn out cars could be overhauled, collision damaged cars rebuilt, faded cars repainted. When necessary too, new cars could be built and the Decatur shops built all the Class B, C and D locomotives entirely within the premises, except for the underframes and trucks. No matter what the condition of equipment going into the Decatur shops, it could not be distinguished from new when it came out again.

On July 24, 1913, this special train was run for ITS shops employees. A second section followed as well. The first section is seen here at Decatur.
Illinois Traction, John Hubbard Collection

Usually the Decatur shops were a busy place, but on this quiet April 16, 1953 Sunday there was little activity. The building at the center of this panoramic view is the carpentry shop. Car 405, normally a St. Louis-Granite City car, was temporarily in use on the Decatur-Forsythe shuttle run.
Paul H. Stringham

The first group of class C locomotives under construction at the Decatur shops, probably in 1924. Trucks were used from dismantled passenger motors, frames were purchased from Commonwealth Steel of Granite City, and the rest of the locomotives were built from scratch.

Illinois Traction, Jack Harry Collection

The Granite City shops took care of the Granite City-St. Louis suburban cars, and later, the St. Louis-Alton cars as well. In addition, many smaller repairs were taken care of on the mainline cars. The shop was opened in 1910, and the photo was probably taken shortly thereafter.
Charles Goethe Collection

Though small in comparison to Decatur, a second major shop was to be found at Granite City. Again a brick and steel structure, its prime function was to look after the St. Louis-Granite City cars though some mainline equipment was dealt with too, and once the St. Louis & Alton Railway became part of the IT system, their cars too were added.

Though an extension could easily be built if needed, that never in fact happened and throughout its life the Granite City shops consisted only of two tracks used entirely for repair work, and the eight track car storage yard along the southeast side of the shop building.

In Champaign and Urbana, the street railway carbarns were used for the interurbans.

At the west end of the Illinois River Bridge in Peoria, a former street railway barn was rebuilt into a combination freight house and car barn; for many years it also contained a small waiting room and ticket office.

A one-track frame carbarn was located at East Belt in Springfield to take care of minor repairs, while at Riverton a brick carbarn was situated near the powerhouse and coal pit. For several years there was a two-track carbarn at Wyatt, at the south side of Lincoln. That however was demolished once the Lincoln-Springfield runs were taken off. At the south side of Staunton was a six track carbarn which took care of the cars for the Hillsboro branch together with the freight locomotives used on main-line freight trains which for many years used Staunton as a division point.

A view of the Federal shops at Alton, originally owned by the St. Louis Troy & Eastern. This circa 1930 view also includes the coaling tower, at left, and the turntable for the roundhouse. These shops were used by the steam, and later diesel, engines which ran on the non-electrified portions of the Illinois Terminal Railroad.   Illinois Terminal, Dale Jenkins Collection

This aerial view shows IT facilities in Peoria. At the lower left is the Illinois River bridge; near the bridge's west end, the old powerhouse is the building with the bay over the tracks, and to the left are two storage tracks for IT equipment. Just beyond the powerhouse, and running to the left for a full block, is the carbarn and freight house. The new Peoria station is to the right of Walnut Street (which the bridge tracks parallel), a block beyond the carbarn and freight house. The date is October 9, 1947.
J. Holling, R.W. Deller Collection

The Peoria carbarn is a busy place in this April 6, 1949 photo. The Purina office occupies the former ticket office, which was closed when the new Peoria station opened just a block away. Between the Purina office and the interurban car are tracks leading to the freight house. Paul H. Stringham

East Belt, in Springfield, was always an interesting spot to view freight locomotives. Minor repairs were handled in the frame shop building, and many locomotives laid up between runs. Behind class C locomotive 1585 are the coal and water towers of the Illinois Central Railroad, seen here on September 5, 1949. Paul H. Stringham

Three different paint schemes can be seen on the four cars present at the East Peoria carbarn on April 14, 1950. This facility was constructed late in the IT's history, as runs were being cut back from Peoria to East Peoria.   Paul H. Stringham

Passenger service had already ended when this shot was taken of the East Peoria yard and carbarn in East Peoria on September 5, 1955. The caboose track is at left; to the right of the cabooses sits the scale house. At the right of the photo, the line car sits on a track where departing passenger cars once awaited leaving time.   Paul H. Stringham

Cars of the Illinois Traction System

Summaries and Rosters

DECEMBER 31, 1928 .

    74-78. Lightweight cars for branch line service.

    138. Old car for branch line service.

    221/3/4. Medium weight branch line cars.

    225-233, 235/6, 238-249, 258, 260-264, 270/1, 273-278, 280-285. Heavy combines, except 233 was an office car.

    300/1/5/6/8. Medium weight cars for branch line service.

    350-352. express motors, formerly combines.

    354, 356-358. Heavy combines.

    503/4, 506-9. Railroad roof passenger trailers.

    510-515. Parlor cars. 510-513 had 2 motors, the rest were trailers.

    516-524, 526-534. Arch roof passenger trailers.

    900-919. Suburban motor cars.

    950-959. Suburban trailers.

    1053/55/57/58/60. Railroad roof express motors.

    1063-1067. Arch roof express motors.

    1200-1203. Heavy combines.

This August 1933 view of car 244 shows one of the last of the Pullman green paint jobs at that time.   Paul H. Stringham

1520. Locomotive with express body.
1521. Locomotive with center cab, flat car.
1524. Locomotive with express car body.
1550-1560. Locomotives with center cab.
1561-1571. Locomotives with express car bodies Class B.
1579-1594. Locomotives with express car bodies Class C.
1700-1705. Line car, half box, half flat.
Unnumbered sleepers St. Louis, Peoria, Decatur, Springfield, Edwardsville and Sangamon.
This last was a sleeper and parlor car.

LOCOMOTIVE AND MOTOR CAR DATA
Main Line.
51-3. 4 GE 285C motors, 65:16 gear ratio.
61. 4 GE 55H motors, 60:17 gear ratio.
70-74. 8 WH 571FD1 motors, 63:16 gear ratio.
233,240,241,248,258. 4 GE 205B motors, 53:21 gear ratio. 234 air-conditioned sleeping car trailer. 233,248,258 field tapped.
260/61/63/64/70/71/73-8/80-85. 4 GE 222G motors, 52:26 gear ratio.
260,261,270,271 field tapped.
263/4/70/1/5/7/8/83-85 air conditioned.
510-513. 2 GE 222G motors, 52:26 gear ratio. Air conditioned.
516-518. Control and trailer jumper.
519-21/3/4/6. Passenger trailers.
528-532. 2 GE 222G motors, 52:36 gear ratio. Air conditioned.
533-535. Control and trailer jumper. Air conditioned.
560,561. Express trailers.
601-605. Express trailers.
1200-1203. 4 WH 303A motors, 56:21 gear ratio. Field tapped.
1551/2/4. 4 GE 73C motors, 73:17 gear ratio.
1560. 4 GE 55H motors, 60:17 gear ratio.
1561-1578. 4 GE 69C motors, 68:18 gear ratio. 1561-70 were classified as switch locomotives, the rest as road locomotives.
1579/82/83/85. 8 GE 73C motors, 73:16 gear ratio.
1586. 8 GE 302B motors, 61:16 gear ratio. Field tapped.
1587/9. 8 GE 73C motors, 73:16 gear ratio.
1590/92/93. 8 GE 205B motors, 72:16 gear ratio.
1594. 8 GE 205B motors, 57:17 gear ratio.
1595-98. 8 GE 205B motors, 72:16 gear ratio.
1700-1706. 4 GE 73C motors, 53:22 gear ratio.
Granite City Suburban 019. Snow sweeper with 2 GE 216A and four GE 201G motors, 71:25 gear ratio.
404-415. 4 GE 265D motors, 67:16 gear ratio.
470-473. 4 GE 275A motors, 50:22 gear ratio.
St. Louis & Alton 100-104. 4 WH 548C motors (except 103 had only two), 61:28 gear ratio. Field tapped.
120-123. 4 GE 205B motors, 53:21 gear ratio. Field tapped.
Alton-Grafton 206. Motor Coach.
Motor ratings
GE 55H - 140 h.p..
GE 216A - 50 h.p..
GE 285C - 255 h.p..
GE 69C - 200 h.p..
GE 222D - 140 h.p..
GE 302B - 120 h.p. blown.
GE 73C - 90h.p. unblown, 125 h.p. blown.
GE 222G - 140 h.p..
WH 303A - 100 h.p..
GE 201G - 65 h.p..
GE 265D - 35 h.p..
WH 548C - 95 h.p..
GE 205B - 110 h.p. unblown,125 h.p. blown.
GE 275A - 60 h.p..
WH 571FD1 - 225 h.p. blown.

SUMMARY OF EQUIPMENT, JULY 1, 1945.
Main Line
27 Passenger motors.
4 combination locomotives.
17 Passenger trailers.
2 class O locomotives (1551/52)
4 Reserved seat coaches.
2 class A locomotives (1554/60)
1 Sleeping car.
18 class B locomotives (1561-1578)
7 Express trailers.
15 class C locomotives (1579/82/83/85-7/89/90/92-98)
5 class D locomotives (70-74).
Total 109
Granite City Suburban, St. Louis & Alton, Grafton lines
25 Passenger motors.
1 motor coach.
1 snow sweeper.
Total 27

ILLINOIS TERMINAL RAILROAD ELECTRIC EQUIPMENT MARCH 3, 1956.

73,74. Class D locomotives.
101,104. Center entrance motor cars.
233,234. Motor and trailer office cars.
274/6/7/80/82-85. Combines.
300-302. Streamlined combines.
330,331. Streamlined coaches.
350-352. Streamlined parlor cars.
404,410,415. Lightweight suburban cars.
450-457. PCC suburban cars.
470-473. Center entrance suburban cars.
530-532,535. Trailers.
1568/70. Locomotives Class B.
1587/90/92-96/98. Locomotives Class C.
1700/02/03. Line cars.

Car 258 is shown here circa 1940, pausing at the Peoria & Pekin Union crossing in East Peoria early in the morning. Note the length of the car.   Bob Mehlenbeck

Car 247 sits in the yard behind the Springfield station, in 1938. Some of the 240-series cars were built to run on either AC or DC.
Bob Mehlenbeck

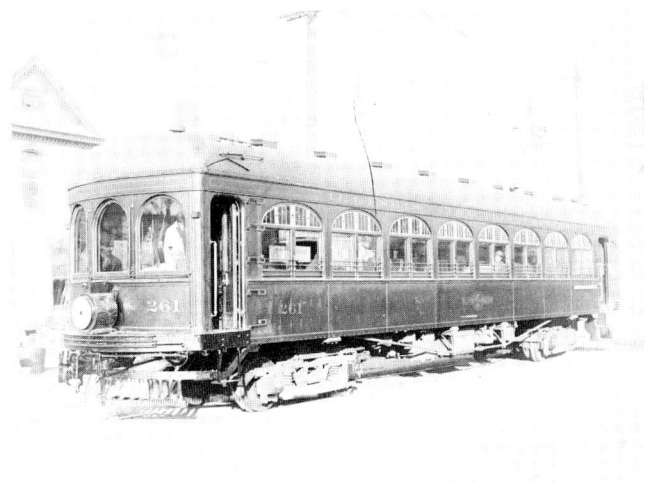

This circa 1920 view shows car 261 heading up a two-car train at Ninth and Monroe, in Springfield.
Illinois Traction, Dale Jenkins Collection

One of the longest IT passenger motors was car 271, shown here at Neil and University Streets in Champaign, en route to Danville on April 18, 1936. Bill Janssen

Awaiting its departure time of 1:10 p.m., car 264 is at Springfield on November 2, 1937. Paul H. Stringham

Car 271 as it appeared circa 1948, at the Wabash station in Champaign. Bob Mehlenbeck

Car 263 was a sister car to the 264, but by the time this August 20, 1948 view was taken, she looked quite a bit different due to "modernization." Paul H. Stringham

When this photo was taken at the St. Louis station in 1916, car 276 was only three years old. John McDermand Collection

Car 284, circa 1930 at Decatur.
Illinois Terminal, Dale Jenkins Collection

This view looks into the baggage compartment of car 284, on December 12, 1955.
Donald R. Kaplan

Table 1 — Mainline Motor Cars

Numbers	Builder & Date	Length	Width	Seats	Weight	Motors	Trucks	Control	Notes
136	American, 1903	51'5"	8'7"	48	78,000	4-GE74D	Bdwn 78-25A	M-C6k	OS Jan. 1924
137	American, 1903	51'5"	8'7"	48	78,000	4-GE74D	Bdwn 78-25A	M-C6k	OS May 1926
220	American, 1905	51'4"	8'7"	50	68,000	4-GE73C	Bdwn 78-25A	M-C6k	OS Jan. 1924
221	American, 1905	51'4"	8'7"	50	69,700	4-GE74A	StL 62	M-C6k	SFS to HM 1/5/43
222(1st)	American, 1905	51'4"	8'7"	50	68,000	4-GE73C	Amer. 15MCB	M-C6k	Wrecked 1906
223-224	American, 1905	51'4"	8'7"	50	69,700	4-GE74A	StL 62	M-C6k	1
225(1st)	American, 1905	51'4"	8'7"	50	68,000	4-GE73C	Amer. 15MCB	M-C6k	Ren. 222(2nd)
225(2nd)	St. Louis, 1907	52'9"	9'0"	58	77,000	4-GE73C	StL 62	M-C6k	SFS to HM 9/23/33
226-227	St. Louis, 1906	52'9"	9'0"	58	77,000	4-GE73C	StL 62	M-C6k	SFS to HM 9/23/33
228	St. Louis, 1906	52'9"	9'0"	58	77,000	4-GE73C	Bdwn 176	M-C6k	SFS to HM 9/23/33
229	St. Louis, 1906	52'9"	9'0"	58	77,000	4-GE73C	ACF 73MCB	M-C6k	2
230	St. Louis, 1906	52'9"	9'0"	58	77,000	4-GE73C	Bdwn 176	M-C6k	No Disposal Data
231	St. Louis, 1906	52'9"	9'0"	58	77,000	4-GE73C	StL 62	M-C6k	3
232	St. Louis, 1906	52'9"	9'0"	58	77,000	4-GE73C	ACF 73MCB	M-C6k	SFS to HM 9/23/33
233(1st)	St. Louis, 1906	52'9"	9'0"	58	77,000	4-GE73C	StL 62	M-C6k	225(2nd) in 1909
233(2nd)	St. Louis, 1906	62'0"	8'11"	27	92,300	4-GE205B	StL 62	M-C6k	4
234(1st)	St. Louis, 1907	52'6"	8'10"	55	81,000	4-GE205B	StL 62	M-C6k	5
234(2nd)	Danville, 1910	52'6"	8'10"	25	67,600	None	StL 102	None	6
235-236	St. Louis, 1907	52'6"	8'10"	55	81,000	4-GE205B	StL 62	M-C6k	SFS to HM 9/30/30
237	St. Louis, 1907	52'6"	8'10"	55	78,000	4-GE205B	StL 62	M-C6k	7
238, 239	St. Louis, 1907	52'6"	8'11"	55	81,000	4-GE205B	StL 62	M-C6k	SFS to HM 9/30/30
240	AC&F, 1908	52'6"	9'2"	52	84,200	4-GE205B	StL 62	M-C6k	SFS to HM 11/30/50
241	AC&F, 1908	52'6"	9'2"	49	85,000	4-GE205B	StL 62	M-C6k	8
242-247	AC&F, 1908	52'6"	9'2"	49	85,000	4-GE205B	StL 62	M-C6k	9
248-249	AC&F, 1908	52'6"	9'2"	36	87,225	4-GE205B	StL 62	M-C6k	10
250, 251	AC&F, 1904	52'7"	8'10"	46	84,000	4-GE73C	ACF MCB	M-C6k	11
252	AC&F, 1904	52'7"	8'10"	46	84,000	4-GE73C	Bdwn 176	M-C6k	12
253	AC&F, 1904	52'7"	8'10"	46	84,000	4-GE73C	StL 62	M-C6k	Retired 1/26
254	AC&F, 1904	52'7"	8'10"	46	84,000	4-GE73C	Bdwn 125	M-C6k	Retired 1/26

Table 1 — Mainline Motor Cars

Numbers	Builder & Date	Length	Width	Seats	Weight	Motors	Trucks	Control	Notes
255-257	AC&F, 1904	52'7"	8'10"	46	84,000	4-GE73C	ACF	M-C6k	13
258, 259	St. Louis, 1906	62'6"	9'6"	60	94,000	4-GE205B	StL 62	M-C6k	14
260	Danville, 1911	55'9"	9'6"	50	94,000	4-GE222	StL 62	C101A	15
261	Danville, 1911	55'9"	9'6"	50	94,000	4-WH303A	StL 62	HL	16
262-264	Danville, 1911	55'9"	9'6"	50	94,000	4-GE222G	StL 62	HL	17, 18
270	Niles, 1906	68'6"	8'9"	47	105,000	4-GE222G	StL 62	HL	19
271	Niles, 1906	68'6"	8'9"	47	105,000	4-GE222G	StL 62	HL	20
272	Holland, 1903	62'0"	8'9"	24	unk.	—	unk.	—	21
273	St. Louis, 1913	57'4"	9'10"	55	100,000	4-GE222G	StL 62	C101A	SFS to CS 1/14/56
274-278	St. Louis, 1913	57'4"	9'10"	55	100,000	4-GE222G	StL 62	C101A	22
279	St. Louis, 1913	57'4"	9'10"	55	94,000	4-GE222G	StL 62	C101A	23
280-283	St. Louis, 1913	57'4"	9'10"	55	100,000	4-GE222G	StL 62	C101A	24
284	St. Louis, 1914	57'4"	9'10"	55	100,000	4-GE222G	StL 62	C101A	24
285	St. Louis, 1914	57'4"	9'10"	55	100,000	4-GE222G	StL 62	C101A	24

1. SFS to HM: 223 on 10/2/23 and 224 on 1/5/34. 2. To Chicago, Ottawa & Peoria (its 258) in 1922. Returned to Decatur 1924. Retired 6/26. 3. SFS to HM 9/23/33. Its body was taken to Roxanna for use as a station. 4. Originally car *Missouri*, rebuilt in 1909. Rebuilt 1940 with arch roof, and arch windows were covered. Also air conditioned. Sold to Illini Railroad Club 4/57. Now at Illinois Railway Museum. 5. To Chicago, Ottawa & Peoria (its 259) in 1922. Returned to Decatur 1924. Retired 6/26. 6. Originally car *Champaign*. Became *Sangamon* on 5/28/27. Rebuilt to 234(2nd) 3/2/36. It was motorized for a short period. Sold to Illini Railroad Club 1/2/56 to Illinois Railway Museum in 1968. 7. Wrecked and burned at Mooney Creek, near Edwardsville, 10/26/16. 8. To National Museum of Transport 7/25/50. 9. 242—Retired 6/9/36 and body sold to Mahan-Maurer Coal Co. in Decatur for an office. 243—Dismantled 10/9/35. 244—Dismantled 10/9/35. 245—Retired 6/15/36. Body sold to Darling & Hess at Bainbridge, Ind. 246—Arch windows covered. Became bunk car 082 on 5/21/41. Dismantled at Federal 6/26/48. 247—Became bunk car 083 on 10/27/41. SFS to HM 5/19/54. 10. 248—Rebuilt with arch roof and arch windows were covered. SFS to Purdy 8/26/52. 249—Became caboose 990 on 2/23/44, then bunk car 0-96 on 12/1/47. SFS to Purdy 9/20/62. 11. 250 rebuilt with arch roof. Wrecked near Carlinville 3/19/25 in a head-on collision with a line car. 12. Became bunk car 15 in Jan. 1925, then car 029 in Sept. 1930. 13. 255—Retired 1926. 256—Became bunk car 7 in March 1925, then car 057 in Oct. 1930. Burned at Decatur 8/15/31. 257—Became bunk car 8 in April 1925, then car 058 in Aug. 1930. SFS to HM 9/30/33. 14. 258—Rebuilt from car *Indiana* in 1910. Steel sheathed in 1923. SFS to HM 11/13/50. 259—Rebuilt from car *Illinois* in 1910. Steel sheathed in 1923. Wrecked at DeLong Siding on 5/31/28 in head-on with 271. SFS to HM 11/13/50. 15. Ex-Chicago, Ottawa & Peoria. Rebuilt 1930 with revolving chairs. Arch windows covered in 1940s. SFS to HM 11/13/50. 16. Ex-Chicago, Ottawa & Peoria. Rebuilt 1930 with revolving chairs. Arch windows covered in 1940s. 17. Ex-Chicago, Ottawa & Peoria. All rebuilt 1930 with revolving chairs. All had arch windows covered in the 1940s. 263 and 264 were air conditioned Aug. 1939. 262—Burned 11/26/30. 263—SFS to HM 7/2/53. 264—Dismantled 4/7/50. 18. The original cars 265-269 were retired Dec. 1926, and the best parts of the entire 260-269 series were used to build five good cars, which were numbered 260-264. 19. Built for the Columbus, Delaware & Marion as its *Glenna*, it was purchased by ITS in 1907 and named *Champaign*. It was rebuilt in 1909 with a baggage compartment at the front (the same as other ITS cars) and renamed *Bloomington*. A new body was built in 1922, and in 1935 the car was rebuilt with field tap shunts, clasp brakes and air conditioning; it acquired multiple-unit control in 1936. It was retired 4/9/51 and SFS to Purdy 7/25/52. 20. Built for the Columbus, Delaware & Marion as its *Mary*, it came to ITS in 1907 and was named *Danville*. It received a new body in 1922, and air conditioning April 1937. It was retired 6/3/52, and SFS to Purdy 8/26/52. 21. Originally sleeping car *Decatur*, it was rebuilt to coach 272 in 1911. In Aug. 1914 it was converted to bunk car 7, renumbered to 14 in July 1922, and in June 1930 renumbered 028. It was retired 2/2/39. 22. 275—Arch windows were covered and air conditioning was added in May 1936. It was wrecked in a head-on collision with locomotive 72 at Kings Siding, near Lincoln, on 8/11/48; it was scrapped 2/2/49. 276—Air conditioned; SFS to CS 3/13/56. 277—Rebuilt inside, with new ceiling lights, a heater room and seats in Oct. 1951. Air conditioned. Sold to Illinois Railway Museum 3/9/56. 278—Air conditioned May 1927. SFS to HM 5/19/54. 23. Burned at Cahokia Creek, near Edwardsville, due to a trolley break on 12/8/13. 24. 280—A "Tangerine Flyer" in 1924, with parlor car seats and orange exterior. Parlor car seats were removed July 1929. SFS to BM 3/13/56. 281—Rebuilt for "Tangerine Flyer" service in 1924. Parlor car seats were removed in July 1929. SFS to HM 10/18/53. 282—To Chicago, Ottawa & Peoria (CO&P) Oct. 1913; returned to ITS April 1922. Rebuilt as "Tangerine Flyer" in 1924, its parlor seats were removed July 1929. SFS to HM 5/16/56. 283—To CO&P Oct. 1913; returned to ITS April 1922. Rebuilt as "Tangerine Flyer" in 1924, parlor seats removed July 1929. Air conditioned Aug. 1939, and received new seats in Oct. 1947. SFS to HM 5/16/56. 284—Rebuilt for "Tangerine Flyer" service in 1924, parlor seats removed Dec. 1928. Air conditioned in July 1936. New seats installed Oct. 1947 and interior remodeled Oct. 1953. SFS to CS 5/16/56. 285—Rebuilt for "Tangerine Flyer" service in 1924, parlor seats removed Dec. 1928. Air conditioned Aug. 1938 and new seats installed Dec. 1952. SFS to HM 5/16/56.

Table 2 — Mainline Motor Cars

Numbers	Builder & Date	Length	Width	Seats	Weight	Motors	Trucks	Control	Notes
350-352	American, 1907	58'0"	8'9"	57	84,000	4-GE205B	StL 62	M-C6k	1, 2
353, 354	American, 1907	58'0"	8'9"	57	84,000	4-GE205B	ACF75MCB	M-C6k	3
355	American, 1907	58'0"	8'9"	57	84,000	4-GE205B	StL 62	M-C6k	Retired 9/19/25
356	American, 1907	58'0"	8'9"	57	84,000	4-GE205B	StL 62	M-C6k	SFS to HM 10/2/33
357	American, 1907	58'0"	8'9"	57	84,000	4-GE205B	StL 62	M-C6k	SFS to HM 9/30/33
358	American, 1907	58'0"	8'9"	57	84,000	4-GE205B	StL 62	M-C6k	2
359	American, 1907	58'0"	8'9"	57	84,000	4-GE205B	StL 62	M-C6k	Disposition Unknown

General—Cars 350-359 were built as double-end straight coaches with air-conditioning equipment and four GE605 motors. In 1909 they were rebuilt to combination passenger-baggage and raised to standard height. At that time they were made single-end. 1. In 1919 Nos. 350 and 351 had most of their seats removed and were made into almost full-length express cars. 2. In October 1928, No. 358 was renumbered to 352 and made into an almost full-length express car; No. 352 became 358. Motors were removed from both and they were used as trailers. 3. No. 353 was retired in Jan. 1929; No. 354 was SFS HM 9/30/33.

Car 350 is shown circa 1930, at Ninth and Monroe in Springfield, serving as a "yard engine" as a parlor car is cut off a Peoria-St. Louis train. The car was painted orange at the time. Bill Janssen

By the time this September 16, 1931 photo was taken, car 352 had been stripped of its seats, motors, and other apparatus, and was being used as an express trailer to haul bread for A&P stores. It was handled on train 88, the Owl, for several years.
Paul H. Stringham

When the 1200-1203 series came out of the McGuire-Cummings Car Company shops in 1910, they were more express than passenger car. Even the numbers fitted into the express series. They were to be used on sleeper trains, but the company underestimated the number of coach passengers that would ride and a trailer had to be added. The cars were rebuilt to ITS standards in 1921 and were used in all types of service after that. Bill Janssen

Car 1201 went through a transitional rebuilding, as shown here. Space was about half passenger, half express.
Illinois Traction, Dale Jenkins Collection

Car 1201, fresh out of the shop after its rebuilding.
Illinois Traction, Dale Jenkins Collection

This view of car 1200 at the foot of the Illinois River bridge in Peoria was taken on October 10, 1938.   Paul H. Stringham

This interior view is believed to show car 1202, probably before its rebuilding to almost all passenger space.
Illinois Traction, Dale Jenkins Collection

Table 3 — Mainline Motor Cars

Numbers	Builder & Date	Length	Width	Seats	Weight	Motors	Trucks	Control	Notes
1200-1203	McGuire-Cummings, 1910	52'6"	9'3"	50	97,000	4-WH303A	Bdwn 78-25A	HL	1

Numbers 1200-1203 were built as express motors, with 20 seats at the rear. They were equipped with Curtis trucks and four GE205B motors. In 1919 they were rebuilt with just a small baggage section at the front, and equipped with Baldwin trucks. At least one car, 1202, had an intermediate rebuilding with seating for 40 and a long baggage compartment at the front. Numbers 1202 and 1203 became Nos. 202 and 203 on 12/28/53.

Parlor car 513, the Clinton *is seen here at Decatur shops in 1925.*
Illinois Traction, Dale Jenkins Collection

Reserve Seat Coach 514, the Lincoln *is viewed at Clyde siding, just east of Allentown, on a May 15, 1938 fan trip.*
Paul H. Stringham

Table 4 — Reserved Seat Coaches

Numbers	Builder & Date	Length	Width	Seats	Weight	Motors	Trucks	Control	Notes
510	St. Louis, 1911	57'6"	9'6"	35	92,800	2-GE222G	StL 62	C101A	1, 4
511-514	St. Louis, 1911	57'6"	9'6"	35	92,800	2-GE222G	StL 102	C101A	1, 4
515(1st)	Danville, 1909	52'9"	9'1"	52	63,000	None	Bdwn	None	2
515(2nd)	St. Louis, 1913	57'6"	9'6"	35	92,800	None	StL	None	3

General—All were built as trailers. In 1928, Nos. 510-513 were equipped with one motor truck from the 260 series—they could be operated in multiple-unit only with a regular motor car. In 1930, No. 514 was equipped with one motor truck from express motor 1063; it was removed in 1937. Numbers 510-514 were rebuilt and equipped with new furniture—and painted orange—in 1930. These cars were rebuilt again in 1936; arch windows were covered and observation platform enclosed (except No. 514, its platform was never enclosed). 1. Names: 510—*Monticello*, 511—*Urbana*, 512—*Cerro Gordo*, 513—*Clinton*, 514—*Lincoln*, 515(1st)—*Homer*. 2. No. 515(1st) was rebuilt from No. 508 (see Table 6) in 1911 and named *Granite City*. After 515(2nd) was acquired, 515(1st) was rebuilt to a trailer and numbered 509(2nd) (see Table 6). 3. No. 515(2nd) was rebuilt to sleeping car *Missouri* in 1929 (see Table 5). 4. Disposal: Nos. 510 and 511 SFS to HM 11/13/50. No. 512 SFS to Purdy 8/26/52. No. 513 was SFS to HM 11/13/50. No. 514 was SFS to HM 10/11/55.

The Sangamon *was originally built as a "party car" named Champaign. It went through several "adaptive reuses" during its service life. It is seen here at Decatur, circa 1927.*
Illinois Traction, Paul H. Stringham Collection

The sleeper Edwardsville, *circa 1930 at Decatur.*
Illinois Terminal, Dale Jenkins Collection

Car 504, the Peoria lays over at Peoria on June 3, 1938.
　　　　　　　　　　　　　　　　　　　　Paul H. Stringham

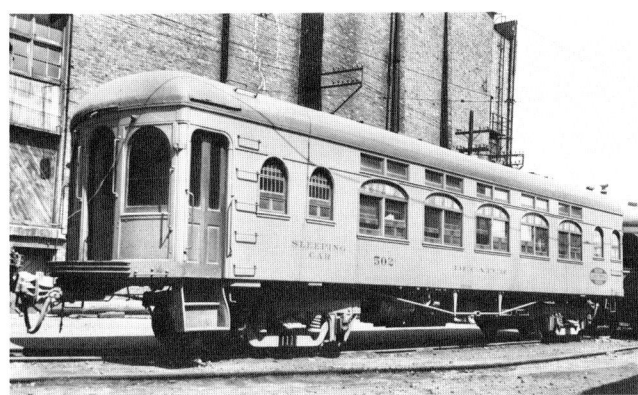

Sleeper 502, the Decatur (2nd) was 3'3" longer than the Peoria, and was built a year later. The added room left space for an extra window in the washroom at the near end of the car. The date is June 3, 1938, the location, next to the Peoria powerhouse.
　　　　　　　　　　　　　　　　　　　　Paul H. Stringham

Sleeping car Illinois brings up the rear on the Owl as it arrives in St. Louis circa 1938.　　　　　　　　　　　　　　Bill Janssen

Rebuilt sleeper Illinois arrived in Peoria on train 88, the Owl, the last sleeping car to do so ever. The date was July 31, 1940. Here, the car is on its way back to St. Louis a few hours later, in Morton.
　　　　　　　　　　　　　　　　　　　　Paul H. Stringham

Sleeping car Missouri was rebuilt from parlor car Homer in 1930. Here she rests between runs at the Granite City shops on September 21, 1939. For most of their years, sleepers carried names only, but on March 2, 1937, the Missouri was assigned number 500.　　　　　　　　　　　　　　Robert Merriman

Trailer 509, circa 1925 at Decatur shops.
　　　　　　　　　　　　Illinois Traction, Dale Jenkins Collection

212 • ILLINOIS TERMINAL

Table 5 — Sleeping Cars

Name	Builder & Date	Length	Width	Berths	Trucks	Notes
Missouri	St. Louis, 1913	55'9"	9'10"	9	StL 102	1
Illinois	St. Louis, 1911	57'4"	9'10"	9	StL 102	2
Decatur (1st)	Holland, 1903	62'0"	8'9"	24	J&S MCB	3
Decatur (2nd)	Barney & Smith, 1911	57'3"	9'10"	20	StL 102	4
Springfield (1st)	Holland, 1903	62'0"	8'9"	24	J&S MCB	5
Springfield (2nd)	Barney & Smith, 1911	57'3"	9'10"	20	StL 102	6
Peoria	AC&F, 1910	54'0"	9'10"	20	StL 102	7
St. Louis	AC&F, 1910	54'0"	9'10"	20	StL 102	8
Champaign	Danville, 1910	52'6"	9'10"	None	StL 102	9
Edwardsville	St. Louis, 1913	52'6"	9'10"	20	StL 102	10

General—In 1937, all remaining sleeping cars were numbered, but retained their names: *Missouri*–500, *Illinois*–501, *Decatur*–502, *Springfield*–503, *Peoria*–504 and *St. Louis*–505. 1. Rebuilt from Parlor Car *Homer* (see Table 4). Became trailer 534(2nd) in 1941 (see Table 6). 2. Rebuilt from trailer 527 in 1929 (see Table 6). Became trailer 535(2nd) in 1942 (see Table 6). 3. Became motor car 272 in 1911 (see Table 1). 4. Became bunk car 052 in 1941. Damaged at Alton and SFS to HM 8/10/60. 5. Destroyed by fire on 5/20/10. 6. Wrecked at Borin Siding on 2/11/38; dismantled on 6/9/38. 7. Became bunk car 049 on 12/16/49. Sold to Cassidy and Ross 8/16/60. Now at Illinois Railway Museum. 8. Became bunk car 050 on 12/21/39. SFS to HM 8/22/57. 9. Built as a trailer "party car" in 1910. A few years later it was motorized and used as an office car. In 1927 it was demotorized and renamed *Sangamon*, and used on Champaign-St. Louis runs. It later returned to a trailer office car. In March 1936 it was numbered 234, the arch windows were covered, and it was rebuilt with an arch roof. It was sold on 2/1/56 to the Illinois Railroad Club and is now preserved at the Illinois Railway Museum. 10. Badly damaged by fire near Morton on 11/30/31, and SFS to HM 9/30/33.

An interior view of car 518, looking at the lavatory end. This view was taken in October 1987; the car has been preserved at the Illinois Railway Museum. Donald R. Kaplan

The interior of car 518, looking away from the lavatory also in October 1987. Donald R. Kaplan

Car 520 was one of the earlier arch-roofed trailers. Note the wood sheathing; most IT cars were steel sheathed. The car is seen here on July 15, 1947. Paul H. Stringham

The 530 is seen here on October 28, 1949, after rebuilding. Paul H. Stringham

Trailer 530 is seen here at Decatur shops, circa 1930. Illinois Terminal, Dale Jenkins Collection

Trailer 535 had a long history. Beginning as trailer 527, she was rebuilt in 1929 to sleeper Illinois, *then in 1942, to trailer 535. In her last rebuilding, the windows did not line up well with the seats. This view was taken on October 28, 1949.* Paul H. Stringham

Table 6 — Trailers

Numbers	Builder & Date	Length	Width	Seats	Weight	Trucks	Notes
500, 501	American, 1906	52'9"	9'1"	52	60,000	Bdwn	Dismantled Aug. 1926
502-509(2nd)	Danville, 1909	52'9"	9'1"	52	63,000	Bdwn	1-8
516	St. Louis, 1911	57'4"	9'10"	56	68,400	StL 62B	SFS to HM 11/13/50
517	St. Louis, 1911	57'4"	9'10"	56	68,400	StL 102	SFS to Purdy 8/26/52
518	St. Louis, 1911	57'4"	9'10"	56	68,400	StL 102	9
519	St. Louis, 1911	57'4"	9'10"	56	68,400	StL 62B	10
520-527	St. Louis, 1911	57'4"	9'10"	56	68,400	StL 62B	11
528	St. Louis, 1912	57'4"	9'10"	56	70,000	Bdwn 78-25	12
529-533	St. Louis, 1912	57'4"	9'10"	56	70,000	StL 102	13
534(1st)	St. Louis, 1912	57'4'	9'10"	56	70,000	StL 102	14
534(2nd)	St. Louis, 1913	55'9"	9'10"	56	70,000	StL 102	15
535(1st)	St. Louis, 1912	57'4"	9'10"	56	70,000	StL 102	14
535(2nd)	St. Louis, 1911	55'9"	9'10"	56	70,000	StL 102	16

1. Nos. 502 and 505 were destroyed in a carbarn fire at Danville in Dec. 1927. 2. Rebuilt to bunk car 45 on 5/10/29; renumbered to 071 in Nov. 1930. Dismantled 6/5/41. 3. Rebuilt to bunk car 46 on 9/13/29; renumbered 063 in Oct. 1930. Burned at Decatur on 8/15/31. 4. Retired 5/10/29 and body taken to Roxanna for use as station. 5. Retired 5/10/29 and body taken to Wood River for use as station. 6. Rebuilt to parlor car 515–*Granite City*. In April 1914, became 509(2nd) (which see). 7. No. 509(1st) renumbered 508(2nd) in April 1914. Retired July 1929. 8. Renumbered from 515(1st) on April 1914 (see Table 4). Became bunk car 048 in Sept. 1930 and retired 12/3/39. 9. Became instruction car 0100 on 12/31/52. Sold to Illini Railroad Club on 6/29/60. Now preserved at Illinois Railway Museum. 10. Retired Nov. 1950 and body taken to Roxanna for yard office. 11. 522—Sent to LeClaire on 4/20/30 for use on Grafton line. Baggage doors cut in and it was equipped with vestibule diaphragms, caboose stove and oil lamps. Returned to electric division in 1934 and retired 12/18/39. 523—Sent to LeClaire (same items as 522). Returned to electric division in 1934 and returned to original condition. SFS to HM 11/13/50. 524—Retired 6/15/54. Body sent to A.O. Smith in Granite City for a yard office. 525—Burned 10/25/23 at Location Siding (on the Chicago, Ottawa & Peoria). 526—Damaged by fire at Riverton on 12/13/50 and SFS to Purdy 7/16/51. 527—Rebuilt to sleeping car *Illinois* in 1930 (see Table 5). 12. Equipped with two motors Dec. 1935; air conditioned on 7/7/37. Retired on 12/23/54 and body used as trainman's room at Decatur. 13. 529—Air conditioned May 1929. Equipped with two motors Dec. 1935. SFS to CS 9/1/56. 530—Equipped with two motors Dec. 1935, and air conditioned on 3/17/37. Received new seats on 11/30/47 and interior upgraded in Dec. 1953. Body to inspection office at Springfield on 4/15/56. 531—Equipped with two motors Sept. 1937, and air conditioned on 3/17/37. Received new seats Aug. 1948 and interior upgraded in Dec. 1953. SFS to CS 9/1/56. 532—Equipped with two motors in Sept. 1937; air conditioned on 6/30/38. SFS to CS 9/1/56. 533—SFS to Purdy 7/17/52. (Nos. 528-533 equipped with GE222G motors.) 14. Sent to St. Louis Car Co. on 12/14/29 to be converted to sleeping cars. Their condition was too poor for rebuilding and they were scrapped in Feb. 1930. 15. Rebuilt from sleeping car *Missouri* in 1941 (see Table 5). SFS to Purdy 8/26/52. 16. Rebuilt from sleeping car *Illinois* in 1942 (see Table 5). Rebuilt to bunk car 098 on 9/18/52. Sold to R.G. Forshaw 8/22/66.

The first, brand-new streamliner is making an exhibition trip over the line on October 29, 1948, running from Springfield to Peoria. The view was taken at Fogarty siding, south of Lincoln, with the train making 76 mph. — Paul H. Stringham

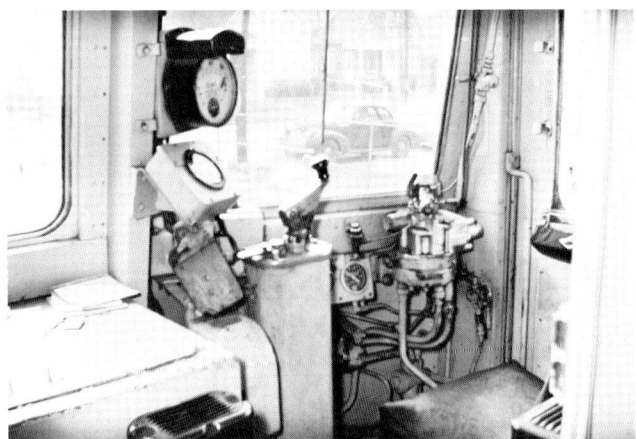

This December 12, 1955 view shows the controls of car 301, at Springfield. — Donald R. Kaplan

Table 7 — Streamliners

Numbers	Builder & Date	Length	Width	Seats	Weight	Motors	Trucks	Control	Notes
300-302	St. Louis, 1948	66'10"	10'0"	44	109,000	4-GE1240A2	1	PCM	2
330, 331	St. Louis, 1948	65'4"	10'0"	56	101,000	2-GE1240A2	1	PCM	3
350-352	St. Louis, 1948	65'4"	10'0"	29	107,000	4-GE1240A2	1	PCM	4

1. General Steel Castings MCB truck. 2. Combination passenger-baggage. 3. Straight coaches, hostler controls only. 4. Reserved seat coaches with buffet section; hostler controls only. Named (in number order) *Louis Joliet*, *Shadrach Bond* and *Pierre LaClede*. Disposition: All SFS to BIMCO in 1956 and kept virtually intact until the early 1980s.

Car 144, one of the early East St. Louis & Suburban cars is at the Granite City shops, about 1935. Bill Janssen

Except for the front trolley pole, car 302 looks the same as it did when in service on the Chicago & Illinois Valley. Here, circa 1934, the car is at the Big Rock wye, just south of Georgetown, serving as the regular Danville-Georgetown car. Bill Janssen

Car 300 is shown while in Danville-Ridge Farm service. It was one of the IT's earliest cars, used mainly in branchline and suburban service. Bill Janssen Collection

Car 403 is seen at Danville in 1934. Bill Janssen

Originally Chicago & Illinois Valley 63, car 414 is seen on a Hillery-Tilton suburban run, in downtown Danville, on April 11, 1937. Bill Janssen

Car 470 came to the IT from the East St. Louis & Suburban. It is seen in the mid-1930s in Granite City. Bill Janssen

Car 415 models the "modernized" look for the ex-C&IV cars. Harre W. Demoro

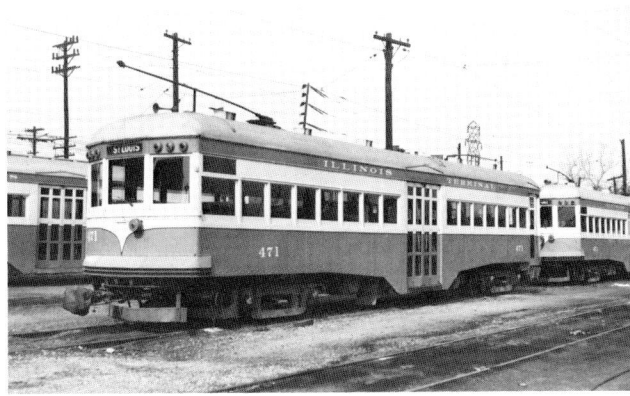

Car 471 shows off its modernized appearance, circa 1955. Harre W. Demoro

PCC 451 is seen in Granite City circa 1955. Harre W. Demoro

The 900-class bridge cars were replaced by rebuilt C&IV cars in 1933, and few pictures seem to exist of them. Here, car 902 sits in storage at the Granite City shops on May 21, 1934.
Paul H. Stringham

Table 8 — Branch Line and Suburban Cars

Numbers	Builder & Date	Length	Width	Seats	Weight	Motors	Trucks	Control	Notes
107	(Secondhand car—no other data)								
134	Stephenson, 1902	39'0"		40		2-GE80	Curtis D-2	K-10	1
135	Stephenson, 1902	39'0"		40		2-GE80	Peckham 14B	K-10	2
138	St. Louis, 1901	45'7"	9'1"	52	61,400	4-GE57A	StL 23	K-14A	3
139	St. Louis, 1901	45'7"	9'1"	52	61,400	4-GE57A	Peckham 14B	K-14A	4
140-142	St. Louis, 1899	43'10"	8'2"	44	36,000	4-WH60	Peckham 30	K-29	5
143-146	Stephenson, 1899	39'0"		40		2-GE80	Brill 27G	K-10	6
147	St. Louis	48'3"				4-GE57A	StL 23A	K-14A	Destroyed 8/26
148	St. Louis	48'3"	8'7"			4-WH69	Peckham 14B	K-14A	Destroyed 1/21
149	St. Louis	48'3"	8'7"			4-GE57A	StL 23A	K-14A	(No data)
150	St. Louis	48'3"	8'7"			4-GE57A	Peckham 14B	K-14A	Retired 1926
151	St. Louis	48'3"	8'7"			4-GE57A	StL 23A	K-14A	(No Data)
152	St. Louis	48'3"	8'7"			4-GE57A	Peckham 14B	K-14A	Retired 1926
160, 163	St. Louis, 1918	41'0"	8'9"	40	38,000	4-GE258C	Comm 101E	K-12A	7
200, 203	St. Louis, 1904	48'0"	8'7"	48	50,000	4-GE74D	Bdwn 78 25A	M-C6k	8
204, 205		(Grafton Railbus)							
206	White, 1939	(Grafton Railbus w/Mack engine)							10
300, 309	St. Louis, 1907	56'3"	8'7"	50	74,000	4-GE73C	StL 62	M-C6k	11
302(2nd)	St. Louis, 1924	48'0"	8'7"	40	39,800	4-GE265D	Comm 69	K35kk	12
303(2nd)	St. Louis, 1924	48'0"	8'7"	40	39,800	4-GE265D	Comm 69	K35kk	13
400	AC&F, 1904	55'0"		44	49,100	4-GE80	Brill 27G	K-28D	14
401-403	Danville, 1910	46'3"	8'10"	44	52,800	4-GE80	Brill 27G	K-28	15
404-415	St. Louis, 1924	46'5"	8'8"	40	39,800	4-GE265D	Comm 69	K-35kk	16
450-457	St. Louis, 1949	50'5"	9'0"	59	42,680	4-GE1220E1	StL B3	GE	17
470-473	St. Louis, 1924	53'8"	8'8"	64	57,260	4-GE275A	Comm 75	C169A	18
900-919	American, 1909	50'0"	9'3"	42	67,000	4-GE201G	Brill 27MCB	K35G	19
950-959	American, 1909	50'0"	9'3"	42	48,500	None	Brill 27MCB	None	20

1. Sold to Danville Railway & Light in June 1914, then to Illinois Power & Light in Peoria in 1928. 2. Sold to Danville Railway & Light in June 1914. Burned in a carbarn fire at Danville on 12/19/18. 3. Acquired from Lehigh Valley Transit in Sept. 1903. Rebuilt to Snow Sweeper 020-1 on 1/13/33. 4. Acquired from Lehigh Valley Transit in Sept. 1903. Retired Dec. 1926. 5. Acquired by predecessor Danville, Paxton & Northern from Third Avenue Railway in New York City in June 1902, becoming DP&N 200-202, then ITS 140-142. 6. Acquired by predecessor Danville, Paxton & Northern from the Metropolitan Railway in Washington, D.C., in 1901. MRy 723, 925, 726 and 727 became DP&N 723, 925, 926 and 927. Order of renumbering to ITS 143-146 unknown. Nos. 143-146 sold to Danville Railway & Light June 1914. No. 146 was resold to Illinois Power & Light in Peoria in 1928. 7. No. 160 purchased from Danville Railway & Light on 8/20/32; Nos. 162 and 163 purchased from Danville Railway & Light on 8/30/32. Nos. 160, 162 and 163 became 360, 362 and 361 on 11/3/32. They were sold to Illinois Power & Light in Peoria on 12/22/34. Nos. 360-362 became Peoria 365-367; all were scrapped in 1946. 8. Retirement dates: 200—Jan. 1924, 201—Dec. 1926, 202—Jan. 1929, 203—Dec. 1926. 9. No. 204 SFS to HM 6/3/40. No. 205 was retired in 1939. 10. SFS to HM 11/16/43. HM donated it to the National Museum of Transport. 11. Disposition: 300—Dismantled 12/31/36. 301—SFS to HM 9/30/33. 302(1st) and 303(1st)—Both retired Jan. 1929. 304—Retired Dec. 1926. 305-307—Retired Jan. 1929. 309—Destroyed by fire on 12/10/09 when East St. Louis freight house burned—Nos. 300 and 301 rebuilt as one-man cars in June 1929. The trucks and electrical equipment from Nos. 302, 305-308 were used in building the class C locomotives. 12. From Chicago & Illinois Valley (its 67) on 8/10/34. Dismantled at Granite City 7/23/41. 13. From Chicago & Illinois Valley (its 69) on 8/17/34. Dismantled at Granite City 7/23/41, its body used for air brake shop at that location. 14. From Bloomington-Normal to Valley Division (as Nos. 52, 81-83) on 1/28/24. Then to Illinois Terminal on 5/22/25. Scrapped 9/11/33. 15. Nos. 401 and 402 SFS to HM 5/31/33. No. 403 was sold on 3/9/35. 16. Histories:

Chicago & Illinois Valley	Illinois Terminal	Renumbering	Chicago & Illinois Valley	Illinois Terminal	Renumbering
60	74 in 1928	404 on 3/25/30	62		410 on 4/30
61	75 in 1928	405 on 3/25/30	68		411 on 11/4/32
74	76 in 1928	406 on 3/25/30	71		412 on 11/4/32
75	77 in 1928	407 on 6/10/30	73		413 on 11/4/32
76	78 in 1928	408 on 9/17/30	63		414 on 10/19/34
70		409 on 9/27/29	64		415 on 9/19/34

Dispositions: 440—SFS to BIMCO on 5/21/56. 405—Wrecked in Granite City on 10/30/45; scrapped 2/14/56. 406—Scrapped 12/7/45. 407—SFS to Purdy 7/11/53. 408—SFS to HM 8/21/50. 409—SFS to HM 8/21/50. 410—SFS to BIMCO 7/24/59. 411—SFS to HM 8/21/50. 412—SFS to HM 8/21/50. 413—SFS to Purdy 7/11/53. 414—Scrapped 10/13/50 and body used as locker room at St. Louis subway 10/13/50. 415—Sold to Illinois Railway Museum on 10/19/56. 17. All sold to BIMCO 7/24/59. No. 450 resold to Ohio Railway Museum in Dec. 1964 and No. 451 sold to Connecticut Electric Railway in Dec. 1964; the balance were scrapped. 18. Nos. 470-473 from ex-St. Louis & Suburban Nos. 70-73, acquired in Feb. 1935. They were all SFS to BIMCO 7/24/59. 19. Disposition: Nos. 900-904 scrapped on 4/4/35. Nos. 905-919 were scrapped on 9/25/33. 20. Disposition: Nos. 950-954 scrapped on 9/25/33. Nos. 955-959 were scrapped on 9/5/33.

Car 120, formerly an East St. Louis & Suburban car, is seen at Granite City on December 1, 1935. Bill Janssen

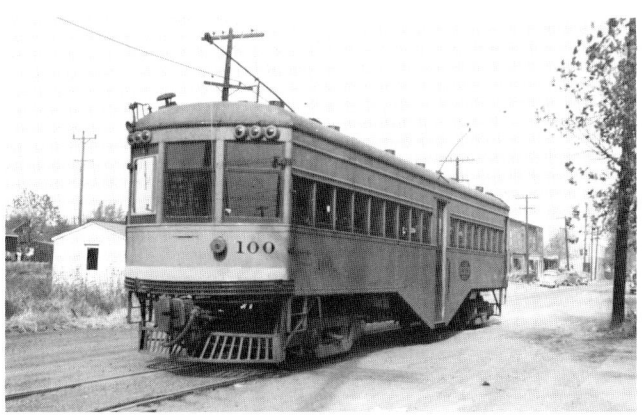

Car 100 models the "modernized" look for the Alton cars.
Harre W. Demoro

A head-on view of car 103 at the Alton station, in the mid-1930s.
Bill Janssen

Table 9 — Alton-to-St. Louis Division Cars

Numbers	Builder & Date	Length	Width	Seats	Weight	Motors	Trucks	Control	Notes
35, 39	American, 1909	45'4"	8'10"	46	54,920	4-GE216A	Br 27	C71C	1
42, 44	American, 1908	45'4"	8'8"	46	55,531	4-GE216A	Br 27	C71C	1
61-68	St. Louis, 1905	52'9"	8'10"	56	76,600	4-GE73	Peck 40A	C23A	2
100-104	American, 1917	53'8"	8'8"	60	58,525	4-WH548C3	Comm 81	HLF	3
120-123	E.St.L&S, 1924	53'8"	8'6"	58	59,000	4-GE205B	StL 62	M-C6k	4
140	American, 1909	45'4"	8'10"	46	55,000	4-GE201	Br 27MCB	C71C	5
141-145	American, 1909	45'4"	8'10"	46	55,000	4-GE216A	Br 27MCB	C71C	6

1. Leased from St. Louis & Alton Railway in June 1930. Returned 4/10/32. 2. Leased from St. Louis & Alton Railway in June 1930. Returned 3/23/33. 3. No. 100—Originally Alton, Granite & St. Louis No. 60, then St. Louis & Alton No. 62. Became IT 100 April 1931. Its original Commonwealth 81 trucks were replaced with St. Louis 62 trucks. 101-104 were originally Alton, Granite & St. Louis 61-64, then St. Louis & Alton 61-64. No. 101 went to Illinois Railway Museum on 3/9/56. 4. Originally East St. Louis & Suburban 4, 5, 11 and 15 (then same numbers on St. Louis & Alton). Became IT cars: 120 in Aug. 1931, 121 in Jan. 1931, 122 in July 1931, and 123 in Aug. 1931. Disposition: 120—SFS to Purdy 7/23/53. 121—SFS to HM 7/23/53. 122—SFS to HM 7/23/53. 123—SFS to Purdy 7/23/53. 5. Was St. Louis & Alton 31, became IT 140 in Sept. 1931. Scrapped at Decatur 12/4/36. 6. To East St. Louis & Suburban on 1/18/35.

Cars 260-269 were the largest cars used on the Valley Division. Car 268 sits on the Ottawa shop lead track in this early 1920s view.
Illinois Traction, Bill Janssen Collection

Valley Division locomotive 1530 sits in the yard at Ottawa shops in January 1934. Three of this series were fabricated at Decatur shops, and shipped to Ottawa in "kit" form to be assembled.
Paul H. Stringham

Table 10 — Chicago, Ottawa & Peoria/Chicago & Illinois Valley

Numbers	Builder & Date	Length	Width	Weight	Motors	Trucks	Control	Notes
41-44	St. Louis	47'0"	9'0"		4-WH306	Brill 27MCB	189D	1
50-53	Stephenson	40'0"	8'6"		4-GE57	Brill 27E-1	K-123	2
54	St. Louis	48'5"	8'4"		4-GE57	StL 23A	K-14	3
55-58	St. Louis, 1903	48'5"	8'4"		4-GE57	StL 23A	K-14	4
59, 62(1st)	Kuhlman	42'9"	8'1"		4-GE57	Peckham	K-14	5
60(1st)	Danville	41'8"	9'4"		4-GE57	StL 23A	K-14	5
61(1st)	St. Louis	41'8"	8'1"		4-GE57	Brill 27E-1	K-14	5
60-62(2nd), 63-76	St. Louis, 1924	46'5"	8'8"	39,800	4-GE265D	Comm 69	K-35kk	6
81, 82	St. Louis	51'0"	8'8"		4-GE57	StL 23A	K-14	7
83	St. Louis	51'0"	8'8"		4-GE57	StL 23A	K-14	7
150-155	Danville, 1908	50'10"	9'2"		None	Danville	None	8
258	St. Louis, 1906	52'9"	9'0"	77,000	4-GE73C	ACF 73-C	M-C6k	9
259	St. Louis, 1907	52'6"	8'10"	81,000	4-GE205B	StL 62	M-C6k	9
260-269	Danville, 1911	47'4"	9'6"	94,000	4-WH303	Bdwn	190-A	10
282, 283	St. Louis, 1913	57'4"	9'10"	100,000	4-GE222	Bdwn	101-A	11
300	St. Louis, 1906	54'0"	9'0"		4-GE57	Bdwn	K-14	12
301	Ill. Valley Ry. '08							12
302(1st)	Ill. Valley Ry. '04				4-GE57			No Other Data
302(2nd), 304	Danville, 1910	51'2"	9'6"		4-WH303A	Bdwn	M	12
522-525	St. Louis, 1912	58'0"	9'8"	68,400	None	Bdwn	None	13
532-535	St. Louis, 1913	58'0"	9'8"	68,400	None	Bdwn	None	14
1505	AC&F, 1907	43'0"	8'5"	78,000	4-GE73C	AC&F	M-C6k	15
1521	AC&F, 1906	43'6"	8'5"	72,000	4-GE73C	AC&F	K14A	15
1523	ITS Decatur, 1907	43'0"	8'8"	73,000	4-GE73A	Curtis	M-C6k	15
1524	St. Louis, 1915	44'0"	8'8"	78,000	4-GE73	Curtis J	M-C6k	15
1530, 1531	ITS Decatur, 1914	43'6"	9'4"	73,000	4-GE73	Curtis J	M-C6k	15

1. Acquired secondhand from Aurora, Plainfield & Joliet and motorized by CO&P. Car 41 was dismantled in 1926 and No. 42 was wrecked at Spring Valley on 1/4/19. 2. No. 50 was wrecked west of Peru on 10/8/04. No. 52 was destroyed on 4/29/13. No. 53 went to the Omaha & Council Bluffs St. Ry. on 12/13/19. 3. Sold to Cairo Ry. & Light Co. on 5/10/11. 4. No. 55 was retired in 1921. Nos. 56 and 57 went to Peoria on 5/11/20 and were returned to the CO&P on 5/19/27; they were scrapped in 1934. No. 58 was sold to the Cairo system on 5/10/11. 5. No. 59 was rebuilt to a line car, and wrecked at Rockwell in April 1912. No. 62 was rebuilt to a line car and was destroyed by fire on 1/7/13. No. 60(1st) was rebuilt to a line car in April 1913 and was retired in 1921. No. 61(1st) burned in 1919. 6. All were sent to ITS (see Roster Table 8 for details). 7. No. 81 became the *Illini* in 1920. No. 82 was rebuilt and renumbered 81, then to line car 93. It was scrapped in 1934. No. 83 was a line car, rebuilt from passenger car 81. It was retired in 1934. 8. Trailers. Nos. 150 and 155 went to Peoria in 1917, then back to CO&P in 1927; they were scrapped in 1934. No. 152 went to Cairo on 5/10/11; No. 154 went to Cairo on 2/2/14. No. 153 was gone by 12/31/23. 9. From ITS (cars 229 and 234[1st]) in 1922. Back to ITS in 1924. No. 229 was retired in June 1926, 234(1st) was retired in Sept. 1926. 10. Went to ITS in Decatur in 1924. There was enough salvage from the 10 cars to make five good cars, which became ITS 260-264. 11. Used only a short time on the CO&P, then returned to ITS. 12. No. 300 was an express motor. No. 301 was an express trailer. Nos. 302(2nd) and 304 were express motors; retired in 1928. 13. Trailers. Nos. 522-524 went to ITS at Decatur in 1926 and No. 525 burned at Location Siding on 10/25/23. 14. Trailers. Returned to ITS in Decatur, probably in 1924 after Nos. 60-76 arrived. 15. These were flat cars with center cabs, or "pull cars." No. 1524 was ex-Illinois Traction 1514, a Pull Car similar to the ITS class B locomotives. All were retired in 1934.

Express motor 1052 still carries the ITS name, even though it had been on the C&IV for a number of years. Another four months would see the end of its usefulness; the shot was taken in January 1934. Paul H. Stringham

Express trailer 601 came to the IT from the Cincinnati & Lake Erie on August 26, 1939. This view shows the car behind motor 276, ready to depart East Peoria on July 11, 1954.
Paul H. Stringham

Express motor 1063, and a former express motor converted to a trailer, sit in the yard beside the Granite City shops in June 1934.
Bob Mehlenbeck

Express trailer 606 began life as express motor 1066. Its motors were removed in February 1935 and it was used as a trailer until July 1942, when it was rebuilt with windows for Illiopolis munitions plant train service. It had four long bench seats for this service. In March 1947 it was restored to being trailer 606. She is seen here on May 12, 1950. Paul H. Stringham

Express trailer 522 was fashioned out of interurban trailer 522 during the Depression, and was used on the line from Alton to Grafton from 1930 to 1934, when a railbus arrived to take over this service. It was pulled in this service by a small 4-4-0 steamer. The car is shown here out of service, in 1938. Paul H. Stringham

An early express trailer, the 1019 is seen at Decatur circa 1920.
Illinois Traction, Dale Jenkins Collection

Illinois Traction had nine of these interurban refrigerator cars; numbers 1800-1803 were constructed by AC&F in 1907, 1804-1808 by Haskell-Barker in 1913. This photo was taken at Decatur circa 1925. Illinois Traction, Paul H. Stringham Collection

Table 11 — Freight Motor Cars (Express Motors)

Numbers	Builder & Date	Length	Width	Weight	Motors	Trucks	Control	Notes
1000	DR&L, 1903				GE 57		K14	No Other Data
1001(1st)	DR&L, 1904							Retired 1912
1001(2nd)	GC Shop, 1912	40'0"	8'6"			Brill 27E2		Line Car 1706 (see Table 13)
1002	Champaign Shop, 1904							Retired 1923
1003								1
1004	—, 1905							2
1005								3
1006	AC&F, 1903	52'8"	8'0"	60,000	4-GE57A		K14a	4
1007	AC&F, 1903	52'8"	8'0"	60,000	4-GE73C	ACF MCB	K14a	Dismantled 10/23
1008-1009	AC&F, 1908				4-GE73C	ACF MCB	M-C6k	5
1050-1051	St. Louis, 1905	44'10"	8'9"		4-GE73C	Brill 27E2	M-C6k	6
1052-1056	St. Louis, 1906-07	51'1"	8'9"	72,000	4-GE73C	Brill 27E2	M-C6k	7
1057, 1058	AC&F, 1908	51'1"	8'9"	77,700	4-GE73C	Brill 27E2	M-C6k	8
1059	AC&F, 1908	51'1"	8'9"	77,700	4-GE205B	AC&F MCB		9
1060	AC&F, 1908	51'1"	8'9"	78,900	4-GE1240A2	GSC MCB	PCM	10
1061-1062	AC&F, 1908	51'1"	8'9"	78,900	4-GE73C	Brill 27E2	M-C6k	11
1063	McG-Cummings, 1910	52'10"	9'6"	88,000	4-GE73C	StL 62	M-C6k	12
1064-1067	McG-Cummings, 1910	52'10"	9'6"	88,000	4-GE222G	StL 62	M-C6k	13

1. Motors removed Nov. 1925, became tool car 36. 2. Motors removed in 1922, became tool car 35. 3. Burned at Danville in 1918. 4. Became locomotive 1520 in Aug. 1925. 5. No. 1008 retired Oct. 1923. 6. To C&IV; No. 1050 on 9/11/28 and 1051 in June 1928. 7. No. 1052 went to C&IV in July 1928. No. 1053 wrecked in Alton on 10/12/30. No. 1054 burned at Staunton on 1/18/18. No. 1055 was dismantled by H-M 1/5/34. No. 1056 was destroyed in Jan. 1921. 8. Both dismantled by H-M 1/5/34. 9. Wrecked on 5/10/10. 10. Dismantled by H-M 1/5/34. 11. No. 1061 burned in March 1926. No. 1062 dismantled by H-M 1/5/34. 12. Its motors went to No. 514 on 8/30/30 and received 1053's motors. It became a trailer on 1/6/45 when its motors went to No. 604. Dismantled at Granite City on 1/26/56. 13. No. 1064 was demotorized in Oct. 1935 and became bunk car 051 on 11/24/39. It was SFS to LB at Peoria 4/19/67. No. 1065 was demotorized in Feb. 1935 and became No. 605 on 1/16/45. It was dismantled at Decatur on 8/14/47 and its body was used as the Madison yard office. No. 1066 was demotorized in Feb. 1935 and became No. 560 on 5/15/42, then No. 606 in March 1947. It was dismantled at Granite City on 1/20/56. No. 1067 was demotorized in Feb. 1935, became No. 561 on 5/15/42, then No. 607 in March 1947. It was wrecked at Hurlbut Siding on 2/1/51. 1001 became line car 1001 in 1921 and renumbered 1706 in 1923. SFS to Purdy 2/10/56.

Locomotive 14182, later numbered 51, was a combination diesel, battery, and electric locomotive, used in its earlier years to switch sidings and yards which were not electrified. Originally a St. Louis Car Co. demonstrator, its batteries were removed in 1940.
Illinois Terminal, John Leisenring Collection

Class A locomotive 1553 is seen at Decatur shops on May 15, 1938. Paul H. Stringham

Locomotive 51 is seen here on April 30, 1955. Paul H. Stringham

Class B locomotive 1564 was brand new when photographed at Decatur shops on October 12, 1910.
Illinois Traction, Paul H. Stringham Collection

Rebuilt from locomotive 1559 in 1939, the 62 was a combination electric/diesel switcher.
Illinois Terminal, Dale Jenkins Collection

Seen at Springfield on January 28, 1950, the 1561 was one of several class Bs which received a coat of orange paint; many kept the dark green their entire service lives. Paul H. Stringham

CARS OF THE ILLINOIS TRACTION SYSTEM • 223

The interior of class B locomotive 1565, photographed in 1987. The locomotive has been preserved at the Illinois Railway Museum.   Donald R. Kaplan

Class C locomotive 1595 at East Peoria, on May 22, 1949.
    Paul H. Stringham

Class D locomotive 70 was photographed brand new at Decatur shops, in 1940.   Illinois Terminal, Dale Jenkins Collection

Class C locomotive 1579 poses for the camera at Decatur, fresh out of the shop on October 27, 1924.
    Illinois Traction, Dale Jenkins Collection

December 5, 1949, finds Class D locomotive 71 "in the hole" at Henry Siding, just west of Morton.   Paul H. Stringham

Table 12 — Electric Locomotives

Classes: Class A—Nos. 1550-1560; Class B—Nos. 1561-1578; Class C—Nos. 1579-1598; Class D—Nos. 70-74

Numbers	Builder & Date	Length	Width	Weight	Motors	Trucks	Control	Notes
51, 52	St. Louis, 1930	48'7"	9'10"	187,000	4-GE285	Comm L92	GE PCL	1
53	Decatur Shop, 1942			196,400	4-GE285	Comm L92	GE PCL	2
61	Decatur Shop, 1939	29'4"	9'9"	112,700	4-GE55H	Alco E52	M-C6k	3
70-74	Decatur Shop, 1940-42	55'5"	9'11"	217,000	8-WH571FD1	StL 82	HLF	4
1550(1st)	Danville Car, 1907	32'8"	11'10"	84,000	4-GE73C	StL 62	M-C6k	5
1550(2nd)	Danville Ry. & Light 1904	32'8"	11'10"	74,240	4-GE73C	Bdwn 78-25A	M-C6k	5
1551(1st)	Danville Car, 1904	32'8"	11'10"	84,000	4-GE73C	StL 62	M-C6k	5
1552-1555	Danville Car, 1907	32'8"	11'10"	84,000	4-GE58	Bdwn 78-25A	M-C6k	5
1556(1st)	Danville Ry. & Light 1904	32'8"	11'10"	74,240	4-GE58	Bdwn 78-25A	M-C6k	5
1556(2nd)	Danville Car, 1907	32'8"	11'10"	84,000	4-GE58	Bdwn 78-25A	M-C6k	5
1557(1st)	Danville Ry. & Light 1904	32'8"	11'10"	74,240	4-GE58	Bdwn 78-25A	M-C6k	5
1557(2nd)	Danville Car, 1907	32'8"	11'10"	84,000	4-GE58	Bdwn 78-25A	M-C6k	5
1558	Danville Ry. & Light 1904	32'8"	11'10"	74,240	4-GE58	Bdwn 78-25A	M-C6k	5
1559, 1560	Alco-GE, 1907	31'1"	9'6"	82,000	4-GE55H	Alco 552	M-C6k	5
1561(1st)	Alco-GE, 1907	32'9"	9'6"	100,000	4-GEA609	Alco 552		6
1561(2nd)-1566	Decatur Shop, 1910	34'0"	9'3"	120,000	4-GE69C	Alco	C83g	7
1567-1578	Decatur Shop[8]	34'0"	9'3"	120,000	4-GE269C	Alco	C83g	8
1579-1584	Decatur Shop[9]	52'5"	9'3"	160,000	8-GE73C8	StL 62	M-C6k	9
1585	Decatur Shop, 1926	52'5"	9'3"	160,000	8-GE73C8	StL 62	M-C6k	10
1586	Decatur Shop, 1926	52'5"	9'3"	160,000	8-WH702	StL 62	HLF	11
1587-1598	Decatur Shop[12]	52'5"	9'3"	160,000	8-GE73C8	StL 62	M-C6k	12

1. No. 51—Trolley, battery and diesel (a 300-hp Buda engine) powered. Batteries removed on 4/19/40. SFS to HM 2/13/56. No. 52 was a duplicate of No. 51. Its batteries were removed on 4/19/54. SFS to CI&M 2/10/56. 2. A duplicate of Nos. 51 and 52, except it had no diesel engine. Its batteries were removed on 4/19/54. SFS to CS 1/14/56. 3. Could be operated on both trolley and diesel power. Rebuilt from No. 1559 on 9/30/39. Sold to Allis-Chalmers 4/24/52. 4. No. 70 built in 1940, No. 71 in 1941, and Nos. 72-74 in 1942. Rebuilt from other locomotives as shown: 70=1580, 71=1581, 72=1591, 73=1584 and 74=1588. Nos. 70-72 SFS to BI&M in Feb. 1956; Nos. 73 and 74 SFS to CS 3/27/56. 5. Nos. 1550(1st) and 1551(1st) became 1556(2nd) and 1557(2nd). Nos. 1556(1st) and 1557(1st) became 1550(2nd) and 1551(2nd). All were built in 1928-1929; 1550(2nd), 1551(2nd) and 1552 became Class O while the other six remained Class A. Nos. 1559 and 1560 were originally Nos. 102 and 103. No. 1560 was SFS to Purdy 7/16/51. 6. Originally No. 104, renumbered about 1904. It was capable of either AC or DC operation. It was returned to GE in 1920 after ITS gave up AC operation, and later went to the Niagara, St. Catherines & Toronto (No. 14); it was scrapped in 1960. 7. Rebuilt as Snow Plow 020 on 12/9/55. SFS to CI&M 9/19/59. No. 1562 was SFS to HM 5/19/54. No. 1563 was SFS to HM 5/25/55. No. 1564 was SFS to CS 5/13/56. No. 1565 was sold to Illinois Power & Light at Champaign 4/10/55; it went to the Illinois Railway Museum in 1960. No. 1566 was sold to Illinois Power & Light at Danville 4/29/52. 8. Nos. 1567-1572 were built in 1914; Nos. 1573-1578 were built in 1918. Nos. 1567 and 1568 were sold to St. Louis Car Co. on 1/17/55 and 2/20/56. No. 1569 was SFS to CS 2/24/56. No. 1570 was SFS to HM 5/10/56. No. 1571 was SFS to HM 11/13/50. No. 1572 was SFS to PD 7/27/51. No. 1573 was SFS to HM 7/2/53. No. 1574 was SFS to HM 10/18/53. No. 1575 was sold to St. Louis Car Co. 6/23/53; it was resold to the National Museum of Transport in Sept. 1963. No. 1576 was rebuilt to snow plow 021 on 12/9/55. It was SFS to CI&M 9/15/59. No. 1577 and 1578 were SFS to HM 10/18/53. 9. Nos. 1579-1581 were built in 1924, Nos. 1582-1584 were built in 1925. No. 1579 was SFS to HM 2/13/56. No. 1580 became No. 70 9/10/40 (see note 4). No. 1581 became No. 71 on 3/27/41 (see note 4). No. 1582 was SFS to CS 1/14/56. No. 1583 was SFS to HM 7/20/53. No. 1584 became No. 73 on 1/2/42 (see note 4). 10. No. 1585 was SFS to HM 7/2/53. 11. No. 1586 was SFS to SBC 6/26/53. No. 1587 was SFS to CS 5/10/56. No. 1588 became No. 74 9/26/42 (see note 4). No. 1589 was SFS to CS 2/20/56. No. 1590 was SFS to CS 3/13/56. No. 1591 became No. 72 on 12/12/42 (see note 4). No. 1592 was SFS to CS 5/10/56. No. 1593 was SFS to PD 4/29/55. No. 1594 was SFS to HM 3/25/56. No. 1595 went to the National Museum of Transport on 12/18/56. No. 1596 was SFS to HM 3/25/56. No. 1597 burned at the East Belt (Springfield) engine house on 8/11/54, its remains were SFS to CI&M 9/13/54. No. 1598 was SFS to CS 4/11/56.

Pull car 1514 was built to resemble a passenger car, and was used to bring freight trailers from Venice into the downtown St. Louis freight terminal. The fenders hooked to the pilot were used only across the McKinley bridge and in the streets of St. Louis.
Illinois Traction, Paul H. Stringham Collection

It would be useful, before presenting the next two tables, to describe each type. Most of the *pull cars* were flat cars with a center cab. Some had narrow cabs so that poles or rails could be carried; others had full-width cabs. Number 1514 was an exception—its appearance was close to a class B electric locomotive except that it was a little longer and had passenger car windows on each side. The *line cars,* after rebuilding, had an enclosed section resembling a boxcar for a little over half their length. Each end had two windows, with a train door in the center. There were two windows on each side. The flat car end had a large framework for a wire spool, plus space for equipment.

Table 13 — Pull Cars/Line Cars

Numbers	Builder & Date	Length	Width	Weight	Motors	Trucks	Control	Notes
1500-1502	Decatur Shop, 1907	44'0"	8'8"	73,000	4-GE73A	Curtis j688-64	M-C6k	1
1503	AC&F, 1906	43'0"	8'5"	78,000	4-GE73C	AC&F	K14a	2
1505	AC&F, 1907	43'0"	8'5"	78,000	4-GE73C	AC&F	M-C6k	3
1506-1507	Danville Ry. & Light 1906	44'0"	8'8"		4-GE73C	Bdwn 78-25A	M-C6k	4
1510	McG-C, 1909	55'1"	9'7"	62,000	4-GE216	McG-C 70A	K35	5
1511-1513	St. Louis, 1914	44'0"	8'8"	78,000	4-GE205B	Bdwn 78-25A	M-C6k	6
1514	St. Louis, 1915	44'0"	8'8"	78,000	4-GE73	Curtis J	M-C6k	7
1520	Danville Ry. & Light 1903	42'8"	8'0"	60,000	4-GE57A	Peckham	K14a	8

1. No. 1500 became line car 1500 in 1922 and was renumbered 1700 in July 1926. It was SFS to HM in May 1956. No. 1501 was renumbered 1523 in Nov. 1925. It went to C&IV in June 1925 and was scrapped by C&IV at Ottawa in Jan. 1935. No. 1502 was scrapped in Jan. 1921. 2. Renumbered to 1521 on 8/19/25. Dismantled on C&IV at Ottawa 3/10/35. 3. Renumbered to 1522 in Nov. 1925. It went to C&IV in June 1925 and was scrapped by C&IV at Ottawa in Jan. 1935. 4. No. 1506 became line car 1506 in 1922 and was renumbered 1701 in Aug. 1925. It was SFS to HM 7/2/53. No. 1507 became line car 1507 in 1922 and was renumbered 1702 in Aug. 1925. It was sold to the Illinois Railway Museum on 10/11/58. 5. A snow sweeper. 6. No. 1511 became line car 1511 in 1921 and was renumbered 1703 in July 1925. It was SFS to HM on 5/16/56. No. 1512 became line car 1512 in 1921 and was renumbered 1704 in July 1925. It was SFS to HM 5/19/54. No. 1513 became line car 1513 in 1921 and was renumbered 1705 in July 1925. It was SFS to Purdy 2/10/56. 7. Renumbered to 1524 in July 1925. It went to C&IV in July 1925 and was scrapped by C&IV at Ottawa in Jan. 1935. 8. Rebuilt from Express Motor 1006.

Other Roster Note—There was a Line Car No. 1707. It was built by the EStl&S as its No. 995, then went to St. Louis & Alton as its 995. It came to IT on 4/10/31, and was dismantled at Federal 2/17/37.

Setting poles was mostly a manpower deal in the early 1920s. This early line car was built with a narrow cab so poles could be carried. Note the unusual rig for lifting poles. The photo was made at Bronson shortly after 1920. John Leisenring

Line car 1700 is seen here on April 30, 1955. Paul H. Stringham

The crew on line car 1703 is replacing some trolley wire near Heyworth, circa 1935. Bill Janssen

Table 14 — Line Cars

Note: All rebuilt from units shown on Table 13. For details and dispositions, see that table and its notes.

Numbers	Date Rebuilt and Unit	Renumbering Date	Numbers	Date Rebuilt and Unit	Renumbering Date
1700	1922 from 1500	July 1926	1704	1921 from 1512	July 1925
1701	1922 from 1506	Aug. 1925	1705	1921 from 19513	July 1925
1702	1922 from 1507	Aug. 1925	1706	1921 from 1001	1923
1703	1921 from 1511	July 1925		(see table 11)	

This April 19, 1953 view shows portable substation 056 on the siding at Mindale, taking care of power requirements until the permanent substation can be overhauled. Paul H. Stringham

Wrecker 830 was constructed by Bucyrus-Erie in 1911; in 1930 it was renumbered 01.
Illinois Traction, Paul H. Stringham Collection

Locomotive 1 was originally Illinois Terminal 9. After being sold to the Alton & Eastern and renumbered 1, it came back to the IT when the Alton & Eastern was acquired, and kept the number 1. This view shows her in the dead line at Alton, in 1934, after being replaced by a railbus on the Alton-Grafton run. In the background is interurban trailer 523, which along with 522 was pulled by loco 1 when it was in service. Paul H. Stringham

The Illinois Traction had many freight cars, such as this 11000-series gondola, built by the Mount Vernon Car Manufacturing Works in August 1925.
Illinois Traction, Dale Jenkins Collection

One of the railbuses which replaced steamer 1 is just leaving the Alton station, in the mid-1930s. Bill Janssen

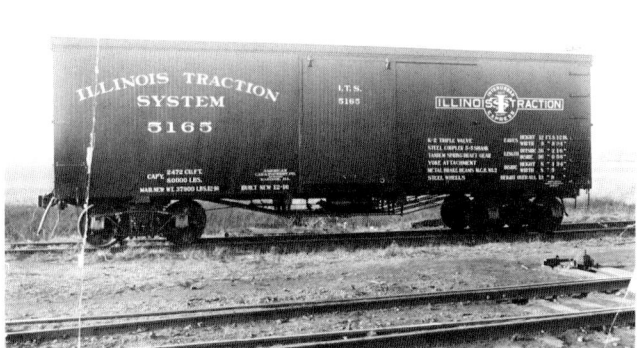

Another example of IT standard railroad freight cars is this boxcar, completed on December 1, 1916, by AC&F.
Illinois Traction, Dale Jenkins Collection

2-6-0 number 16 leads a string of tank cars from the refinery at Roxanna. Note the headlight placement and the pilot, which date the photo circa 1930.
Illinois Terminal, Paul H. Stringham Collection

This January 8, 1949 view shows engine 23 at Federal. Tex Prusia

Illinois Terminal 27 was acquired in the acquisition of the St. Louis Troy & Eastern. This view was taken at the Federal roundhouse on October 29, 1939. Robert W. Merriman

December 14, 1948, finds engine 32 about ready to pick up its train for Edwardsville. Tex Prusia

Locomotive 34 came to the IT from the Florida East Coast. It is seen here at Federal on December 14, 1948. Tex Prusia

Illinois Terminal 36 is at Federal on December 21, 1948. Tex Prusia

Table 15 — Steam Locomotives

Numbers	Type	Drivers	Cylinders	Builder	Builder No.	Date	Notes
1(1st)	0-4-0	50"	17 x 24"	Baldwin	17082	Sept. 1889	1
1(2nd)	4-4-0	62"	18 x 24"	Baldwin	31229	July 1907	2
2	0-6-0	50"	17 x 24"	Baldwin	21563	Jan. 1903	3
3	0-6-0	50"	18 x 24"	Baldwin	24042	Apr. 1904	3
6(1st)	4-4-0	56"	17 x 24"	Baldwin	17340	Jan. 1900	4
6(2nd)	2-6-0	52"	20 x 24"	Baldwin	40954	Nov. 1913	SFS to Purdy 7/23/48
7(1st)	4-4-0	64"	17 x 24"	C&A Ry.		1887	5
7(2nd)	2-6-0	52"	20 x 24"	Baldwin	39935	June 1913	SFS to HM 7/30/48
8(1st)	2-6-0	56"	18 x 24"	Baldwin	23354	Dec. 1903	6
8(2nd)	2-6-0	52"	20 x 24"	Baldwin	39009	Jan. 1913	Retired 6/10/40
9(1st)	(also numbered 2, which see)						
9(2nd)	0-6-0	51"	22 x 26"	Baldwin	52986	1920	7
10	2-6-0	52"	20 x 24"	Baldwin	35261	Sept. 1910	8
11	2-6-0	52"	20 x 24"	Baldwin	37438	Jan. 1912	SFS to Purdy 7/23/48
12	2-6-0	52"	20 x 24"	Baldwin	38968	Dec. 1912	SFS to HM 8/3/35
14	2-6-0	52"	20 x 24"	Baldwin	43852	Aug. 1916	SFS to HM 8/3/35
15	2-6-0	52"	20 x 24"	Baldwin	47390	Dec. 1917	SFS to HM 8/3/35
16	2-6-0	52"	22 x 26"	Baldwin	53162	Apr. 1920	SFS to HM 7/31/48
17	2-6-0	52"	22 x 26"	Baldwin	53163	Apr. 1920	SFS to HM 11/27/48
18	2-6-0	52"	22 x 26"	Baldwin	55860	Dec. 1922	SFS to Purdy 10/6/48
19	2-6-0	52"	22 x 26"	Baldwin	59073	Mar. 1926	SFS to HM 5/29/50
20	2-6-0	52"	22 x 26"	Baldwin	60003	May 1927	SFS to HM 5/29/50
21	2-6-0	52"	20 x 26"	Baldwin	60487	Apr. 1928	SFS to HM 6/9/50
22	2-6-0	52"	22 x 26"	Baldwin	60678	Oct. 1928	SFS to HM 6/30/50
23	2-6-0	52"	22 x 26"	Baldwin	60679	Oct. 1928	SFS to HM 6/29/50
27	2-8-0	51"	21 x 28"	Brooks	47773	1910	9
28	2-8-0	50"	21 x 30"	Pittsburgh	27894	June 1903	10
29	2-8-0	50"	21 x 30"	Pittsburgh	26331	Mar. 1903	10
30	2-8-2	55"	25 x 30"	Baldwin	60924	July 1929	SFS to HM 5/12/50
31	2-8-2	55"	25 x 30"	Baldwin	60925	July 1929	SFS to HM 4/13/50
32	2-8-2	55"	25 x 30"	Baldwin	60926	July 1929	SFS to Purdy 2/23/50
33	0-8-0	51"	24 x 28"	Richmond	66375	June 1925	11
34	0-8-0	51"	24 x 28"	Richmond	66372	June 1925	12
35	0-8-0	51"	24 x 28"	Richmond	66373	June 1925	13
36	0-8-0	50"	22 x 28"	Schenectady	66399	June 1925	14
37	0-8-0	51"	24 x 28"	Richmond	65771	Feb. 1924	15
38	0-8-0	51"	24 x 28"	Richmond	65772	Feb. 1924	16

1. Sold to Granite City & Mississippi River July 1913. 2. Also shown as 9(1st). To Alton & Eastern (A&E 1) March 1925. When A&E was acquired by IT, the A&E number was retained. 3. Sold to List & Gifford Construction Co. 6/11/21. 4. Sold to Creston, Winterset & Des Moines in 1912. 5. Sold to Peoria & Pekin Union (P&PU 16) March 1919. Became Chicago & Alton 112. 6. To Missouri & Arkansas (M&A 9) in Feb. 1907. Retired 1929. 7. Purchased from Goodyear Tire & Rubber Co. (its No. 1), then to St. Louis, Troy & Eastern (No. 9). In 1928, when T&E was acquired by IT, it became No. 27. 8. Sold to Rapid City, Black Hills & Western in 1927 (became its No. 55). 9. Built for Buffalo & Susquehanna, but never delivered. Purchased by St. Louis, Troy & Eastern (its No. 6). When T&E was acquired by IT in 1928, it became IT No. 27. 10. Purchased from Pittsburgh & Lake Erie (their Nos. 188 and 180) by St. Louis, Troy & Eastern (becoming their Nos. 11 and 10). In 1928, when IT took over T&E, they became Nos. 28 and 29. 11. Ex-Florida East Coast 267; SFS to HM 4/28/50. 12. Ex-Florida East Coast 264; SFS to HM 5/12/50. 13. Ex-Florida East Coast 265; SFS to HM 3/23/50. 14. Ex-Alton & Eastern 2; SFS to HM 4/28/50. 15. Ex-Florida East Coast 254; SFS to Purdy 10/6/48. 16. Ex-Florida East Coast 255; SFS to HM 4/13/50.

Alco S-2 710 is at the Decatur shops on September 30, 1952. Painted black with white lettering, it was brought to the area long before the overhead was removed to serve industries with non-electrified sidings. Paul H. Stringham

EMD GP-7 1605 is shown here at the Illinois Railway Museum, where it has been preserved, in 1987. Donald R. Kaplan

Table 16 — Diesel Locomotives

Orig. Numbers	1967-1968 Numbers[1]	Builder	Date	Model	HP	Notes
700-705	1001-1006	Alco	1948	S-2	1,000	2
706-711	1007-1012	Alco	1950	S-2	1,000	3
751-752	1051-1052	Alco	1948	RS-1	1,000	4
753	1053	Alco	1948	RS-1	1,000	5
754-756	1054-1056	Alco	1950	RS-1	1,000	6
725	801	EMD	1950	SW8	800	7
775-786	1201-1212	EMD	1955	SW1200	1,200	8
	1220-1221	EMD	1950	SW7	1,200	9
	1507	EMD	1949	F7B	1,500	10
	1508	EMD	1950	F7B	1,500	10
1600-1605	1501-1506	EMD	1953	GP7	1,500	11
	3419	EMD	1954	GP9	1,500	12
	1750	EMD	1952	GP7u	1,750	13
	1509-1515	EMD	1970	SW1500	1,500	14
	2001-2004	EMD	1977	GP20	2,000	16
	2008-2009	EMD	1970	SW1500	1,500	15
	2301-2306	EMD	1969	SD39	2,300	17

1. In 1967-1968, IT renumbered all of its locomotives; the new numbers were to correspond with horsepower available. This practice was also following on most new power subsequently purchased. 2. No. 700 traded in to EMD Feb. 1970. No. 701 to BR&L became Weirton Steel Co. 223 at Weirton, W. Va. Nos. 702 and 703 traded in to EMD May 1969. No. 704 to BR&L (Boyle Co.) Aug. 1969 for Universal Atlas Cement Co. at Hudson, N.Y. In 1982 it went to the Morristown & Erie Ry. No. 705 to BR&L Aug. 1969, then to Weirton Steel Co. (its No. 225) at Weirton, W. Va. 3. No. 706 to BR&L Aug. 1969, to United Ry. Supply Co. then to Dominion Steel & Coal. No. 707 to BR&L Aug. 1969, became No. 226 of Weirton Steel Co. at Weirton, W. Va. No. 708 traded in to EMD Aug. 1969. No. 709 to BR&L Aug. 1969; became No. 476 of Washington Western R.R. at Franklinton, La. Sold Jan. 1981 to RELCO. No. 710 traded in to EMD Aug. 1969. No. 711 to BR&L March 1970, then to Duval Sierrita Corp. at Sahaurita, Ariz. 4. To GM&O (its No. 1051) Nov. 1969. Became ICG 1261. Sold 1976 to Lone Star Industries at Eagle Lake, Texas. No. 752 to BR&L Aug. 1969. Became No. 58 of C&K Coal Co. at Rimersburg, Pa. 5. Originally No. 753. To GM&O March 1970, ICG 1263. Sold to Green Mountain Ry. July 1976, becoming its No. 400. 6. No. 754 became GM&O 1054 March 1970, then ICG 1264. Sold 1976 to Lone Star Industries, Eagle Lake, Texas, becoming Texas & Northern No. 43. No. 755 became GM&O 1055 March 1970, then ICG 1265. Sold 1976 to H.O. Forgey, Jackson, Tenn. No. 756 became GM&O 1052 March 1970, then ICG 1252. Sold July 1976 to Green Mountain Ry. becoming its No. 401. 7. Originally EMD 800. Became N&W 2115. Retired 5/12/82, SFS 8/19/83. 8. No. 775 became N&W 1201. No. 776 became N&W 1202. To Southern Aggregates, Postell, Ga., June 1987. No. 777 became N&W 1203. No. 778 to Archer-Daniels-Midland (No. 1) at Peoria, June 1981. In 1987 moved to A-D-M at Decatur. No. 779 became N&W 1205. No. 780 became N&W 1206. In 1987 sold to Atlantic Steel Co., Atlanta, Ga. No. 781 became N&W 1207. No. 782 became N&W 1208. Sold to Rail Link, Petersburg, Va., in 1987. No. 783 became N&W 1209. No. 784 became N&W 1210. No. 785 became N&W 1211. SFS May 1984. No. 786 became N&W 1212. Sold to Brenco Bearings, Petersburg, Va., May 1987. 9. No. 1220 became N&W 1220. No. 1221 became N&W 1221. From C&O (No. 5228) via Chrome Crankshaft Aug. 1979. Both were sold Aug. 1986 to George Silcott (locomotive broker) who sold them Oct. 1986 to Cahokia Terminal in Illinois. No. 1507 and 1508 were from RF&P (Nos. 1557 and 1559) in 1966 via PECo. Both were traded in to EMD May 1969. 11. No. 1600 became N&W 3401. SFS 8/19/83. No. 1601 became N&W 3402. SFS 12/29/82. No. 1602 became N&W 3403. Retired 4/9/84. SFS to Pielet 1984. No. 1603 became N&W 3404. Retired March 1983 after being wrecked in 1982. No. 1604 became N&W 3405. Retired 4/9/84. SFS to Pielet 1984. No. 1605 to Illinois Railway Museum, Union, Ill., in Nov. 1984. 12. Became N&W 3419. Originally T&NO 284, to GE-PNC, in 1974 to IT. To PNC 3/5/82. 13. Originally Wabash 475, became N&W 3475, then PNC 3475. To IT June 1976. Back to PNC in 1981. 14. No. 1509 became N&W 2290. No. 1510 became N&W 2291. No. 1511 became N&W 2292. No. 1512 became N&W 2293. No. 1513

became N&W 2294. No. 1514 became N&W 2295. To Manufacturers Ry. (No. 257) in 1985. No. 1515 became N&W 2296. 15. No. 2008 became N&W 2008. From PNC, ex-UP 712 (482). To IT in 1980. No. 2009 became N&W 2009. From PNC, ex-UP 710 (480). To IT in 1980. 16. Nos. 2301-2303 became N&W 2961-2963. To Boston & Maine (its Nos. 690-692) in Aug. 1985. No. 2304 became N&W 2964. To K. Gibbs in Sept. 1984. April 1985 to AT&SF, its slug 140(2nd). No. 2305 became N&W 2965. Aug. 1984 to K. Gibbs, then to Morrison-Knudsen for parts. No. 2306 became N&W 2966. Aug. 1984 to K. Gibbs, then to Morrison-Knudsen. Later to Guilford Industries, becoming Maine Central 693.

Builder Serial Numbers — Diesel Locomotives

700	75654	711	77055	778	20669	1507	10166	1602	17986	2301	34883
701	75655	725	12463	779	20670	1508	10170	1603	17987	2302	34884
702	75656	751	75840	780	20671	1509	35823	1604	18706	2303	34885
703	75657	752	75841	781	20672	1510	35824	1605	18707	2304	34886
704	75672	753	73839	782	20673	1511	35825	1750	17076	2305	34887
705	75673	754	77055	783	20674	1512	35826	2001	766065-1	2306	34888
706	77050	755	77056	784	20675	1513	35827	2002	766065-2	3419	19480
707	77051	756	77057	785	20676	1514	35828	2003	766065-3		
708	77052	775	20666	786	20677	1515	35829	2004	766065-4		
709	77053	776	20667	1220	10761	1600	17984	2008	26057		
710	77054	777	20668	1221	8435	1601	17985	2009	26055		

Roster compiled by James J. Buckley, with minor revisions by Paul H. Stringham.

Abbreviations

BIMCO: Biermann Iron & Metal Co.
CI&M: Clerman Iron & Metal Co.
CS: Compressed Steel Co.
HM: Hyman-Michaels
LB: Lipsett Bros.
Purdy: Purdy Co.
SFS: Sold for Scrap
E.St.L.&S. = East St. Louis & Suburban

A Colorful Interurban

The Illinois Terminal was many things to many people. It lived a remarkable and innovative life, and when it died, it took with it a different way of life from those whom it once served. Come with us now, as we bring this truly special interurban system to life in a colorful way.

On the last day of operation for the Bloomington line, car 278 crosses Salt Creek, south of Clinton. The date was February 21, 1953.
Bill Janssen

Car 241 is seen at Springfield on January 15, 1946. J.P. Shuman

Class D locomotive 72 heads a northbound freight along East Jefferson Street in Morton, on August 23, 1952. Bill Janssen

Just a few minutes later, locomotive 72 is seen with its train, number 72, at the west end of Morton.   Bill Janssen

Train 97 is seen at East Peoria on August 23, 1952.   Bill Janssen

A COLORFUL INTERURBAN • 235

Car 282 ducks under the Gulf Mobile & Ohio overpass on Western Avenue in Bloomington, en route from Peoria to Decatur. The date was October 11, 1952. Bill Janssen

The date is October 12, 1952, as car 103 stops at Mitchell en route from Alton to St. Louis. The track behind the car makes a reverse curve onto the viaduct over the Gulf Mobile & Ohio and New York Central tracks. Bill Janssen

On the same day—October 12, 1952—car 101 has just arrived at Granite City from Alton. An IT bus awaits passengers headed for East St. Louis; after the transfer is completed, car 101 will round the curve and head for St. Louis. Bill Janssen

It's a beautiful evening as car 280 does station work at Bloomington, circa 1952.

T. Hefner, Bill Janssen Collection

Looking north at the Maroa trolley stop, circa 1952. T. Hefner, Bill Janssen

Train 91 streaks over the Gulf Mobile & Ohio at Mindale, in January 1952. Bill Janssen

The date is February 14, 1953, as car 278 rounds the curve from Madison to Lincoln Street in Bloomington.
Bill Janssen

Car 278 is about to enter North Monroe Street in Clinton, on a Peoria-Decatur run. It was February 21, 1953, the final day of operation for the Mackinaw Junction-Decatur line.
Bill Janssen

A COLORFUL INTERURBAN • 239

Car 278 continues on its way through Clinton, on this last day of operation. Bill Janssen

A northbound streamliner clatters across the double-track Illinois Central, and is about to cross the Wabash as well, at Starne tower just outside Springfield on September 12, 1953. Bill Janssen

Fall of 1953 finds car 453 stopping at North Broadway station in St. Louis on a Granite City-St. Louis suburban run. The IT elevated structure can be seen in the distance.   Bill Janssen

A two-car train of PCCs has just crossed the McKinley bridge and is curving onto the elevated, headed towards downtown St. Louis. The old street route into St. Louis went straight ahead at this point. The date is February 22, 1954.   Bill Janssen

Granite City, May 1954. T. Hefner, Bill Janssen Collection

A three-car streamliner flies over the GM&O and IC tracks at Springfield on September 11, 1955. Bill Janssen

The end is near for interurban service as train 81 rolls over the McCambridge Avenue bridge in Madison, on February 22, 1956. Bill Janssen

The last scheduled southbound interurban train is just south of Virden on March 3, 1956. Bill Janssen

The last train pauses in Gillespie. Bill Janssen

The last train pauses at Edwardsville. (A special run followed.) Bill Janssen

244 • ILLINOIS TERMINAL

An ink blotter from the mid-thirties.   Bill Janssen Collection

Suburban service continued to run for a few more months. Here, PCC 452 is on State at 19th in Granite City, in March 1956.   Bill Janssen

Although printed in only orange and black, this mid-'teens promotional folder looked as though it was printed in color through skillful lithography.   Bill Janssen Collection

PARLOR CARS

All the convenience of modern railway travel without the smoke and cinders is offered by Traction Parlor Cars operating between Peoria, Springfield and St. Louis. They are luxuriously furnished with large, comfortable, leather upholstered chairs. Besides the observation compartment, they contain club compartment with tables for writing or card playing and men's smoking compartment. The wash rooms are large and commodious.

Cafe service is provided at reasonable prices.

PARLOR CAR
Length—55 feet, 9 inches
Weight—80,000 pounds
Seats—Thirty-five passengers

SLEEPER
Length—57 feet, 6 inches
Weight—80,000 pounds
Berths—Ten uppers, ten lowers

SLEEPERS

In addition to the conveniences found in the standard Pullman sleeper the Illinois Traction sleeper contains many innovations that add comfort for the passengers. Upper berths are provided with windows, insuring perfect ventilation. The berths are about six inches longer than those in the ordinary sleeping car. Each is provided with a safety deposit vault for valuables. The entire car and each berth is lighted with electricity, and electric fans keep the car cooled when needed. Toilet rooms are equipper with the most modern conveniences.

Nightly between St. Louis, Springfield, Peoria

STANDARD ELECTRIC LOCOMOTIVE AND FREIGHT TRAIN ON "THE ROAD OF GOOD SERVICE"

An Illinois Traction Xpress stub, from the mid-twenties. Bill Janssen Collection

A COLORFUL INTERURBAN • 247

An Illinois Terminal stock certificate, from 1947-1948. Dale Jenkins Collection

Appendix A

NOTES ON THE ILLINOIS TRACTION SYSTEM'S CORPORATE HISTORY.

Although Illinois Traction System was lettered on all of the line's equipment, and was used by everyone who spoke of it, there was never a time when that was its official title. The system instead was made up of many companies, financed by the same syndicate, organized as the Illinois Traction Company in 1904. Each company constructed about 50 miles of line and operated them as such for a few years. But as time went by, some of the smaller companies consolidated with each other until in 1923, all electric lines became Illinois Traction Incorporated, as near to the commonly used name as was ever legalized.

1). The main lines to 1937.

First of the interurban companies was the Danville Paxton & Northern Railroad Co., incorporated December 2, 1899. Construction began at Danville in July 1901, and by September 1902, the DP&N had completed 10.43 miles from Danville to Georgetown and 6.4 miles from Danville to Catlin.

The DP&N was acquired by deed of sale on April 24, 1903, by the Danville Urbana & Champaign Railway Company. This latter incorporated July 31, 1902. From August 1902 to September 1903, the DU&C built 31.4 miles from Danville west to Urbana. The 5.5 mile Homer branch was built between October 1903 and May 1904, and in 1905 the ex-DP&N Georgetown branch was extended to Ridge Farm. The DU&C maintained its separate existence until consolidation into Illinois Traction Inc. on May 23, 1923.

Illinois Central Traction Company incorporated December 10, 1903, constructing a 39 mile line from Springfield to Decatur between June 1904 and September 1905. The 3.5 mile Mechanicsburg branch was built in the summer of 1905. ICT maintained its separate corporate existence until consolidation into Illinois Traction Inc. in 1923.

Decatur Springfield & St. Louis Railway Co. incorporated May 25, 1903, name changed December 28 to St. Louis & Springfield Railway Co. Between June 1903 and March 1906, this company built a 60.5 mile line southwest between Springfield and Staunton. On January 8, 1910, the SL&S was sold to the St. Louis Springfield & Peoria Railroad Co.

St. Louis & North Eastern Railway Co. incorporated December 22, 1904, building 53.9 miles Hillsboro-Granite City between May 1904 and January 1907. February 4, 1907, bought Danville & Edwardsville Terminal Railroad Co., incorporated January 17, 1906, to build a short stretch of line in Venice, Illinois but had not done so.

On December 21, 1907, St. Louis & North Eastern was broken up. The 17.2 miles between Staunton and Edwardsville was sold to the new St. Louis & Staunton Railway Co. (incorporated November 4, 1907). On the same day, 13.6 mile Granite City- Edwardsville line sold to Tri-City Traction Co., incorporated April 26, 1907.

St. Louis & North Eastern retained 22.8 miles between Hillsboro and Staunton. All three companies were bought by St. Louis Springfield & Peoria Railway January 8, 1910.

Springfield Lincoln Bloomington Pekin & Peoria Electric Railway Co. incorporated March 7, 1904, changing its name December 23 to Springfield & North Eastern Railroad Co. Some construction done on 29.8 mile Springfield-Lincoln line, but money ran out. Springfield & North Eastern Traction Co. incorporated April 28, 1906, and on September 1st purchased the moribund S&NE, completing unfinished line Springfield-Lincoln. S&NE Traction sold to St. Louis, Springfield & Peoria October 1, 1913.

Peoria Lincoln & Springfield Traction incorporated April 18, 1907, building 27.6 miles from Mackinaw Junction to Lincoln between March 1907 and January 1908. It was sold to the St. Louis Springfield & Peoria March 22, 1912.

Peoria Bloomington & Champaign Traction Co. incorporated April 19, 1905. Between January 1906 and April 1907, 37 miles of line were completed between Peoria and Bloomington. Sold to St. Louis Springfield & Peoria March 23, 1912.

Springfield Belt Railway Co. incorporated November 24, 1906. Between 1909 and March 1911 it built a 5.9 mile belt line round the south and east side of Springfield, but was sold to the St. Louis Springfield & Peoria November 14, 1910.

Edwardsville Belt Railway Co. incorporated October 16, 1909. Between August 1909 and August 1911, it built 2.9 miles of belt line around the south and east side of Edwardsville, then sold to St. Louis Springfield & Peoria July 13, 1911.

When incorporated January 6, 1910, St. Louis Springfield & Peoria had built no lines itself, but in a few years had, as we have seen, consolidated under its banner no less than eight companies. Another large consolidation company was Bloomington Decatur

Champaign Railway, incorporated November 28 1910, which within a short time had absorbed three further lines.

These were the Chicago Bloomington & Decatur Railway, incorporated April 19, 1905, the St. Louis Decatur & Champaign Railway Co. incorporated April 25, 1906, and the Decatur Belt Railway, incorporated October 16, 1909. The CB&D built 45.5 miles between Bloomington and Decatur between June 1905 and July 1906, being sold to the BD&C Railway December 27, 1913. The St. Louis Decatur & Champaign built 50.6 miles between Champaign and Decatur between May 1906 and June 1907 before sale to the BD&C at an unknown date. The Decatur Belt Railway built 5.3 miles of belt line around the west and north side of Decatur between 1907 and June 1911. It was sold to the BD&C December 30, 1912.

By the outbreak of World War One, only the Bloomington Decatur & Champaign, Danville Urbana & Champaign, Illinois Central Traction, and the St. Louis Springfield & Peoria companies were functioning over the main interurban lines, and these were consolidated May 23, 1923, into Illinois Traction Inc. (Main Division), which continued operations until April 26, 1928 when it was leased to Illinois Terminal Railroad Co. This ended use of the name Illinois Traction.

2). The Valley Division to 1934.

Illinois Valley Traction Co. incorporated December 27, 1901, building 9.29 miles from Peru to Ladd in 1902. In 1903 and 1904, 21.2 miles was built from Marseilles to LaSalle, before being sold to the Illinois Valley Railway Co. July 1, 1904. Their line was built across the Garden City Sand Co., east of LaSalle under what turned out to be defective powers of condemnation. The Sand Company tested those powers in court, and the court agreed Illinois Valley Traction had no such powers. The new Illinois Valley Railway Co. was able to settle a new condemnation suit in August 1904.

Ottawa Marseilles & Morris River Railway Co. incorporated December 29, 1902, already building from Ottawa to Marseilles. After some grading was done, the company failed, and was sold December 20, 1904 to the Illinois Valley Railway Co.

Marquette Spring Valley & Northwestern Railroad incorporated July 17, 1901. Financed by C. J. Devlin, and intended to be a steam operated coal-hauler, 4.13 miles were built between Marquette and Spring Valley. Devlin died before construction was complete and his heirs had no interest. A Receiver was therefore appointed, and the railroad sold June 15, 1907, to the Illinois Valley Railway.

Illinois Valley Railway incorporated June 27, 1904, mainly to acquire Illinois Valley Traction Company, in trouble over the condemnation suit noted earlier. With that settled, 1905 saw the IVR build 5.56 miles Marseilles-Seneca, and 14.09 miles between May 1906 and February 1907 from end of Marquette Spring Valley & Northwestern tracks, to Princeton, completing Hicks Junction-Princeton. On June 1, 1907, the IVR was leased to Chicago, Ottawa & Peoria Railway, being sold to CO&P April 15, 1908.

Chicago, Ottawa & Peoria incorporated April 19, 1907, making its first acquisition September 30 when Peoria Streator & Ottawa Railway (incorporated March 1, 1906) was taken over. The PS&O had done a little preliminary construction work, but nothing really noteworthy. The CO&P did not resume work on the 17.20 mile Ottawa-Streator line until 1909, but then had a major burst of activity when in 1909 and 1910 it built 10.28 miles Seneca-Morris, plus in 1911 21.82 miles Morris-Joliet. Also aquired the Illinois Valley Railway on April 15, 1908.

CO&P consolidated into Illinois Traction Inc. May 23, 1923, as Illinois Traction Inc. (Valley Division).

Chicago & Illinois Valley Railroad Company incorporated January 22, 1929, after buying Valley Division the day before, and remained in control of the line until abandonment May 14, 1934.

3). The Illinois Terminal Railroad Company and subsidiaries to 1937.

Illinois Terminal Railroad incorporated July 8, 1895. In 1896 built 1.35 miles from Alton (Henry Street) to Illinois Glass Company plant, extending 4.7 miles in 1899 to Edwardsville Crossing (Hartford). It then leased the Wabash Railroad branch from Edwardsville Crossing to Edwardsville, making a 14.7 mile Alton-Edwardsville line. December 20, 1922, changed name to Illinois Terminal Company, but became Illinois Terminal Railroad Company again January 22, 1937, the date of the great merger.

Illinois & Mississippi Valley Terminal Railroad Co. incorporated June 23, 1899. Built no line, merged with Illinois Terminal Railroad September 21, 1899.

St. Louis Troy & Eastern Railroad incorporated August 16, 1899, building 13.12 miles from East St. Louis to Donkville (Collinsville) in 1899. Leased to Illinois Terminal Co. from January 1, 1928.

Collinsville & Troy Railroad Co. incorporated September 25, 1899, building 6.86 miles from Collinsville Junction to Troy in 1899 and 1900. Acquired by St. Louis Troy & Eastern Railroad October 27, 1902.

St. Louis & Illinois Belt Railway Co. incorporated October 4, 1905, building 6.8 miles Formosa-Edwardsville between 1906 and 1908. Leased to St. Louis Troy & Eastern and on January 1, 1928, acquired by the Illinois Terminal Co.

St. Louis Electric Terminal Railway incorporated March 8, 1906. Between 1907 and 1910 built 6.7 miles between St. Louis and Granite City, including the mighty McKinley Bridge and standard gauge street railway tracks in St. Louis. Citizens' Railway Co. of Venice incorporated January 10, 1910, deeded to St. Louis Electric Terminal Railway immediately. Electric Terminal Railway leased to Illinois Terminal Company January 1, 1928.

Alton Terminal Railway Co. incorporated March 25, 1899, building a mile of track that year in the City of Alton. From January 1, 1930, leased to Alton & Eastern Railroad.

This latter incorporated December 16, 1924, and bought that part of the Chicago, Peoria & St. Louis between Grafton and Granite City, 30.4 miles long.

Leased to Illinois Terminal Co. from January 1, 1930. Consolidated into Illinois Terminal Railroad January 22, 1937.

January 22, 1937, Alton & Eastern, St. Louis & Illinois Belt, St. Louis Troy & Eastern, and Illinois Traction Inc. (Main Lines and Valley Division) consolidated into Illinois Terminal Railroad Company group, itself renamed that day from Illinois Terminal Company.

4). Alton Electric Lines to 1940.

Alton & Southern Railway Co. incorporated September 8, 1904, changing name September 20 to Alton Granite & St. Louis Traction Company. In 1904 and 1905 it built a 23.81 mile line between East St. Louis and Alton.

Edwardsville Alton & St. Louis Railway Co. incorporated January 14, 1905, building 8.87 miles Edwardsville-Mitchell, connecting with Alton, Granite & St. Louis. Edwardsville, Alton & St. Louis merged with Alton Granite & St. Louis January 4, 1907.

St. Louis & Alton Railway Co. incorporated June 21, 1926, and on December 1 acquired Alton, Granite and St. Louis Traction.

Illinois Terminal leased St. Louis & Alton June 4, 1930, effective July 1, 1930.

St. Louis & Alton bought by Illinois Terminal December 27, 1940.

5). All Lines 1940-1982.

December 14, 1945, Illinois Terminal Railroad changed name to Liquidating Railway Corporation, on same day selling property to Purchaser Railway Corporation (incorporated September 21, 1945). PRC then changed name to Illinois Terminal Railroad. This was one of the moves necessary in order to separate the railroad property from the hitherto closely associated Illinois Power & Light Corporation and was done on the order of the Securities and Exchange Commission.

Illinois-Missouri Terminal Railway Company incorporated November 8, 1954, by the Baltimore & Ohio, Chicago & Eastern Illinois, Chicago, Burlington & Quincy, Gulf Mobile & Ohio, Litchfield & Madison, Illinois Central, Nickel Plate, St. Louis & San Francisco and Wabash Railroads, to purchase Illinois Terminal Railroad.

Acquisition complete June 15, 1956, three months after last main line passenger runs.

Name of Illinois Terminal Railroad changed to Illinois-Missouri Terminal Railroad.

That lasted ten days only, for on June 25, name reverted to Illinois Terminal Railroad. Later, the New York Central and the Chicago, Rock Island & Pacific Railroads joined the initial consortium of IT owners. This remained the position until 1980, when the Norfolk & Western Railroad studied the notion of an outright purchase of the IT from the owning group. Though the Rock Island's receiver objected initially, an agreement was worked out and the sale to Norfolk & Western took place December 1, 1981.

At this time, the Illinois Terminal Railroad operated over 420 miles of track, of which only 149 miles were still owned. The rest were trackage rights on other lines. The acquisition however meant the loss of IT's separate identity and with the Norfolk & Western acquisition, the property was merged into the larger road.

B. UPGRADING THE SYSTEM, 1906-1951.

As the McKinley System gradually switched to long-haul passenger services and began to carry more freight, so over the years the lines had to be modified and upgraded. One of the first such changes was in May 1906, when construction of a high-level bridge was begun over the Vermillion River at Danville. This boasted two 128 foot long deck truss spans, one 75 foot long span, one 30 foot span, and sixteen 50 foot spans, carrying the line across a deep ravine. On October 6, 1906, car 134 made the first crossing, with Superintendent Mike Connors at the controls. Rails on the Gilbert Street Bridge were then removed.

Attention then turned to the line south of Springfield, where in 1907 a number of sharp curves were eliminated. A downtown station and Dispatcher's office was opened at Wood and South Water Streets in Decatur March 10, 1908, and on August 17 the station at Ninth and Monroe in Springfield was opened. By this time, 134 trains used Springfield station daily.

Some time in 1909, Mr. Chubbuck came up with the notion of a uniform station style for the system, something which he said had come to him in a dream. The day after he had the dream, he discussed it with an architect, who then came up with a design for neat buff brick stations and substations, nicely finished with red tile roofs.

Illinois Traction System's main division was completed when the McKinley Bridge was opened October 3, 1910. A week later, two cars met head-on north of Staunton, due to the northbound motorman overlooking his orders. 38 people were killed. As a result, the company immediately began a study on block signal systems. John Leisenring was brought to Illinois from New York's Hudson & Manhattan Railroad to oversee the installation, and so pleased was he with the ITS, he remained with them as Signal Engineer and Electrical Superintendent until the line was dieselized.

A bottleneck at Lincoln was eliminated April 4, 1913, when the first car used the new line at Athol Tower, crossing the Chicago & Alton and Illinois Central. The old route had right-angle turns that could be negotiated only by freight trailers.

The new line could be used by any type of freight equipment. A month later, the timber trestle over the Wabash Railroad at Bement was replaced with a steel viaduct, and during 1914 no less than fourteen additional timber trestles were replaced with concrete or steel structures. Mechanical interlocking plants were installed at Wabash and Chicago & North Western Railroad spurs near Staunton in 1915. Another was put in during 1916 at the Chicago & Illinois Midland Railroad crossing near Auburn.

The Venice high-line was begun on March 1, 1927, and took a year to finish. An 894 foot long timber trestle was followed by 734 feet of steel trestle, then two trusses spanning the Terminal Railroad, 125 and 145 feet long respectively, then another 2640 feet of timber trestle connecting with the McKinley Bridge. Over $1 million was spent, but it eliminated all freight movements in Granite City, Madison and Venice.

This was but a preliminary to one of the largest construction projects ever attempted by an interurban, when in March 1930 work began in St. Louis on removing the old freight and passenger terminals. A new subway was built (several blocks long) together with a mile of new elevated structure and a large new terminal building. The elevated line opened July 4, 1931, and the subway into the terminal station October 4, 1932. This eliminated all but two blocks of street running in St. Louis.

New stations were opened October 1, 1930 in Peoria, May 24, 1931 in Decatur and February 26, 1933 in Springfield. Passenger runs used the belt lines in both Decatur and Springfield when the stations opened.

In the late 1940s, East Peoria yard was raised above the flood crest of the Illinois River and in August 1949 a new carbarn was built there to replace the Peoria carbarn, followed in November 1951 by the opening of the new East Peoria Station.

Appendix B

PRESIDENTS OF THE ILLINOIS TRACTION SYSTEM AND ILLINOIS TERMINAL RAILROADS.

1). William Brown McKinley 1900-1924.

Born in Petersburg, Illinois on September 5, 1856, son of George and Hannah (nee Finley). The family moved to Champaign in 1858 where his father became Pastor of the Presbyterian church. He studied at the University of Illinois for two years, (entering at age 14!) but had to drop out when money ran short. He then served as a drug store clerk, then as bookkeeper in the country real estate and farm mortgage business of his uncle, renamed J. B. and W. B. McKinley, when he was taken on as a partner. In 1884 he became interested in the Champaign-Urbana horse railway and a local waterworks, attracting eastern capital into both operations. Later, he bought an interurban between Springfield and Defiance Ohio, and a Bay City Michigan utility property. His next interests were at Danville, Illinois where he bought the street railway system and other utilities.

Here the Illinois Traction system had its beginnings. In February, 1881, he had married Kate Frisbee, but the childless couple were separated by 1896.

The 1893 Depression curtailed his activities, but in 1896 he was involved in an early Illinois interurban which ran for 11 miles out of Joliet. It failed to reach Chicago and soon after, he sold the road, purchasing instead street railways in Quincy and Galesburg, IL. In the next two decades the syndicate expanded mightily both by constructing its own interurban lines and by acquiring existing properties. Details of the syndicate's composition are not clear, but there was considerable Canadian cash involved, principally that of Toronto's Sun Life Insurance Company which sold its ITS shares in 1923 for $30 million. Other stockholders were based in Montreal, and they probably acted for British stockholders. Such investors don't drop in uninvited off the street; McKinley made the initial contacts through his long experience in the farm mortgage business, and these financial relationships stood him in good stead as his plans for an interurban empire developed. He was always known as a scrupulously honest businessman, a reputation he jealously guarded all his life.

By 1918 McKinley Syndicate rail properties (under the Illinois Traction System name) were as follows: Bloomington & Normal Railway & Light. 22 miles.

Bloomington Decatur & Champaign Railroad. 98 miles linking the three towns.

Cairo Railway & Light. 22 miles.

Danville & Eastern Illinois Railway. 2 miles in Danville.

Danville & Southeastern Railway. 3 1/2 miles of street railway from Danville.

Danville Street Railway & Light. 15 miles.

Danville Urbana & Champaign Rlwy. 61 miles linking the three towns plus Catlin, Ridge Farm and Homer branches.

Decatur Railway & Light. 15 miles.

Galesburg. Galesburg Railway Light & Power. 20.75 miles linking Galesburg, Knoxville and East Galesburg.

Galesburg. People's Traction Company. 12.5 miles linking Galesburg and Abington.

Illinois Central Traction. 46 miles between Decatur & Springfield.

Jacksonville Railway & Light. 8 miles.

Kewanee Public Service Company. (Kewanee streetcars--not acquired until mid-1920's).

Ottawa. Chicago Ottawa & Peoria Railway. 107 miles.

Ottawa Northern Illinois Light & Traction. 8 miles.

Peoria Railway Company. 53 miles.

Quincy Railway Company. 23 miles.

St. Louis Springfield & Peoria. 223 miles from Venice to Hillsboro, Bloomington and Peoria via Springfield.

Urbana & Champaign Rlwy Gas and Electric. 12.5 miles.

Western Railways & Light Company.

Iowa Oskaloosa Traction & Light. 9 miles linking Oskaloosa and Beacon.

Kansas Atchison Railway Light & Power. 9.84 miles.

Topeka Railway Company. 41.233 miles.

Wichita Railroad & Light Company. 33.6 miles.

Missouri Jefferson City Bridge and Transit Co. 7 miles.

St. Louis Electric Terminal Railway Co. 14.5 miles.

Nebraska Omaha & Lincoln Railway & Light Company. 13.8 miles linking Omaha, Ralston & Papillion.

(This list does not include the impressive portfolio of McKinley-held electric, gas and water utility companies.) Between 1902 and 1934, the McKinley Syndicate also controlled the street railways in LaSalle-Peru and Hillsboro and through the years was never a static entity, buying and selling properties as needed. McKinley however, while retaining overall control, left much of the day-to-day operations to H. E. Chubbuck, a man far more experienced in the nitty-gritty of operating street railways. Instead, McKinley turned to politics, half-jokingly commenting that he'd blundered into it because his business was running so smoothly, he had nothing to do. A Republican party member, he was elected to the U.S. House of Representatives in 1904. In 1912, he became William H. Taft's campaign manager. Taft was not re-elected, and neither was McKinley, but McKinley did return to Congress in 1914. In 1920, he was elected to the U.S. Senate, dying of prostate cancer December 7, 1926. As a Senator, he was Chairman of the Committee on Manufactures, and a member of the Senate Appropriations Committee.

On election, and for years thereafter, he was rumored to be one of the wealthiest men in Congress, worth more than $12 million. When he died, all but $500,000 had been donated to charity, mostly religious. His alma mater (the University of Illinois) was one of the largest beneficiaries. There he built the first church in the U.S. intended solely for students, established a scholarship fund for seniors, donated a hospital, endowed a chair in the economics of public utilities and paid for the building of the University YMCA and YWCA. Though they remained separated, he never divorced his wife, and bequeathed $100,000 to her.

H. E. Chubbuck, while never Company President, was McKinley's right-hand man for decades and ran the system during McKinley's absences in Washington, DC. Born in Utica, New York, on March 23, 1863, he began his public utilities career with the Thomson-Houston Company, then of Providence, Rhode Island. He joined McKinley at Quincy in the 1890s, after some years with General Electric. He started by putting the Quincy street railway system in good order, then went on to Galesburg to upgrade that line. When that was complete, the Joliet-Princeton section (Chicago Ottawa & Peoria) was under way and he was assigned to supervise that project. In 1910 Chubbuck was appointed General Manager of the Illinois Traction System and in 1911 became the Executive Vice- President, retiring in 1923 when the Studebaker interests assumed control. He died in Peoria June 4, 1931.

2). Clement Studebaker 1924-1928.

Though Chubbuck was McKinley's right-hand man, the Congressman's increasingly frequent absences in Washington began to interest outside investors, and at some point the Studebaker family of South Bend, Indiana (the automobile Studebakers) began to buy into the ITS group. At the same time Clement Studebaker became more deeply involved in the ITS and its management, so that once the Sun Life sold its shares in 1923, and the Studebakers became majority shareholders, Clement assumed direct management control as President, while McKinley become Chairman of the Board. In 1926 there was a larger deal in which equal minority control of McKinley's North American Power & Light Company (the holding company which owned the ITS system) was divided between the North American Company and the Insull-owned Midland United-Midwest Utilities system. These latter two companies were among the largest utility holding companies in the country, with vast portfolios of profitable (and not so profitable) traction securities. Once firmly installed, Studebaker immediately began to upgrade the Illinois traction system. The best cars were remodeled, and orange paint began to replace the Pullman green. Schedules were speeded up and freight locomotives were built in the company shops. On McKinley's death in 1926, Studebaker became Chairman of the Board, assuming that role early in 1927. He died in Chicago December 3, 1932.

3). L. E. Fischer 1928-1933.

During Fischer's term, the Illinois Traction System continued its massive upgrading.

Many new passenger stations were built, the Champaign, Urbana and Ottawa Belts were completed and cars taken off the streets in several of the larger cities. The passenger equipment continued to be upgraded, and he both began and completed the most massive of all interurban projects of that time, the $16 million St. Louis Elevated and Subway terminal project. With that in operation by late 1932, he resigned effective May 26, 1933, and died in 1952.

4). A. P. Titus 1933-1948.

Titus came to the Illinois Terminal Railroad as executive Vice-President in 1928 from the Chicago & Alton Railroad. Under his administration an abortive attempt was made to abandon the 151 miles of line between Mackinaw Junction Decatur and Danville in 1942, at the behest of the U.S. War Production Board. But at the same time, it was under his administration that attempts were made for the final time to rebuild the passenger business. At the height of the wartime passenger boom in 1944, the Illinois Terminal made informal inquiries of the St. Louis Car Company concerning PCC cars for suburban service and new streamlined interurban cars of steam railroad quality, to run on the main lines. Though ordered in 1946, a lengthy strike at the Westinghouse plant, and slow delivery from other suppliers, plus their own bulging order books, meant St. Louis Car Company could not deliver the new cars until 1948/49, a time when the long ridership boom of the 40s was already well past its peak. Worse, the operational difficulties with the streamliners in the Peoria area, which ought to have been foreseen by the IT people, made their running a fiscal disaster. This of course was no reflection on Titus, who resigned as President May 1, 1948, to become Chairman of the Board. He died in St. Louis November 9, 1950.

5). H. W. Ward 1948-1954.

Elected May 1, 1948, he was previously Minneapolis & St. Louis Railroad Vice- President-Traffic. Under his administration, interurban passenger services were run down towards abolition and freight services dieselized. He retired December 1, 1954.

6). Vacant (F. L. Dennis, Vice-President 1954-1956).

7). Arthur K. Atkinson 1956-1958.

With the purchase of the Illinois Terminal by 11 railroads, Atkinson, who was President of the Wabash Railroad, was elected President of the Illinois Terminal also, becoming Chairman of the Board in 1958 and retiring July 1, 1960.

8). Fred L. Dennis 1958-1960.

After 45 years' service with the Illinois Terminal, Dennis was elected President and General Manager January 1, 1958, after having served as Vice President of Operations and Maintenance since 1955. He was caught up in the Board's instructions to abandon trackage, an idea which he opposed. He retired August 1, 1960.

9). Earl. L. Keister 1960-1968.

Elected President July 1, 1960, he had been with the Alabama State Docks Railroad.

Under his administration, trackage rights were obtained on several railroads and many miles of Illinois Terminal track were taken up. He retired August 31, 1968, and returned to his home in Knoxville, Tennessee.

10). E. B. Wilson 1968-1977.

Elected President September 1, 1968, he had served as Vice President for several months. He attempted to restore the line's financial and physical health and succeeded in posting the largest net profit in Company history. He retired December 31, 1977, because of a worsening heart condition. He came to the Illinois Terminal from the Chicago & North Western Railroad.

11). Walter J. Cassin 1978-1981.

Elected president February 22, 1978, coming from the Illinois Central Gulf Railroad, where he had been a Vice President. He made a valiant effort to revive the line but with most of the IT's trains being operated over foreign tracks under trackage right agreements, getting cooperation from the owner companies was an impossible task.

However the Norfolk & Western Railroad was anxious to get Illinois Terminal switching facilities in the Granite City-Madison area, and to guarantee that would happen, they applied to purchase the entire line. The other ten owning companies agreed and Cassin remained as President until September 1, 1981, when the Norfolk & Western took over.

Appendix C

GRAIN ELEVATORS

1). Peoria-St. Louis Line

Miles from Peoria		Miles from Peoria		Miles from Peoria	
Belsley	11.3	Richmond	28.5	Fogarty	48.4
Walnut (two)	19.9	Burt	29.9	Hurlbut	55.8
Fravert	22.1	Union	33.3	Mt. Fulcher	57.1
Mindale	24.1	Wilmert	37.0	Woodside	79.9
Sutter	26.1	Evans	38.3	Hamel	143.0

2). Mackinaw Junction-Decatur Line

Miles from Peoria		Miles from Peoria		Miles from Peoria	
Stuckey	26.7	Carle Springs	53.2	Crawford	70.5
Elkins	29.9	Ducey	55.9	Emery	72.5
Earls	49.3	Craig	64.8	Martin	73.5
Buck	52.5	Maroa	68.5		

3). Springfield-Danville Line

Miles from Spfld.		Miles from Spfld.		Miles from Spfld.	
Hessar	9.0	Illiopolis	23.2	State Road (from Ogden on branch)	2.5
Mechanicsburg	2.8	Harristown	31.9		
Mason	53.0	Homer	5.5		
Lanesville	17.7	Lark	64.1		
Haynes	20.3	Ogden	105.2	DeLong	107.8

Appendix D

PRINCIPAL COAL MINES

1). Peoria-St.Louis line

Miles from Peoria		Location
Urbandale Mine	3.2	Near East Peoria
Capitol Mine	72.4	Springfield
Brewerton Mine	-	On Springfield Belt
Peabody #57 Mine	-	On Springfield Belt
Black Diamond Mine	91.6	Solomon Siding
Chicago Wilmington and Franklin Mine	94.2	Thayer
South Mine	114.4	Carlinville
Little Dog Mine	123.3	Gillespie
Kerens and Donnewald Mine	139.8	Worden
East Side Mine	150.9	Edwardsville Belt

2). Danville-Springfield line

Miles from Danville		Location
Electric Mine	4.1	Hillery
Chicago Colliers Mine	5.6	Dolan
United Electric Coal Company #1, #6 Mines	6.6	Grays
United Electric Coal Company #4 Mine	7.2	Missionfield
Dawson Mine	96.4	Dawson
Sharon Mine	12.3	On Ridge Farm line
Carbon Hill Mine	2.2	On Tilton line

Appendix E

ILLINOIS TERMINAL ABANDONMENTS

Date	Segment	Miles	
March 31, 1924	Litchfield downtown loop, less than 1 mile		
Jan. 31, 1928	Catlin to Danville	3.8 miles	
July 17, 1928	Homer to State Road	3 miles	
June 21, 1930	Champaign to Staleys	3.2 miles	TR
Sept. 30, 1930	Street trackage, Peoria	0.5 miles	
April 23, 1931	Decatur street trackage	5.5 miles (trains use Belt)	
Feb. 26, 1933	Springfield Street track	5.8 miles (trains use Belt)	
Sept. 30, 1933	Ridge Farm to Georgetown	4.9 miles	
Sept. 30, 1933	Hillsboro to Litchfield	8.9 miles	
April 26, 1936	Georgetown to So. Danville	9.6 miles	
Dec. 18, 1937	Street track, Edwardsville	About 3 miles (trains use Belt)	
Aug. 1, 1937	Street track, Champaign-Urbana		TR
May 1946	Danville-So. Danville	1.5 miles (included high bridge)	
June 7, 1950	Peoria to East Peoria	0.5 mile	
Sept. 12, 1951	State Road to Ogden	2.5 miles	
Apr. 26, 1952	Danville to DeLong	15.5 miles (first main line aban.)	
May 6, 1952	Troy Junction to Troy	2.5 miles	
Feb. 21, 1953	Mackinaw Jct. to Forsythe	59.7 miles	
Mar. 7, 1953	Granite City to Alton	17.4 miles	
May 23, 1953	Alton to Grafton	14.9 miles	
Dec. 19, 1955	Morton street track	2.0 miles	TR
Aug. 4, 1956	McKinley Jct. to Stallings	7.2 miles	
June 22, 1958	Venice to Granite City	About 3 miles	
Dec. 1, 1959	Decatur to Springfield	35.0 miles	TR
April 1, 1962	Lincoln to Sherman	22.1 miles	TR
April 30, 1961	DeLong to Urbana	16.2 miles	TR
Oct. 16, 1961	Decatur to Champaign	44.0 miles	TR
Aug. 1, 1966	East Peoria to Morton	7.0 miles	TR
Spring 1967	Edwardsville to Stallings	7.3 miles (long unused)	
Sept. 22, 1968	Springfield to Nilwood	38.9 miles	TR
July 11, 1970	Edwardsville to Benld	24.3 miles	(Note A)
Fall 1971	Emery to Crawford	2.0 miles (long unused)	
May 2, 1972	Benld to Wilson	12.0 miles	TR
Oct. 1, 1973	Nilwood to Sheeps	7.5 miles	
Sept. 21, 1976	Worden to Hamel	2.6 miles	
Aug. 6, 1977	Allentown to Lincoln	29.7 miles	TR
1980	Sheeps to Wilson	8.0 miles (long unused)	
1981	Troy Jct to O'Fallon	10.0 miles (long unused)	

Note A: 2.6 miles Worden to Hamel left when Benld to Wilson line was abandoned.

TR: Trains shifted to parallel railroads under trackage rights.

Feb. 24, 1988: Norfolk Southern abandoned 60.2 miles ex-Penn Central line, East Peoria to Maroa, only ex-IT track in St. Louis area.

Bibliography

1. Original Sources:
   Illinois Terminal records on file in St. Louis offices
   Illinois Traction Annual Reports
   Illinois Terminal Annual Reports
   Illinois Power & Light Corporation Annual Reports
   Illinois Public Utilities Commission Annual Reports
   Illinois Commerce Commission Annual Reports
   Interstate Commerce Commission Valuation Reports
   Interstate Commerce Commission Finance Reports

2. Second Sources – Magazines:
   Current Topics Magazine (Illinois Power & Light Corporation)
   Electric Railway Journal
   Electric Traction Magazine
   Street Railway Journal
   Various thumbnail histories published by the Illinois Traction and Illinois Terminal Publicity Departments

3. Secondary Sources – Newspapers:
   Alton Telegraph
   Bloomington Pantograph
   Bureau County Republican (Princeton)
   Carlinville Democrat
   Clinton Register
   Danville Commercial News
   Danville News
   Decatur Herald
   East St. Louis Journal
   Edwardsville Intelligencer
   Girard Gazette
   Granite City Press Record
   Hillsboro Journal
   Illinois State Journal (Springfield)
   Illinois State Register (Springfield)
   Joliet Republican
   Lincoln Courier
   Litchfield Union Monitor
   Morris Herald
   Ottawa Republican Times
   Peoria Evening Journal
   Peoria Evening Star
   Peoria Transcript
   St. Louis Globe-Democrat
   Staunton Star Times
   Streator Free Press

Index

Legend:
Italics indicate caption references.
Appendices and the Roster are not indexed.

A

ACF Industries 50
Advance Thresher Co. 182
Allen, Fred 85, 86
Allentown, Ill. 26
Alternating current lines 24, 35
Alton & Eastern Railroad 90, 98
Alton Granite & St. Louis Traction Co. 21, 23, 29, 86, 87, 98, 126
Alton, Ill. 85-87, *88, 89*, 90, *90, 92*, 95, 96, 98, 114, 123
Alton Light & Traction 86
Alton Railway Co. 90
Alton Terminal Railway 98
Alvey's Drug Store 24
American Bottoms, Ill. 128
American Car Co. 15, 26
American Locomotive Co. 107
American Railroad Association 108
Atchison Topeka & Santa Fe Railway Co. 74, 76
Athol Tower 143
Auburn, Ill. 18, 173
Aurora Plainfield & Joliet Ry. 82
Aux Sable River 82

B

Baltimore & Ohio Railroad 98
Bells, Ill. 104
Bement, Ill. 26, 182
Benld, Ill. 173
Big Four Railroad (NYC) 11, 12, 14, *21, 22, 23*, 86, 126
Black Bridge 86
Black Diamond Mine 108
Bloomington & Normal 26
Bloomington, Ill. 24-26, 107, *110*, 111, *113*, 116, *117*, *179*,
                                                                    180, 186, 193
Bloomington *Pantagraph* 117
Bondville 183
Bosenbury, J.M. 39
Broadwell, Ill. 24, 170
Bronson, Ill. 107, 183
Brooklyn, Ill. 86
Buffalo, Ill. 21, 180
Bunker Hill, Ill. 18
Bureau, Ill. 78, 82
Burlington Railroad (see *Chicago, Burlington & Quincy*)
Bus service *42, 43*

C

Cahokia Creek Valley 19
Caldwell Hill 138
Caldwell Siding 119, *139*
Caldwell Substation 101
Cantrall 20
Capitol Limited 35, 42, 47, *47*, 52, *138*, 146
Carlinville, Ill. 18, 19, 42, 123, 126, 131, 173

Catlin, Ill. 13, 59, *60*
Catlin line 16
Champaign 37, 126
Champaign, Ill. 15, 26, 27, 56, 105, 123, 127, *153-155*,
                                                                  182, 183, 193
Champaign Powerhouse 186
Champaign Shops 198
Chatham, Ill. 107, 173
Chautauqua Park *75*
Center Grove Park 22, *22*
Central Electric Railroad Association *41*
Central Railway Co. of Peoria 25
Cerro Gordo *47*
Cerro Gordo, Ill. 27, 182
Certain-Teed Plant 80
Chicago & Alton Railroad 18, 19, 26-28, 76, 86, 95, 96, 103, 170
Chicago & Eastern Illinois Railroad 11, 13, 107, 110, 116, 183
Chicago & Illinois Valley *61*, 65, 70
Chicago & Joliet Electric Railway 78
Chicago & North Western Railway 74, *79*, 80, 82, 123, *146*
Chicago Bloomington & Decatur 24, 26, 103
Chicago Burlington & Quincy Railroad 74, 76, 82, 95, 173
Chicago, Ill. 78
Chicago Ottawa & Peoria Railway Co. 73, 74, *75*, 77
Chicago Peoria & St. Louis Railroad 19, 96, 98
Chicago Rock Island & Pacific Railroad 74, 78, 80, 107, 133
Chubbuck, H.E. *11*, 167
Cincinnati Hamilton & Dayton 19
Citizens' Coach Co. 90
City of Decatur 52, *54*, 55
Clinton *41*
Clinton, Ill. 24, 25, 128, *179*, 180
Clover Leaf Railroad 15, 96, 104
Collinsville & Troy Railroad 96
Collinsville, Ill. 29
Conrail 123, *123*
Corn Belt Limited service 19, 23, 34, 126
Coon Creek 25
Cotters 96

D

Danvers, Ill. 26, *160, 161*, 175
Danville & Edwardsville Terminal Railroad 29
Danville Car Co. 77
Danville, Ill. 11, 14-16, *16*, 39, 55, 56, 73, 98, *105*, 108, 111,
                                                      114, 125, *157*, *159*, 184, *185*, 193
Danville lines 59
Danville Paxton & Northern 11, 12, *12*, 13
Danville powerhouse 186, *186*
Danville Street Railway & Light Co. 12, 63, 105, *105*
Danville Urbana & Champaign Railway . . . *12*, 13, *14*, 16, 19, 26, 105
Danville-Westville line 13
Davis siding 128

Dawson, Ill. 20, 180
Decatur 35, 36, 126
Decatur Belt Railway 103, *104*
Decatur, Ill. *17*, 19, 24-27, 37, 50, 56, *104*, 107-110, 112, *113*,
   116, *116*, 123, 180, *180*, *181*, 182, 193, *193*
Decatur powerhouse 186, *196*, *197*
Decatur shops 39, 193, *193-195*, 195
Decatur Street Railway & Light Co. 16, *17*
Decatur Springfield & St. Louis Railway 16, *17*, 18-20
De Long, Ill. 56, 118, 129
De Pue, Ill. 74, 82
Direct current lines 35
Donk Brothers' Coal Mine 96
Donkville, Ill. 96
Donovan, Ill. 180
Duncan, James 98

E

Eads Bridge 22, 87
East Alton, Ill. 86
East Belt (Springfield) 198, *200*
East Peoria, Ill. ..25, 26, 52, 56, *57*, 123, 130, 131, *137*, 138, *170*, 201
East Peoria yard *137*
East St. Louis & Suburban Railway *67*, *68*, 70, 98
East St. Louis, Ill. 22, 23, 29, 30, 35, 86, 87, 90, 96, 98, 107
East Springfield 20
Edwardsville *41*
Edwardsville Alton & St. Louis Railway 86, 96
Edwardsville Belt Railway 104
Edwardsville Crossing 95, 96
Edwardsville, Ill. 18, 21, 22, 86, 87, 95, 96, 98, 104, 108,
   114, 123, 129, 173
Electro-Motive Division (EMD) 118, *120*
Elgin Joliet & Eastern Railway 80
Elkhart, Ill. 24, 131, 170, 172
Elsah, Ill. 98
Emery, Ill. *11*, 24, 180
Evans, William 27
Everett-Moore Syndicate 16

F

Farm Creek 131
Farm Creek Bridge 26
Farm Creek yard 111, 137
Farmdale Junction 123
Federal 96, 123
Federal Shops (Alton) 199
Fischer, L.E. 26
Fithian, Ill. 15, 183, *188*
Fithian substation 15
Ford's Crossing 112
Formosa Junction 96, 98
Forsythe, Ill. 24, 25, 56, 180
Fort Creve Coeur 52
Fox & Illinois Union Railway 82
Fox River, Ill. 74, 78
Frankfort, Ill. 102, 130

G

Garden City Sand Co. 74
Georgetown, Ill. 13, 15, 16, 59, 185, *185*
Gilbert Street bridge 12, 13
Gillespie, Ill. 18, 35, 127, 173
Girard, Ill. 19, 107, 125, 173, *173*
Glennon, John 31

Glover 110, 116
Goat Hollow 19, *115*, 126, *129*
Grafton, Ill. *89*, 98
Grand Ridge, Ill. 76, 82, *83*
Granite City & St. Louis Railway Co. 86, 87
Granite City, Ill. 18, 19, *22*, 29-31, 59, 64, *67*, 69, 70, 85, *85*,
   86, 87, 123, 126, 173
Granite City shops *198*
Granite City Venice & East St. Louis Railway Co. 86
Gray's siding 111
Greenwood, Ill. 82
Gulf Mobile & Ohio Railroad *143*, *144*, *146*, 173
Gunthers Crossing 82

H

Hamel, Ill. 127, 173
Harlan & Hollingsworth Co. 34
Harristown, Ill. 21, 182
Hartford, Ill. 95
Henry siding *120*
Hessar 20
Heyworth, Ill. 25, *164*, *179*, 180
Hicks Junction, Ill. 74, 78, 80, 82
Hillery, Ill. 59
Hillsboro Chautauqua 126
Hillsboro, Ill. 23, 24, 185
Hoeschan WigWag 131
Holland Palace Car Co. 34
Homer branch 15, 16
Homer, Ill. *15*, 185
Horseshoe Lake, Ill. 86, 126
Hurlbut siding 131
Hyman-Michaels 56

I

Iles, Ill. 103
Illini 42
Illini Beach Park 82
Illiopolis, Ill. 21, 50, *151*, 180
Illinois 34, 49, 126
Illinois & Michigan (I&M) Canal 74, 80
Illinois & Mississippi Valley Terminal Railroad 96
Illinois Central Gulf Railroad 123
Illinois Central Railroad 13, 19, 20, 24, 25, 27, 28, 80, 82,
   103, 104, 127, *143*, *145*, *154*, 155, 200
Illinois Central Traction Co. 16, 19, 20, 21
Illinois Commerce Commission 78, 96
Illinois Glass Co. 95, 96
Illinois Light & Traction Co. 76, 78
Illinois Power & Light Corporation 78, 98, 114, *184*, 186
Illinois Railroad and Warehouse Commission 76, 102, 107
Illinois River 80
Illinois River Bridge (Verdin) 25, 26, *49*, *52*, 198
Illinois River Railway 74
Illinois River Valley 25, 26, 81, 82
Illinois Terminal Co. (name) 98
Illinois Terminal (last electric passenger service) 99
Illinois Terminal Railroad (1895) Origin ...85 (and many references)
Illinois Terminal Railroad Co. (1937) Formation 98
Illinois Terminal Railroad (steam) 86
Illinois Terminal Transportation Co. 90
Illinois Traction, Incorporated (Main Lines) 98
Illinois Traction, Inc. (Valley Division) 78
Illinois Traction System ....22 (and many references)
Illinois, University of 13

Illinois Valley Railway Co. 74
Illinois Valley Traction Co. 73, 74
Illmo Limited 45, *45*, 47, 52, 130, *139*, *140*, *144*
Indiana 34
Interstate Commerce Commission 108, 114

J

Jacksonville & St. Louis Railroad 18
Joliet & Southern Traction 82
Joliet, Ill. 77, *77*, 82

K

Kankakee & Urbana Traction Co. 112
Kelly Coal Co. 15
Kenney, Ill. 123
Kickapoo Creek bridge 24
Kickapoo Creek Valley 25, 28
Kings siding 131

L

Lanesville, Ill. 180
Ladd, Ill. 73, 74, 82
LaSalle, Ill. 74, 77, 80, 82
LaSalle powerhouse 186
LaSalle-Peru City Electric Co. 73
LeClaire, Ill. *95*, 96, 104, 114
LeClede Steel 97
Lincoln, Ill. 24, 27, 28, 131, 170
Lincoln Sand & Gravel *144*
Lincoln Street Railway 27
Litchfield & Madison Railroad 21, 95, 96, 104, 126
Litchfield, Ill. 23, 24, 85
Little Vermillion bridge 16
Little Vermillion River 74, 82
Lock Haven, Ill. 98
Long Point 21
Louisville & Nashville Railroad 23, 87, 98
Loveless siding 35, 126

Mc

McCullis, L.K. *164*
McKinley Bridge 29, *30*, 31, 64, *64*, *71*, 87, 98, 110, 114, *148*
McKinley Junction 49, 90, 123
McKinley Syndicate 12, 15, 16, 19, 20, 24-27, 74
McKinley Syndicate Co. 21
McKinley System (ITS) . . . . 33 (many references)
McKinley, William B. 12-14, 21

M

Mackinaw, Ill. 26, *160*, 167, 175
Mackinaw Junction *28*, *52*, 56, *106*, 107, 111, *116*, *142*, 170, *171*
Mackinaw River 26
Macoupin County Grand Jury 126
Madison County Ferry 31
Madison County Highway Commissioners 21
Madison, Ill. 29, 31, 49, *68*, 85-87, 90, 96, 98, 114, 123
Maroa, Ill. 24, 25, 123, 129, *165*, 180
Marquette Spring Valley & Northwestern Railroad 74
Marseilles, Ill. 74, 77, 80
Mattis, Julia 31
Mayview, Ill. 14
Mechanicsburg & Buffalo Railroad 21
Mechanicsburg branch 21, 114
Mechanicsburg, Ill. 21, 42, 114
Mechanicsburg Junction 37, 180

Merchant's Bridge 22
Merriam substation 190
Metals Reserve Co. 116
Metropolitan Street Railway (Washington, D.C.) 13
Midwest Terminal Building (St. Louis) *174*, *176*, *177*
Milliken University *37*
Milmine, Ill. 27, 182
Mindale, Ill. 170
Minooka, Ill. *73*, 77, 80
Middle Fork Valley 16
Missouri 19, 34, 49, 126
Missouri Illinois Belt & Bridge Railroad 95
Missouri Kansas Texas Railroad 95, 96
Mitchell, Ill. 86, 87
Monterey Mine 123
Mont 123
Monticello *50*
Monticello, Ill. 26, 27, *153*
Morris, Ill. 76, 77, 82
Morton, Ill. 25, *25*, 26, *115*, *117*, 140, 141, *170*
Mound City 52
"Mt. Fulcher" 24
Mt. Olive, Ill. 24
Muncie, Ill. 183
Myers, L.E., Construction Co. 24

N

Nameoki Transit Co. 130
National Hotel (Peoria) 170
New York Central System 76, 86, 95
New York, Chicago & St. Louis Railroad
  (Nickel Plate) 95, *123*, 130, 131, 180
Niantic, Ill. 16, 182
Nickel Plate Road (see *New York, Chicago & St. Louis Railroad*)
Nilwood, Ill. 18, 19, 173
Norfolk & Western Railway 99, 123, *123*
Norfolk Southern 123
North Carlinville, Ill. 18
Northern Illinois Light & Traction Co. 76, 77

O

Oakley, Ill. 26, 182
Oakwood, Ill. 183
O'Fallon, Ill. 98
Ogden-Homer branch 13
Ogden, Ill. 15, *157*, 183, *184*
Ottawa, Ill. 73, 74, 77, 79, 80, 82
Ottawa Marseilles & Morris River Railway 74
Ottawa shops *81*
Owl 42, *46*

P

Pait, Ill. 98
Paxton, Ill. 15
Penn Central 123, *123*
Pennsylvania Railroad 96, 98, *119*, *123*, 128, 139
Peoria 35
Peoria & Eastern Railway 11, 13, 15, 16, 28, *153*, 156, 178
Peoria & Pekin Union Railroad 49, 108, 111, *138*, 168
Peoria Bloomington & Champaign Traction 25, 28
Peoria, Ill. 25, 26, *41*, *45*, *46*, 52, *54*, 98, *109*, 111, 112, 114,
                  118, *137*, *168*, 169, *170*, 171, *198*, *199*, *200*
Peoria powerhouse 186, *187*
Peoria Lincoln & Springfield Traction 26, 27
Peoria Railway Terminal 110, 112

Peoria Streator & Ottawa Railway Co. 74
Peru, Ill. 74, *79*, 82
Pinson...20
Pontiac, Ill. 98
Porter, J.F. 86
Possum Trot, Ill. 14-16
Princeton, Ill. 74, 77, 78, 80, *81*, *82*

R
Railbus (Alton-Grafton) *89*, *90*
Railway Post Office 49
Ridge Farm, Ill. 15, 185
Ridge Farm line 16
Ridgely 122, 170
Riverton bridge 16
Riverton, Ill. 16, 20, 21, 107, *150*, 180, 193, 198
Riverton powerhouse 186
Rock Run siding 77
Rock Island (see *Chicago, Rock Island & Pacific Railroad*)
Rockwell siding 74

S
St. Ellen, Ill. 98
St. Joseph, Ill. 13-15, 105, *156*, 183
St. Louis 35
St. Louis Alton & Springfield 98
St. Louis & Alton Railway Co. 52, 87, 90, *91*, 98, 173, 198
St. Louis & Eastern 18
St. Louis & Illinois Belt Railway Co. 96, 98
St. Louis & North Eastern Railway 18, 21, *21*, 23, 29
St. Louis & San Francisco Railway (Frisco) 107
St. Louis & Springfield Railway 16, 18, 19, 21
St. Louis Car Co. 40, 78, 126
St. Louis Chicago & St. Paul Railroad 98
St. Louis Decatur & Champaign Railway 26
St. Louis Electric Terminal Railway 29, 98, 110, 114
St. Louis Jerseyville & Springfield 98
St. Louis, Mo. 29-31, 42, 64, *64*, 66, *110*, *111*, *115*, 175, *176*, *177*
St. Louis Public Service Co. *66*
St. Louis subway 65, *89*, *149*, *174*
St. Louis Troy & Eastern Railroad *91*, 96, *97*, 98, 114, *119*
St. Nicholas Hotel (Decatur) 21
Salt Creek 24
Salt Creek Valley 25
Salt Fork 16
Salt Fork bridge 14
Sangamon 54, 59
Sangamon River 16, 27
Sangamon River Bridge 20, *150*
Sangamon Valley 21
Santa Fe Railway (see *Atchison Topeka & Santa Fe Railway*)
Seneca, Ill. 74, 76
Seymour, Ill. 26
Sharmon, C.H. 85
Sharon Mine 108
Sharps 112
Sheldon Brick Co. 108
Sixth Avenue Elevated (New York) 50
Smith, B.D. 23
Solomon siding 108, *122*
South Danville, Ill. 12, 13
South Ottawa, Ill. 76
Southern Railroad 110
Spencer, E.J. 85
Springfield 35, 36, *36*, 126

Springfield & North Eastern Railroad 24, 26
Springfield & North Eastern Traction 24
Springfield Belt.....................................102
Springfield Consolidated Railway 18, 20, 21
Springfield, Ill. 16, 18, 19, 24, 34, 35, 37, 39, 46, 50, 55, 107,
                    108, 110 *111*, *146*, 170, 171, *172*, 180, 198
Springfield yard 103
Springfield, Lincoln, Bloomington, Pekin &
  Peoria Electric Railway............................24
Spring Creek, Ill. 74, *79*, 82
Spring Valley, Ill. 74, 78, 82
Split Rock, Ill. 74, 78, 82
Starnes 20, 24, 145
Starved Rock, Ill. *75*, 82
Starved Rock State Park 75
Staunton, Ill. 18, 19, *19*, 22, 24, *68*, *92*, 126, *148*, 173, 185
Stevens Creek 21
Stone Creek 16
Streator, Ill. 76, 78, 82
Substations (Table) 189
Summit, Ill. 28
Summit substation *190*
Sun Life Insurance Company of Canada 170

T
Taft, William Howard 31, 37, *37*
"Tangerine Flyers" 39, 40, 45, 47
Terminal Railroad Association 19, 22, 23, 29, 87, 96, 108,
                                           110, *118*, 173
Terre Haute Indianapolis & Eastern *41*
Thayer, Ill. 173
Thomasboro 112
Thompson, A.T. 21
Tilton, Ill. 16
Third & Washington Terminal (St. Louis) 90
Toledo Peoria & Western Railroad...............26, *50*
Transfer House (Decatur) 21
Troy, Ill. 96
Troy Junction 96, 98
Twin Grove *162*, *178*

U
Union Electric Co. 98, 186
Union (Logan County), Ill. 111, 121, 170
Urbana & Champaign Railway 13
Urbana, Ill. 13, 14, 108, *155*, 183, *183*, 198
U.S. Mail Limited 47, 138
U.S. War Production Board 116, *116*
Utica, Ill. 74, 77, 78, 82

V
Vandalia Railroad 19, 24, 28
Venice, Ill. 29, 31, 49, *71*, 85, 86, 110, 114, *118*
Venice, Ill.-St. Louis, Mo. ferry 86
Venice Madison & Granite City Railway 29, 85, 86
Venice powerhouse 186
Vermillion County, Ill. 11
Vermillion County Board 12
Vermillion Heights, Ill. 14, 126
Vermillion River 13, 14, *14*, 16
Vermillion River bridge 61, *157*, *158*
Vermillion River Valley 16
Virden, Ill. 18, 19, 107, 173

W

Wabash Railroad 11-14, 19, 21, 22, 24, 27, 95, 96, 103, 104,
110, 123, 126, *145*, 155, *183*, 183
Wall siding *19*, 126
Wapella, Ill. 180
Washington, Ill. *163*
Webster Park 82
West Alton, Ill. 96
Westclox factory (Peru, Ill.) *79*
Western Brick Co. 14, 108
Westville, Ill. 12, 13, 185
White Heath, Ill. 26, 183
Williamsville, Ill. 24, 170, *190*
Wilson 123
Wood Run, Ill. 85, 86, 90, *91*, 96, 123
Woodruff siding *163*
Worden, Ill. 18, 21, 22, 107, 173
World War II 116
Wyatt, Ill. 198
Wyatt Wye 122
Wycles 20

XYZ

Yager Park (Alton, Ill.) 86